D1606229

The Seminars of Alain Badiou

Kenneth Reinhard, General Editor

Alain Badiou is widely considered to be one of the most important Continental philosophers of our time. Badiou has developed much of his thinking in his annual seminars, which he delivered in Paris from the late 1970s to 2017. These seminars include discussions that inform his major books, including *Being and Event, Logics of Worlds,* and *The Immanence of Truths,* as well as presentations of many ideas and topics that are not part of his published work. Some volumes of the seminar investigate individual thinkers and writers such as Parmenides, Plato, Nietzsche, Heidegger, Beckett, and Mallarmé. Others examine concepts such as infinity, truth, the subject, the present, evil, love, and the nature of change. These seminars constitute an essential part of Badiou's thinking, one that remains largely unknown to the non-Francophone world. Their translation is a major event for philosophers and other scholars and students in the humanities and social sciences and for the artists, writers, political theorists, and engaged intellectuals for whom Badiou's work has rapidly become a generative and inspiring resource.

For a complete list of seminars, see page 247.

The One

Descartes, Plato, Kant

Translated by
Jacques Lezra with Susan Spitzer

Introduction by Kenneth Reinhard

Columbia University Press
New York

Columbia University Press
Publishers Since 1893
New York   Chichester, West Sussex
cup.columbia.edu

First published in French as *Le Séminaire – L'Un: Descartes,*
Platon, Kant (1983–1984)
© 2016 Librairie Arthème Fayard

Library of Congress Cataloging-in-Publication Data
Names: Badiou, Alain, author. Spitzer, Susan (Susan Jane), 1946– translator. |
Badiou, Alain Séminaire. English
Title: The one : Descartes, Plato, Kant, 1983–1984 / translated by Jacques
Lezra with Susan Spitzer ; introduction by Kenneth Reinhard
Description: New York : Columbia University Press, 2023. |
Series: The seminars of Alain Badiou | Includes index.
Identifiers: LCCN 2022053577 | ISBN 9780231194129 (hardback) |
ISBN 9780231550666 (ebook)
Subjects: LCSH: Badiou, Alain—Themes, motives |
One (The One in philosophy) | LCGFT: Lectures.
Classification: LCC B2430.B272 E5 2023 | DDC 111/.82—dc23/eng/20230316
LC record available at https://lccn.loc.gov/2022053577

Printed in the United States of America

Cover design: Julia Kushnirsky
Cover image: Shutterstock

Contents

Editors' Introduction to the English Edition of the Seminars of Alain Badiou

KENNETH REINHARD, SUSAN SPITZER, AND JASON E. SMITH

With the publication in English of Alain Badiou's seminars, we believe that a new phase of his reception in the Anglophone world will open up, one that bridges the often formidable gap between the two main forms in which his published work has so far appeared. On the one hand, there is the tetralogy of his difficult and lengthy major works of systematic philosophy, beginning with a sort of prelude, *Theory of the Subject*, and continuing with the three parts of *Being and Event*, *Logics of Worlds*, and *The Immanence of Truths*. On the other hand, there are his numerous shorter and occasional pieces on topics such as ethics, contemporary politics, film, literature, and art. Badiou's "big books" are often built on rather daunting mathematical ideas and formulations: *Being and Event* relies primarily on set theory and the innovations introduced by Paul Cohen; *Logics of Worlds* adds category, topos, and sheaf theory; and *The Immanence of Truths* expands into the mathematics of large cardinals. Each of these great works is written in its own distinctive, and often rather dense, style: *Theory of the Subject* echoes the dramatic tone and form of a Lacanian seminar; *Being and Event* presents a fundamental ontology in the form of a series of Cartesian "meditations"; *Logics of Worlds* is organized in formal theories and "Greater Logics," and expressed in richly developed concrete examples, phenomenological descriptions, and scholia; and for reading *The Immanence of Truths*, Badiou suggests two distinct paths: one short and "absolutely necessary," the other long and "more elaborate or illustrative, more free-ranging." Because of the difficulty of these longer books, and their highly compact formulations, Badiou's shorter writings—such as the books on ethics and Saint Paul—often serve as a reader's first point of entry into his ideas. But this less steep path of induction brings its own problems, insofar as these more topical and occasional works often take for granted their relationship to the fundamental architecture of Badiou's thinking and thus may appear to have a greater (or smaller) role in it than they actually do. Hence the publication of Badiou's seminars from 1983 through (at least) 2012 makes available a middle path, one in which the major lines of Badiou's thinking—as well as its many extraordinary detours—are displayed with the remarkable clarity and the generous explications and exemplifications that always characterize his oral presentations. It is extraordinarily exciting to see the genesis of Badiou's ideas in the experimental and performative context of his seminars, and there is a great deal in the seminars that doesn't appear at all in his existing published writings.

The first volume of the seminars to be published in English, on Lacan, constitutes part of a four-year sequence on "anti-philosophy" which also includes volumes on Nietzsche, Wittgenstein, and Saint Paul. The second volume, on Malebranche, is part of a similar cluster on being, which also involves years dedicated to Parmenides and Heidegger. And the later volumes, beginning in 1996, gather material from multiple years of the seminars, as in the case of *Axiomatic Theory of the Subject* (which is based on the sessions from the years 1996–97 and 1997–98), and *Images of the Present Time* (which was delivered in sessions over three years, from 2001 to 2004).

Isabelle Vodoz and Véronique Pineau are establishing the French text of the seminar on the basis of audio recordings and notes, with the intention of remaining as close as possible to Badiou's delivery while eliminating unnecessary repetitions and other minor artifacts. In reviewing and approving the texts of the seminars (sometimes as long as thirty years after having delivered them), Badiou decided not to revise or reformulate them, but to let them speak for themselves, without the benefit of self-critical hindsight. Given this decision, it is remarkable to see how consistent his thinking has been over the years. Moreover, each volume of the seminars includes a preface by Badiou that offers an extremely valuable account of the political and intellectual context of the seminars, as well as a sort of retrospective reflection on the process of his thought's emergence. In our translations of the seminars into English, we have tried to preserve the oral quality of the French edition in order to give the reader the impression of listening to the original recordings. We hope that the publication of Badiou's seminars will allow more readers to encounter the full scope of his ideas, and will allow those readers who are already familiar with his work to discover a new sense of its depths, its range, and its implications—perhaps almost as if reading Badiou for the first time.

The Seminars of Alain Badiou (1983–2016): General Preface

ALAIN BADIOU

The Seminars in English

It is a great pleasure for me to write this preface to the English-language edition of the entire collection of thirty years of my seminars. The information below is intended simply to shed some light on what these thirty years of public speaking have meant, to me and my various audiences, and why there may be some interest, or even pleasure, to be found in reading the seminars.

I. A Few Historical Reference Points

The word "seminar" should, in principle, refer to collective work around a particular problem. Instead, where these seminars are concerned, it refers to my own individual, albeit public, work on many different problems, all of which were nonetheless united by a philosophical apparatus explicitly claiming to be systematic.

Admittedly, the word "seminar" was already used in the latter sense with reference to Lacan's famous seminar, which, for me and many other people, has raised the bar very high when it comes to this sort of thing.

That a large part of my teaching took the form of such a seminar—whose ongoing publication in French, and now in English and Spanish, will show that it remained virtually free from any institutional authority—was originally due to pure chance.

At the beginning of the academic year 1966–67, while I was the senior class teacher at the boys' high school in Reims, I was appointed lecturer in an establishment that had just been created and that testified to the rapid expansion of higher education in the supremely Gaullist France of those years: the Collège universitaire de Reims, affiliated with the University of Nancy. Initially, only so-called propaedeutic [i.e., college preparatory] teaching was to be provided there (at the time, there was a first year of studies with that name, validated by a final exam that, if successfully passed, allowed students to begin their first year of university). So I was asked to teach the philosophy option in this preparatory year. But all of a sudden, thanks to one of those nasty betrayals so typical of academic life, the University of Nancy announced that, for the time being, it couldn't relinquish its philosophical powers to Reims and that there wouldn't be any philosophy option for the preparatory program to which my position was attached.

So there I was, a teacher of a nonexistent discipline. Given these circumstances, what else was there to do but hold an open seminar? And that's what I did for two years (1966–67 and 1967–68), before—I have to brag a bit here—an increasingly large audience and, what was even more flattering to me, one that was there out of pure interest since there was no final exam to reward their faithful attendance.

If I'd had the energy to look for my notes from that time long ago (when no one had either the idea or the means to bring in one of those big, clunky tape recorders to record my improvisations) and to revise those notes and turn them into a written text, I could have proudly begun this edition of the seminars with the one from 1966–67—fifty years of free speech!—, the year devoted to Schopenhauer, and then continued with the 1967–68 seminar, when my syllabus was focused on Mallarmé, Rimbaud, and Lautréamont, in that order. The *Chants de Maldoror*, however, which I had intended to begin dealing with in early May, was sacrificed on the altar of the mass movement.

And then, as a result of that May upheaval, which was to drastically change my life and my thinking about many issues other than academic appointments, I was appointed (since those appointments continued to be made nonetheless) Assistant Professor at the Experimental University of Vincennes, which soon became Paris 8.

The context in which I began teaching courses there was so feverish and politically so intense, the actions afoot there so radical, that the government decided that the philosophy degrees granted by Paris 8 would have no national accreditation! So there I was again, forced to give an open seminar since there was no state validation of our teaching efforts, despite the fact that they were highly innovative, to say the least.

This marginalization lasted for years. So—if, once again, the documentation really allowed for it—I could give an account of the free and open seminars of the 1970s, which, when all the exciting, frenetic collective action going on at the time allowed them to take place, were devoted in particular to the Hegelian dialectic, to Mallarmé again, to my beloved Plato, and to Lacan, always before audiences that were there out of pure interest alone, since there was no exam and therefore no academic credit to validate their attendance.

Actually, a synthetic account of that period does exist: my book *Theory of the Subject*, published by Seuil in 1982 under the editorship of François Wahl (English translation published by Continuum, 2009). It provides an admittedly very freely rewritten account of the seminars that were held between January 1975 and June 1979.

Beginning in those years, as a result of the so-called political normalization, things calmed down in the universities, even in the one in Vincennes, which had incidentally been moved to Saint-Denis. In the early 1980s, the government authorities decided that we of the glorious Department of Philosophy—where you could hear lectures by Michel Foucault, Michel Serres, François Châtelet, Gilles Deleuze, Jean-François Lyotard, and Jacques Rancière—deserved to have the national accreditation we'd lost gradually restored. It was from that time on, too, that the seminars began to be systematically recorded by several different attendees. Little wonder, then, that I decided to publish all of the seminars between 1983 and the present: for these thirty-odd years, abundant, continuous documentation exists.

Not that the locations, the institutions, and the frequency didn't change. Indeed, starting in 1987 the seminar moved to the Collège international de philosophie, which owed its creation in large part to the determined efforts of everyone in "living [i.e. non-traditional] philosophy" who felt put down and badmouthed by the University, Lyotard and Derrida being the two most emblematic names at the time. In that setting, I rediscovered the innocence of teaching without exams or validation: the seminar was now officially open and free of charge to everyone (for the reasons I mentioned above, it had actually always been so). It was held in the locales that the Collège secured or bargained hard to secure for its activities: the old École polytechnique on the rue Descartes, the École normale supérieure on the boulevard Jourdan, an industrial institution on the rue de Varenne, the Institut catholique on the rue d'Assas, and the main auditorium of the University of Paris 7 at Jussieu.

In 1998, when my seminar had been held under the auspices of the Collège international de philosophie for ten years, a crisis of sorts erupted: one faction of the Collège's administration viewed with suspicion both the form and the content of what I was doing. As far as the form was concerned, my status in the Collège was an exceptional one since, although I'd initially been properly inducted into it under Philippe Lacoue-Labarthe's presidency, I had never been officially re-elected as a member of the Collège. The content was viewed with suspicion because in those times dominated by the antitotalitarian ideology of human rights, rumors were going around that my teaching was "fascist." As I was unwilling to put up with such an atmosphere, I broke off my seminar midyear, thereby causing a lot of confusion.

I set it up the following fall at the École normale supérieure, where I'd been appointed professor. It remained there for fifteen years, which is pretty good, after all.

But this seminar was fated to always end up antagonizing institutions. I had to use the largest lecture halls at the ENS due to the sizeable audiences the seminar attracted, but at the start of the 2014 school year there was a dark plot afoot to deny me all access to those rooms and recommend that I accommodate around 250 people in a room that held only 80! After driving Lacan out, the prestigious ENS drove me out too! But, after all, I told myself, to suffer the same fate as Lacan was in its own way a glorious destiny. What happened to me next, however, can literally be called a "coup de théâtre," a dramatic turn of events. My friend Marie-José Malis, the outstanding theater artist and great renovator of the art of directing, was appointed artistic director of the Théâtre de la Commune in the Paris suburb of Aubervilliers. She offered to let me hold my seminar there, and I enthusiastically accepted. For two and a half years, in the heart of a working-class suburb, I stood on the stage before a full house and interspersed my final seminars, which were connected with the writing of my last "big" book, *L'Immanence des vérités*, with actual theatrical presentations. I was generously assisted in this by Didier Galas, who created the role of Ahmed in my four-play cycle, written in the 1980s and 1990s for the artistic and stage director Christian Schiaretti: *Ahmed the Subtle*, *Ahmed Gets Angry*, *Ahmed the Philosopher*, and *The Pumpkins*. On January 16, 2017, my Final Seminar took place in the Théâtre de la Commune in Aubervilliers, where pure philosophy, congratulatory messages, anecdotes, and theatrical productions all combined to celebrate the seminar's long history for one last time.

—•—

I'd always wanted the seminar to be for people who worked. That's why, for a very long time, it took place between 8 and 10 PM, on Tuesdays for a few years, on Wednesdays for probably twenty years, if not more, and on Mondays between 2014 and the time it ended in 2017, because theaters are dark on Mondays . . .

In these various places, there was a first period—five years, from 1987 to 1992—when the seminar had a feeling of spontaneity to it as it ran through philosophy's "conditions," as they're called in my doctrine: poetry, the history of philosophy (the first seminar on Plato's *Republic* dates back to 1989–90), politics, and love. It was over the course of those years, especially during the sessions on the rue de Varenne, that the size of the audience increased dramatically.

From 1992 on, I began putting together large conceptual or historical ensembles, which I treated over several consecutive years: anti-philosophy, between 1992 and 1996; the Subject, between 1996 and 1998; the twentieth century, between 1998 and 2001; images of the present time, between 2001 and 2004; the question of subjective orientation, in thought and in life, from 2004 to 2007. I dealt with Plato, from 2007 to 2010; then with the phrase "changing the world," from 2010 to 2012. The final seminar, which was held, as I mentioned above, in a theater, was entitled "The Immanence of Truths."

I should point out that, although it was a more or less weekly seminar at the beginning, it was a monthly one for all of the final years of its existence.

II. The Seminar's Form

As I mentioned at the outset, my seminar ultimately took the form of an ex cathedra lesson, the venerable old form known as the "formal lecture" [*cours magistral*]. But this was the outcome of a long evolution. Between 1969 and, let's say, the late 1980s, there were questions from the audience. It was obviously a lot easier to entertain questions in a room with 40 people at Vincennes than in a theater with 300. But it was also a matter of the time period. Initially at Vincennes, every "class" was a sort of steeplechase in which the hedges, which had to be jumped over elegantly and efficiently, were the constant hail of questions. It was there, as well as in the tumultuous political meetings I attended, that I learned how to stay unfailingly focused on my own thinking while agreeing with perfect equanimity to answer any question calmly, even if it was clearly a side issue. Like Claudel's God, I took crooked paths to reach my goal.

I must admit that, little by little, with the "normalization," I was able to rely on the audience's increasing unwillingness to listen to overly subjective rambling, rants with no connection to the subject under discussion, biased ideological assaults, complaints about not understanding or boasts about already knowing it all. Ultimately, it was the dictatorship of the masses that silenced the frenzied dialectic of interruptions without my having to change, on my own, my relationship with the audience. In the Jules Ferry auditorium at the ENS or in the Théâtre de la Commune, nobody interrupted anymore, or even, I believe, considered doing so, not out of fear of a stern refusal on my part but because the ambient opinion was no longer in favor of it.

I never ruled out having someone else come and speak, and thus, over time, I extended invitations to a number of people: François Regnault, to speak on theater; Jean-Claude Milner, to speak on

Lacan; Monique Canto, to speak on Plato; Slavoj Žižek, to speak on orientation in life, etc. These examples give you a sense of my eclecticism.

But in the final analysis, the seminar's form, solidly in place for about twenty-five years, remained by and large that of a one-man show. Session by session, I began with careful preparation, resulting in a set of lecture notes—I never really wrote out a seminar—that provided the basic outline, a few summary sentences, and the quotations or references used. Often, I gave out a handout containing the texts that I would read and comment on. I did this because my material was nothing like philosophical references in the traditional sense of the term. In particular, I had frequent recourse to the intellectual concentration that poetry allows for. Naturally, I also engaged in logico-mathematical formalism. However, it's very difficult to make extensive use of that resource before large audiences. I usually reserved it for another seminar, one that could be called arcane, which I held for a long time on Saturday afternoons and which contributed directly to my densest—and philosophically most important—books: *Being and Event* and *Logics of Worlds*. But for the time being there are no plans to publish these "other" seminars.

III. What Purpose Did the Seminar Serve?

It's hard for me to say in what respect my seminar was useful for people other than myself. What I noticed, however, was that its transmission of sometimes very complex subjects was of a different sort from that of my writings on these same subjects. Should it be said that the seminar was easier? That's not exactly the point. Clearly, philosophy has always combined oral activity and writing and has often privileged the oral over the written, as did its legendary founder, namely, Socrates. Even those—like Derrida—who promoted the primacy of writing were very careful never to overlook physical presence and the opportunities oral presentation provides for transference love, which Plato already theorized in his *Symposium*.

But I think that the oral presentation, as far as I myself and no doubt many attendees were concerned, conveyed the movement of thought, the trajectory of the investigation, the surprise of discovery, without having to subject them to the pre-established discipline of exposition, which is largely necessary whenever you write. It had the musical power of improvisation, since my seminar was not in fact written out. I met many seminar attendees who hadn't read my books. I could hardly commend them for it, obviously. But I understood that the thinking-on-the-spot effect of the oral presentation had become the most important thing to them. Because if the seminar "worked" as it should—which was naturally not guaranteed—the audience felt almost as if they themselves had thought up what I was talking to them about. It was as though all I'd done, in Platonic parlance, was trigger a recollection in them, whereas philosophical writing per se demanded sustained and sometimes unrewarding effort. In this respect, the seminar was certainly easy, but such easiness also left traces, often unconscious ones, of which attendees who thought they'd understood everything would have been wise to be wary.

For me, there's no question that the seminar served as a laboratory. I tested out ideas in it, either already established ones or even ones that emerged during my public improvisations, by presenting them from a variety of perspectives and seeing what happened when they came in contact with texts, other ideas, or even examples from contemporary situations in politics, art and public opinion. One of the great advantages of oral presentation is to be able to repeat without really boring your audience—which would be very difficult to do in writing—because intonation, movements, gestures, slight accentuations, and changes in tone give repetition enough charm to make it not just acceptable but even retroactively necessary. So the seminar went hand in hand with the inner construction of my thought, something Deleuze would have called the moment of invention of the concept, and it was like a partly anarchic process whose energy could later be captured by prose in order to discipline it and incorporate it into the philosophical system I've created, whose final, and I daresay eternal, form, is nonetheless the written form.

Thus, some of the seminars directly became books, sometimes almost immediately, sometimes later. For example, *Saint Paul: The Foundation of Universalism* (the 1995–96 seminar, published by Presses Universitaires de France in 1997; English translation published by Stanford University Press in 2006); *Wittgenstein's Antiphilosophy* (the 1993–94 seminar, published by Nous in 2009; English translation published by Verso in 2011); *The Century* (the 1998–2001 seminar, published by Seuil in 2005; English translation published by Polity in 2007). In all three of these cases, the content of the books is too similar to that of the seminars for there to be any need for the latter to be published for the foreseeable future.

But all the seminars are in a dialectic with books, sometimes because they exploit their effects, sometimes because they anticipate their writing. I often told my seminar attendees that I was without a doubt throwing myself on the mercy of their attention span (a two-hour seminar before such an audience is truly a performance), but that their presence, their degree of concentration, the need to really address my remarks to them, their immediate reaction to my improvisations—all of that was profoundly useful to my system-building efforts.

The complete set of volumes of the seminar may, in the long term, be the true heart of my work, in a dialectical relationship between the oral and the written. Only the readers of that complete set will be able to say. It's up to you now, dear reader, to whom every philosopher addresses himself or herself, to decide and pronounce your verdict.

Introduction to Alain Badiou's seminar *The One* (1983–1984)

KENNETH REINHARD

Alain Badiou's seminar of 1983–1984, *The One: Descartes, Plato, Kant*, is the earliest of his seminars that he has chosen to publish. He began delivering an annual lecture series in 1966 while teaching at a lycée in Reims; in 1969, when he became a professor at the newly created University of Paris 8 at Vincennes, the seminar shifted there.[1] The earliest seminars were largely investigations of specific concepts and figures in the history of philosophy, but the seminars of 1975–1979 provided the basis for his first major philosophical statement, *Theory of the Subject*, published in 1982. The seminar on the One continues lines of thought from *Theory of the Subject*, but it leans forward toward the publication in 1988 of *Being and Event*, which opens with a discussion of the One.[2]

Badiou's essential philosophical project is to establish a general theory of change: how does one state of being (a "situation") and the specific conditions of appearing that it supports (as a "world") change into another? The question of change, however, presupposes an ontology, a theory of the nature of the beings that change. Like Martin Heidegger, Badiou strives to free being from the normative grip of ontotheological metaphysics, which located being squarely under the sway of the One. In the opening meditation of *Being and Event*, Badiou describes the paradox of the one and the multiple that haunts philosophy: "Since its Parmenidean organization, ontology has built the portico of its ruined temple out of the following experience: what *presents* itself is essentially multiple; what presents itself is essentially one" (23). Our phenomenal experience is of a world of multiplicity: we perceive a plurality of different things, and every apparently single thing presents itself in the guise of many different elements, properties, and conditions. Is the truth of being, as Parmenides argued, its unchanging oneness, beneath or behind the appearance of its manyness? Is Leibniz right when he claims, in the famous statement that Badiou refers to in *Being and Event*, that "what is not *a* being is not a *being*"? For Badiou, this is a question that requires not an argument—for what prior certainty or evidence could it be based on?—but a decision. The decision in favor of the primacy of the One, produced by the convergence of the monotheistic traditions and certain readings of Parmenides and Plato, leads to the ontotheological framing of the world that, according to Heidegger, has concealed Being from human beings for more than two millennia. Badiou's decision is that "the one *is not*"—a decision, that is, in favor of the multiple, or "inconsistent multiplicity," as he will term the underlying strata of being as such. There is no fundamental particle of being: to be is to be multiple, and multiples are themselves multiples of multiples.

Nevertheless, a crucial function of oneness remains: in a formulation in *Being and Event* that he borrows from Lacan, Badiou insists that even though there is no One, "*there is* some Oneness" [*il y a de l'Un*]: "What has to be declared is that the one, which is not, solely exists as *operation*. In other words: there is no one, only the count-as-one" (24). To be human is to gather together elements of the inconsistent multiplicity and delimit such groupings—that is, to *count* them as a multiplicity of singular entities, or ones. In doing so, we produce "consistent multiplicities," or multiplicities of multiplicities-counted-as-one; moreover, it is only by positing such consistent multiplicities that we can retroactively apprehend the absolute inconsistency of being itself, since any presentation of inconsistent multiplicity will always already have counted it as one. To count the multiple "as one" is to enter into the symbolic order of structures; Badiou writes, "the generic essence of a structure is to count as one in given multiplicities and thereby to overcome apparent separations" (Session 1). Nietzsche's understanding of concept formation in his early essay "On Truth and Lies in a Nonmoral Sense" is another version of the function of the count-as-one: "Every concept arises from the equation of unequal things."[3] Counting-as-one is the fundamental yet undefined operation at the heart of set theory, and for Badiou it is the operation that gives any "situation" its consistency. So we begin with a crucial distinction: having decided that there is *no One*, that being is fundamentally multiple and inconsistent, and that the One is a theological belief masquerading as a philosophical concept, there is still the crucial conceptual operation of "counting-as-one" through which human beings collect and grant unity to some subsets of that multiplicity.[4]

Two years after delivering the seminar *The One*, Badiou launched a three-year sequence of seminars on the topic of being, beginning with a year on Parmenides. In the first session of that seminar, Badiou presents a brief recapitulation of *The One*, which clarifies the centrality of the concept of the subject in it, and the relationship of the subject to the count-as-one. Badiou argues that the essential object of philosophy is not being, as Heidegger claims, but the subject—as long as we understand the subject not as the "subject matter" of philosophy but as the object *cause* of philosophy, parallel to the way that Lacan describes the *objet a* not as the object "of" desire but as the object that *causes* desire. As Badiou argues, "philosophy's object, even in the absence of its signifier, is the subject" (Session 5). So the sessions here on Descartes, Plato, and Kant all involve discussions of the subject (or "the subjective process"), even in the case of Plato, where there is no explicit reference to such a concept. Here, in the opening of the *Parmenides* seminar, Badiou argues that the subject emerges out of the failure or undecidability of the count-as-one of being: "Basically, the subject-process assumes that something has not been counted as being, or that something has been subtracted from being counted as one. In other words, the mode of appearing of the lack-of-being [*manque-à-être*] is always subtraction from a count." Badiou borrows Lacan's expression "manque-à-être" to indicate that the conditions for a subject arise when something is missing in being—that is, in the terminology of *Being and Event*, when there has been an "event" in which the consistency of being in a situation has been rendered uncertain by the undecidable lack or excess of some element. For Lacan, "manque-à-être" refers to the lack instituted by castration as the structural condition of the neurotic subject, and for Badiou it is the failure to count as one that opens up the possibility of a "truth procedure" that investigates the connections between that ontological aberration and other elements in the surrounding situation. For Badiou, such a work of gathering and elaborating is the condition of possibility of a subject, which is the local instantiation of such a procedure, which is potentially infinite. Hence the count-as-one of being and its eventual failures are the conditions of a truth procedure, or a subjective process. And these truth procedures, which for Badiou will ultimately be four—politics, science, art, and love—are themselves the conditions, or the "cause," of philosophy.

1. Descartes

In this seminar, Badiou examines three philosophers whose thinking involves reflections, implicit or explicit, on the One: Descartes, Plato, and Kant. All three will be central to Badiou's work in the coming decades, but while Badiou's relationship with Kant's philosophy will be ambivalent, Descartes and especially Plato remain close to his heart, against the grain of much French philosophy in the second half of the twentieth century. Descartes once had a special place in French intellectual life, primarily for his rejection of all dogmatism and his naïve belief in experience. But in the wake of Heidegger's attacks on Descartes and the notion of the subject, anti-Cartesianism became increasingly dominant in Continental thought.[5] Badiou's positive account of Descartes owes much to Lacan, who regarded the Cartesian subject as the subject of science and the origin of the subject of psychoanalysis. Descartes's methodical doubt in his *Meditations* of all his previously held beliefs and experiences, leading finally to the one indubitable conclusion that there must be *someone* who is doubting, was often regarded as the triumphal establishment of the modern subject as self-conscious, as an "ego." For Lacan, however, the importance of Descartes's reflections lies in the difference or gap between the utterance "I think" and any statement or meaning such as "I am" that may be extrapolated from it: the subject is not a foundation or self-presence to be deduced from the fact that I cannot doubt that I am doubting; it is something that emerges momentarily in the discursive act of thinking only to immediately disappear. For Lacan, the Cartesian subject is punctual and evanescent, and the subject of psychoanalysis that he locates in that vanishing is intrinsically divided between the act of saying and the possibility of meaning. Badiou understands the essence of this Cartesian aperçu to be "*The point of truth is of the order of the event*" (Session 1). That is, the Cartesian vanishing point does not define a stable subject but an *event of subjectivation*, the sudden decompletion of being and knowledge in a world through which the possibility of a subject emerges. In psychoanalytic theory, this is when the imaginary wholeness of the body is shattered by castration anxiety, leaving a signifier of primal repression in its place. Such an event of momentary "subjectivation" may be followed by a "subjective process" in which the traces and implications of that primal wound expand into the more enduring and intractable structures of, for example, obsessive neurosis or hysteria.[6] It is only from the vantage of such a process that the event of subjectivation, whether understood as the performative utterance of the cogito or the inscription of a primal signifier, can be counted as one. Badiou understands this to be Descartes's true modernity: the introduction of the truth of an *event*, something punctual that transpires over time, in opposition to the truth of statements, or knowledge. This is one origin of Badiou's distinction between "being" and "event": for Badiou, the decision that there is no One implies that the work of ontology cannot be sutured to theology but belongs to *mathematics*, as the science of being as pure multiplicity; the "event," on the other hand, is "not of the order of being as such" but is a subtraction from or irruption within being. If for Descartes the cogito is the evental something-of-one that constitutes the subject as the foundation of all knowledge (with a little help from God), for Badiou the subject only emerges *after* the event, which is the condition of possibility of truths, and in the creative process of exploring its implications.

For Badiou, it is Descartes's movement from the subject of the cogito to God, the Other he sees as implied by the existence of the subject, that will be problematic. Like Descartes, Badiou thinks that another term is necessary for thinking: an event cannot mean or be anything in itself but only in relation to and from the perspective of the new linkages that will be made between it and elements of the world in which it occurs. But there can be no "sufficient reason" that links the two: Badiou sees the Other not as a being that is implied by the subject of the cogito but as a *place*, the locus of being, and the path followed through that place in the process of investigating the event's implications is undetermined and aleatory. In order to establish the possibility of real knowledge, Descartes connects the One of the subject and the One of God: "Descartes will suture the

Two to the One of the order of reasons; he'll stitch together these two existences—the 'I's' existence and God's existence—through the proof sequence. . . . The proof is very interesting because it will allow us to define what suturing is, namely, an operation aimed at thinking the Two as One" (Session 2). Badiou argues that "thinking the Two as One" via an imaginary suture is to eliminate the Two, to return to the primacy of the One, and thus to deny dialectics as such, in which the Two *precedes* the One, and any claim of Oneness must be divided into two. Moreover, Descartes's principle of sufficient reason, that everything (except God) has its cause, leaves no room for the causality of *lack*, which will be key to both Lacan's theory of the subject of desire and Badiou's account of mathematical ontology, which begins with no more than the empty set, the mathematical name of the void. For Badiou, this is not merely a formal question but also, and essentially, a *political* one: difference for Descartes is always a difference between beings, and this leads, according to Badiou, to ontological hierarchies, nonegalitarian conceptual orders of being. Badiou argues that egalitarian thinking requires both a nonessentialized account of difference and an account of the causality of lack, something akin to the Atomism of Lucretius (which Descartes rejected) for whom, Badiou writes, "atoms are hierarchically indistinguishable, of equal value as far as being is concerned, and what differentiates them causally is a disappearance, the *clinamen*" (Session 4). Nevertheless, while Descartes's account of the order of reasons involves a hierarchy of concepts, he makes no claims for a hierarchy of the world based on experience, and he provides no cosmologies; for Badiou, this makes him a profoundly original and still urgent thinker.

2. Plato

In the sessions of the seminar devoted to Plato, Badiou focuses on the *Sophist* and the *Parmenides*. Both Plato and Badiou regard Parmenides as the father of Greek philosophy, and both consider the sophists to be philosophy's greatest adversaries. But in the process of criticizing the sophists, Plato also seems to criticize Parmenides's assertions that being is One and that nonbeing simply is not and should not be entertained as a concept. According to Plato, the sophists use the power of rhetorical language to present the false as true and the true as false. But the fact that the false can be presented at all suggests that it must have some being—hence the division between being (as true) and nonbeing (as false) cannot be as clear as Parmenides would like. The philosopher can only combat sophistry by utilizing the concept and linguistic possibility of nonbeing, rather than denying it categorically. In the *Parmenides*, Plato problematizes the assertion of the Oneness of being by demonstrating the linguistic paradox it involves: if language names being, does it do so as something other than what it names? If we say yes, then we imply the Two; if we say no, then the name and the thing named are indistinguishable, and being is no more than a name, hence less than One. For Plato, Badiou argues, the paradox implies that there must be a *place* for being—not a geometrical space, but an intelligible topos or structure in which being is located: "The concept of the One necessarily implies the concept of the place for which there is One. As a result, the Parmenidean thesis is untenable because it purports to be exclusively punctual, to give the point without the place of the point" (Session 5). And if this is the case, then the One cannot be originary but is the result of the one as *placed*, that is, the count-as-one.

The concept of the Whole raises a similar problem for an ontology of the One: the whole implies that it is composed of parts. Hence if being is whole, then it is multiple, more than one; if it is not whole, then it is lacking something and is less than one. Badiou argues that the concepts of the One and the Whole work on different planes of signification, and their connection is not a correlation but, in a key concept from *Theory of the Subject*, a *torsion*, like a mobius strip twisting back onto itself; moreover, such a torsion is the topological condition of the subject—to return to a Lacanian vocabulary, this is the link between a primary signifier and all the other signifiers of a symbolic order. Thus, Badiou argues that Plato rejects both monism and dualism: being cannot be understood as a rigid One, but neither can it be regarded simply as Two, or even as radical multiplicity. Rather, Badiou shows that for Plato, being is what is *counted as one*, and this implies the concept of an intelligible place, of a structure of dialectical thought that allows being to be sayable—and capable of change. For Badiou, this notion of an intelligible place of being is located in Plato's theory of the "greatest kinds" (*megista gene*) in the *Sophist*, the five meta-forms, or what Badiou calls in Session 6 "the syntax of the Ideas": being, motion, rest, the same, and the other (or the different). These greatest kinds either combine with each other or don't, depending on the case; rest and motion are mutually contradictory and cannot be combined, while being and rest can. The other is distinct from being, according to Plato, but it exists in combination with or as the limit of all the greatest kinds, insofar as they are all other (or different) from each other; Badiou understands this as suggesting that Plato's notion of the other is something like an "empty class" or spectral "void" that is included everywhere but present nowhere.

Badiou uses Plato's concept of the other and his implicit critique of Parmenides's argument that being is One, without parts or gaps, to argue that being is made up of nothing more than the void itself—an argument he will develop in *Being and Event* and elsewhere.[7] And in a striking formulation, Badiou argues that the "ontological gesture" of counting the void as one is itself an event (Session 10).

The structure of the event is always of this sort: there is an unpresentable that's the index of being, and there is the count-as-one that's in a place. That's what an event is, and, of course, there is, strictly speaking, only the event. There's no point in saying that there is being. There is never anything but the Two, a Two constituted by the event (1) counted as one (2). . . . The nexus between the structure and the event is the fact that the event is the count-as-one of the unpresentable, therefore the Two, but that this Two is always counted as one. The structure is what counts the event as one. The formula of any structure is: two combine into one. One, on the other hand, divides into two, and this irreducible Two is always the count-as-one of the unpresentable.

The unpresentable void in being and at the heart of every situation is counted as one, or named (in the language of *Being and Event*) or it leaves a trace (in the terminology of *Logics of Worlds*).[8] It is an *event* for the void or the unpresentable to suddenly be counted and thus presented. Moreover, it is not that first there is "being" and then, occasionally, there are "events" that irrupt within it; rather, in Badiou's formulation here, structured being is constituted in the situated count-as-one of the event, which is itself the count-as-one of the unpresentable void. It is only from the vantage of structure, of course, that the event can be perceived as such, and once it has been counted in this way, it has already disappeared, leaving only the count, the name, the trace. Structured being is the count-as-one of two, as in the understanding of the dialectic as the "synthesis" of two into one. The event, on the other hand, involves the dialectic in which the one divides into two—the two of the unpresentable void and its count, naming, or trace—and thereby opens a fissure in being itself.[9] The event opens up the possibility of a truth procedure, insofar as the unpresentable void is *generic*, in the formulation that will become dominant in *Being and Event*—that is, it is everywhere present in the situation, and thus both anonymous and inseparable from its essential structure: "Whenever there is an event, a part that is universal, a part that's a part of everything in the whole, emerges in the structure" (Session 10). Thus, the event both exposes the underlying state of being of the situation and allows for an investigative procedure that can generate a new truth and the possibility of a new situation.

3. Kant

In the final part of the seminar, Badiou investigates the concept of the One and the subject in Kant, whom he regards as the beginning of the second phase of the modern thinking of the subject and the critical retroactivation (or, he suggests, the "deconstruction") of its Cartesian origins. Badiou argues that the system of Kant's three *Critiques* involves a pattern wherein the solution to one difficulty requires a split of faculties that itself calls for resolution, a way to recover the One (Session 13):

> Underlying the system of the three *Critiques* is that of a recovery of the One where the immediate solution of the problem had resulted in a split, a manifold of faculties. This movement of recovery is characteristic of the Kantian trajectory and of this thinking that divides, splits apart, discriminates, and immediately wonders how the One can be recovered in the element of this scission.

As we will see, in the first *Critique*, the necessity of dividing the supersensible from representation will itself be "counted as one" in the figure of what Kant calls "the transcendental unity of apperception," which Badiou describes as Kant's name for the subject as the trace left from the subtraction of supersensible being from its sensible representations.[10] Kant's crucial gesture, Badiou argues, is to desubstantialize Descartes's reified subject, and then to ask, what is the nature of the being of such a subject? For Kant, Descartes's "I think" cannot be understood as leading to the conclusion

"I am" if that implies *what* I am or any other knowable predication. The cogito as the "unity of apperception" is the transcendental condition of possibility of all experience but is itself empty and objectless. For Badiou, this is the "point of the real" of the subject, as opposed to the empirical experiences of the self that for Lacan are the "imaginary" aspects of the ego. Badiou argues, however, that it is also necessary to distinguish a third term, that of the transcendental "place": the symbolic structure from which the two of Kant's transcendental and empirical subjects are counted as one. Badiou points out that Kant's distinction between this transcendental point of consciousness and all empirical experience will open the history of philosophy's ongoing separation from its own psychologistic tendencies and is a condition of possibility for psychoanalysis.

One conventional narrative has it that for Descartes the subject is an ontological entity, whereas Kant's critical gesture is to desubstantialize the subject, to reduce it to a structure for the production of knowledge, at the expense of the noumenal "thing-in-itself" which is foreclosed from possible experience. This reading often leads to the rejection of Kant as an idealist thinker of the subject, unmoored from any materiality. But Badiou follows Heidegger in arguing that Kant's "fundamental question is the question of being, and that the movement of critique is itself a movement toward this question" (Session 12).[11] While it is true that the Kantian thing-in-itself, which Badiou calls "the existential index of representation," is not available to cognition, it is its condition of possibility and, as such, it can be *thought*. Thus, the transcendental place is not simply a logical system of categories but constitutes what Badiou calls an "onto-logic" where being is not formalized but presented as the *impasse* of logical formalization: "Being, which was subtracted, underpinned, *as subtracted*, the objectivity of the object" (Session 13). Badiou argues that this is Kant's implicit return to and extension of Parmenides's thesis of the reciprocity of being and the One: that which is counted as one is being insofar as it is subtracted from representation, in relation to the subject as void, empty point of apperception.[12] And Badiou poses the question, "Are subtraction and void the same thing? . . . Can the subtractive and the void really be counted as one?" (Session 13).

To respond to this question, Badiou shifts his attention to the *Critique of Practical Reason* and the question of freedom, which for Kant involves the relationship of the subject to the supersensible. Badiou points out that the connection between the supersensible subtracted from representation and the unity granted to representation by the count-as-one of the structural subject is how Kant will conceptualize the will and its formalization in the categorical imperative. Just as the first *Critique* limited the faculty of the understanding to knowledge of the object as it appears, as distinguished from the pure being of the thing-in-itself, so in the second *Critique* the exercise of freedom by means of a formal moral law excludes the possibility of knowledge or consideration of situational particularities or mitigating circumstances. To act freely, in accord with a law of reason, is to proceed lawfully but without the guidance of the understanding, which is limited to the sensible realm of nature. For Kant the will is *subtracted* from the transcendental categories, especially causality, and in this sense it is "unfettered, free will" (Session 14). Freedom, Badiou argues, is the way Kant strives to reconcile the split between the subject as void in representation, counted as one as "unity of apperception," and being as subtracted from representation, as noumenal "thing-in-itself"—that is, the way void and subtraction can be counted as one.

The gap between our knowledge of the natural world and the unknowable supersensible realm of things-in-themselves (as well as the three unknowable noumena: the soul, God, and the universe as a totality) is bridged by the possibility of moral action, which links supersensible being with sensible existence, attesting to the supersensible without producing any knowledge of it. Badiou argues that the third *Critique*, Kant's *Critique of Judgment*, is motivated by the question of whether the noumenality that exceeds representation in our experience of nature is the same as the noumenality that constitutes freedom in our practice of the moral law; that is, can they be counted as one? This cannot be done in terms of either knowledge of nature or our respect for reason and the moral law but occurs at the level of *feeling*, as experienced in aesthetic judgment: "Art can make me feel that certain sensible forms of nature, due to their purposive perfection, touch being as revealed by the moral law, and therefore freedom. That is why the work of art realizes the count-as-one of the supersensible: it is ultimately the key to general ontology" (Session 15). The pleasure connected with the sense of "purposiveness" in a judgment of the beautiful, Badiou argues, derives from an immediate experience of oneness within the heterogeneity of the sensible world, a higher purpose that links the being excluded from our sensible experience and the supersensible source of our practical existence.

The distinction between the One (that is not) and the count-as-one (as the perhaps definitive human operation) will continue to be central in Badiou's teaching and writing after this early seminar, as will discussions of Descartes, Kant, and especially Plato. Read this earliest of Badiou's published seminars, however, not only for the sake of finding the seeds of later discussions or to track the various modifications that emerge but also for the intrinsic pleasure and elucidation provided by its singular readings, breathtaking theorizations, and frequently astonishing offhand remarks. The great adventure of Badiou's seminars begins here!

About the 1983–84 Seminar on the One

ALAIN BADIOU

Between 1982, when *Theory of the Subject* was published, and 1988, when *Being and Event* appeared, my annual seminar was devoted almost exclusively to the study of texts from the great tradition that constitutes the history of philosophy, which was at the time, and largely still is today, the backbone of the academic teaching of our discipline. The purpose of this wide-ranging investigation was to consolidate the construction of a number of fundamental concepts of my ontology as expounded in *Being and Event*. This is how Parmenides, Malebranche, and Heidegger, the subjects of three seminars from 1985 to 1987 that have already been published,[1] contributed (unwittingly!) to my mathematical and subtractive theory of being qua being. Before then, in 1984–85, I had focused on Aristotle, Spinoza, and Hegel to introduce the concept of Infinity, which has since continued to play a key role in my thinking. That seminar will be published in the fall of this year (2016). Finally, in 1983–84, drawing on Descartes, Plato, and Kant, I had reflected on the One, a concept I intended to show should be divested of its metaphysical preeminence and reduced to an operation I have called "the count-as-one."

Over the course of those few years, I gave an oral account of a kind of voyage through the history of philosophy. It was quite comprehensive in a way, since it dealt with the great thought of antiquity (Parmenides, Plato, and Aristotle), with French Classicism (Descartes and Malebranche), and with the German tradition (Kant, Hegel, and Heidegger).

What I am presenting here is the very first seminar in this series, the seminar on the One, dating back more than thirty years. The text, meticulously edited by Isabelle Vodoz, is the result of an effort that was all the more remarkable in that it presented serious challenges: the primary sources were rare and incomplete, whereas the often highly technical nature of the arguments required implacable precision. Furthermore, it was necessary to find the versions of the foundational texts by Descartes, Plato, and Kant that were used at the time.

What is the seminar about? It is about putting to the test the central metaphysical concept, the One, which usually connotes the existence of God, and replacing it with the operation called "the count-as-one," which is now just a particular and secondary determination of the multiple. It is therefore a critical step on the path that has led me to an ontology of the multiple "without-One," or inconsistent multiple.

I begin with Descartes because he inaugurated his thinking with a radical shift in the point of departure: it is no longer being but the Subject, no longer transcendence but the pure, indisputable immanence of the "I am." In other words, Descartes reduces the original certainty to a mere point of existence, experienced negatively as resistance to doubt. Using my terminology, we could say that Descartes attempts to base his whole project on the fact that *we can count on the One of the thinking subject*, in both senses of "to count": it's a simple point counted as one, and on this One we can count in order to move forward to both the transcendence of God and the existence of the world. The path thus leads from the count-as-one to the One.

After Cartesian existential certainty, I examine Plato's conceptual uncertainties about the One—namely, the mind-boggling pirouettes of the *Parmenides* dialogue, expressly devoted to the One, and the trenchant assertions of the *Sophist*, where the question of the One, though more indirect, is no less central. From all this I derive the justifications for what will be one of the fundamental tenets of my ontology: *the One is not, there is only the count-as-one.*

I reserve special treatment for Kant, for the following reason: I think the move from one *Critique* to another (from scientific knowledge to morality and from morality to aesthetics) always stems from *having to count as one what was previously separated in a seemingly definitive way.* Thus, the *Critique of Pure Reason* guarantees a certain type of universality to scientific statements about phenomena but blocks all access to the supersensible. The *Critique of Practical Reason* provides access to the supersensible, but only so long as nothing sensible is involved, or acts as a cause, in this access. Only the *Critique of the Power of Judgment* manages to count as one the sensible and the supersensible, science and morality, the law of true cognition and that of right action without subsuming them under the One.

Thus, this historical exploration leads to a strict distinction between what we assume to be One and what we can know is counted as one. The most important axiom is contained in this distinction: being, as such, is pure multiplicity; it does not participate in the One, except that it is still, locally, counted as one. This count is empirical when it is only a mode of presence of the multiple. It is rational when it concerns a generic multiplicity—the type of multiplicity that, since it has a universal value, deserves to be called truth.

But that's a different story, which, in 1983, had only just begun.

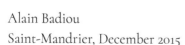

Alain Badiou
Saint-Mandrier, December 2015

The One: Descartes, Plato, Kant

Session 1

November 11, 1983

A s far as the question of the subject is concerned, roughly three ages of modern philosophical thought can be distinguished. The first one explicitly articulated the notion of the subject as the primary referent of modern thought. Remember that this articulation, which occurred in the seventeenth century, is unthinkable outside the context of the Scientific Revolution. Indeed, the modern notion of the subject developed on the basis of what Koyré and others studied, namely, the break with the hierarchical and stable view of the universe, which led to the representation of the world becoming unstable and infinite.[1] This intellectual moment linked a break in the representation of the world with the emergence of the concept of subject as such. It was therefore a decentering/recentering movement. The image of the universe was decentered; its hierarchical consistency was undermined, and the concept of subject rearranged the representation of the world by recentering it on subjective experience. Descartes proposed the first systematization of this movement. He thus ushered in the modern age of philosophy: his work was truly a revolution in philosophy.

The second modern age of the question opened with Hegel. He included *historicity* in the notion of the subject, whereas the

Cartesian concept of the subject was transhistorical. This work began prior to Hegel, with Rousseau, for example. And its completion was contemporary with the political revolution of the years 1789–1794, just as Cartesianism had been contemporary with the Scientific Revolution.

As for us, we are contemporary (at least we can assume as much) with the third modern age of the question of the subject, a period whose contours are not yet completely clear. We are contemporary not with a political revolution but with a revolution *of* politics, with a new foundation of politics, which is establishing an unprecedented relationship between politics and history.

In the context of this periodization, the text by Descartes that you have before you is an inaugural one since it represents the charter, as it were, of the first modern period. Within Descartes's own work, it is moreover the inaugural text of this inauguration. Let me read it to you.

THE NATURE OF THE HUMAN MIND, AND HOW IT IS
BETTER KNOWN THAN THE BODY

[1] So serious are the doubts into which I have been thrown as a result of yesterday's meditation that I can neither put them out of my mind nor see any way of resolving them [. . .]

[2] Archimedes used to demand just one firm and immovable point in order to shift the entire earth; so I too can hope for great things if I manage to find just one thing, however slight, that is certain and unshakeable.

[3] I will suppose then, that everything I see is spurious. I will believe that my memory tells me lies, and that none of the things that it reports ever happened. I have no senses. Body, shape, extension, movement and place are chimeras. So what remains true? Perhaps just the one fact that nothing is certain.

[4] Yet apart from everything I have just listed, how do I know that there is not something else which does not allow even the slightest occasion for doubt? Is there not a God, or whatever I may call him, who puts into me the thoughts I am now having? But why do I think this, since I myself may perhaps be the author of these thoughts? In that case am not I, at least, something? But I have just said that I have no senses and no body. This is the sticking point: what follows from this? Am I not so bound up with a body and with senses that I cannot exist without them? But I have convinced myself that there is absolutely nothing in the world, no sky, no earth, no minds, no bodies. Does it now follow that I too do not exist? No: if I convinced myself of something then I certainly existed. But there is a deceiver of supreme power and cunning who is deliberately and constantly deceiving me. In that case I too undoubtedly exist, if he is deceiving me; and let him deceive me as much as he can, he will never bring it about that I am nothing so long as I think that I am something. So after considering everything very thoroughly, I must finally conclude that this proposition, *I am, I exist*, is necessarily true whenever it is put forward by me or conceived in my mind.[2]

This passage is from the Second Meditation. *Meditations on First Philosophy* was published in 1641, in Latin. It was translated by the Duc de Luynes as soon as it was published, and this translation was approved by Descartes, who made only a few alterations to it. The publication in French dates from 1647.

The linguistic status of this text is interesting in itself, since even here there's a side effect. Prior to this, there was only one philosophical language, Latin. So this text also marked a new linguistic age of philosophy, its national age. In a place that had heretofore been insulated from the national dimension of thought there emerged the need, which Descartes accepted, to consider the French text as the true one. Philosophy would thereafter be written in national languages, even though some works would remain in Latin even in philosophies of the eighteenth century. So this was a kind of linguistic manifesto, which assigned philosophy the right, and increasingly the duty, to be written in the mother tongue, the national language, and thus to entertain a new relationship with universality. Moreover, from then on, to gain access to philosophical systems written in foreign languages would mean to be increasingly faced with the very complicated problem of the meaning and scope of translations.

There are six Meditations, and Descartes summarized them in a sort of preface that he entitled "Synopsis of the following Six Meditations." This is what he says about the Second Meditation: "In the Second Meditation, the mind uses its own freedom and supposes the non-existence of all the things about whose existence it can have even the slightest doubt; and in so doing the mind notices that it is impossible that it should itself not exist during this time." (2:9)

So it's a question of the freedom to deny, and this freedom proves to be the original principle on the basis of which a question of existence is decided.

It has often been noted that something about the conclusion of the passage (the existence of the mind) presupposes itself (in the form of the freedom of this mind). To get to the "I exist," you have to be in the element of the full use of freedom and therefore of its existence. It is the mind, using its freedom, that determines that it is impossible for it not to exist. It is consequently from the subject's existence in freedom that the statement of its own existence stems: the approach moves from existence to existence. Strictly speaking, the "I exist" can only be a conclusion of itself.

There is a second point, which is important for anyone with even a minimally Lacanian ear. Descartes says that the mind realizes that it is absolutely impossible for it itself not to exist. So it's in the form of an invocation of the impossible that something of the existent appears. It's only in *this* existence alone—that of the (subject's) mind—that Descartes finds a point of the real that can be asserted as such. Based on which symbolic order is there a move here from the impossible to the real? This is an extremely difficult question.

Next comes something having to do with strategy:

> But since some people may perhaps expect arguments for the immortality of the soul in this section, I think they should be warned here and now that I have tried not to put down anything which I could not precisely demonstrate. Hence the only order which I could follow was that normally employed by geometers, namely to set out all the premises on which a desired proposition depends, before drawing any conclusions about it. (2:15)

Descartes gives us two pointers here. The first is tactical and shows his awareness of the revolutionary nature of his doctrine. As an impetuous yet cautious man, he implements a system of precautions. No way was he going to get into trouble like Galileo. It is well known that he would sometimes even forgo publishing (his *Treatise on the World*, for example), and he took refuge in Holland and Sweden. Here, then, he warns us that he won't be dealing with the immortality of the soul. This tactical concern anticipates any religious, that is to say statist, objection.

The second pointer concerns a point of method. A certain order, based on mathematics, will be followed, and so the importance of things won't be presupposed, only their sequence. It's an order in which things follow one another in a deductive way. This is the famous distinction, presented in a letter to Father Mersenne, between the order of topics and the order of reasons. Already in 1641, then, Descartes writes that he will follow the order of reasons and not that of topics. It's important to note that it is here that the idea of the break with the hierarchical vision slips in. Indeed, all objects are subjected to the order of reasons, and their preeminence of being should not be taken into account. This tactical precaution already implies that more important, or even sublime, objects (God, for example) themselves remain linked to the order of reasons, whose paradigm is mathematical.

Freedom ∧ Order of reasons So let's bear in mind these two main ideas: freedom, as the original practical dimension of philosophy, and the order of reasons, which frees us from the hierarchy of beings.

The essence of freedom is the negative, which is very modern. It is the ability to deny. At the heart of the approach there is negativity itself. The same idea is found in the letter to Father Mesland that dates from February 1645: "For it is always open to us to hold back from pursuing a clearly known good, or from admitting a clearly perceived truth, provided we consider it a good thing to demonstrate the freedom of our will by doing so" (3:245).

Thus, it is always possible to deny a good, even a clearly known one. This affirmation of freedom is for Descartes a principle higher than moral values and those of knowledge, higher than both the good and the true. This is a complete break with the Greek classical view: remember that for Plato no one is deliberately evil; evil is always ignorance. Descartes, however, says that evil and falsity are not necessarily errors; the Good has no authority in itself, and we have the freedom to deny it. He thus puts forward a radical principle of negative freedom, which, at the time, constituted an enormous break.

Father Mesland had very serious concerns about this, and he pressed Descartes on how his philosophy could be compatible with Christ's presence in the host, an issue that, truth be told, he had a lot of trouble fitting into the order of reasons. Descartes in fact asserted that he could prove that the materiality of a thing was its extension, in the geometric sense of the term. As a result, it had no qualitative principle. This reduction of everything to its spatiality necessarily raised the problem of Christ's, and therefore the Holy Spirit's, presence in a thin piece of wheat. Before Descartes, and in the language of Aristotle, what was referred to was formal presence: Christ was present as a form, of which the host was only the spatial surface, i.e., matter. But the form/matter opposition was not part of Descartes's demonstrative toolkit. So in the correspondence with Father Mesland we can see Descartes using all his cunning to assert indirectly what could not be asserted according to the order of reasons. The cunning was moreover sincere, since everything suggests that Descartes was a good Catholic—albeit a good Catholic who defended the preeminence of subjective freedom, the absolute and foundational authority of negativity.

Descartes's point of departure is in the context of two things, the subject and its place. In his eyes, freedom is truly infinite: as the power to say no, nothing can restrict it, not even God. Freedom is formally infinite, whereas a particular free act is always finite. This point involves the whole approach since it leads to the possibility of doubting everything. As for the second principle, the order of reasons: things should be arranged in philosophy according to a demonstrative order that has nothing to do with a "real" order, which is presumed to be hierarchical.

As a result, we find as the latent cause of Descartes's text these two things: freedom, which is not restricted by any value, and the order of reasons, which is immanent. The *Meditations* is based on this double principle of rupture, and Descartes embarks on an enterprise as far as possible from a phenomenology—by which I mean as far as possible from a description or an investigation of experience. The practical operator of the rupture is freedom, its theoretical operator, the mathematical order. So, even before things begin, we've got something like a dialectics of the subject (negation) and its place (necessity, reflected in the order of reasons).

The order of reasons presupposes that the problem of the beginning will be resolved. An initial point of certainty is absolutely necessary, and this point cannot itself be deduced. In other words, this first point can't come from the order of reasons. Where can it come from? There's no alternative but to bring the other principle, the infinite nature of freedom, into play, in the guise of something that would impede it. Paradoxically, having posited freedom as unrestricted, I can only find my first "real" term in the form of a restriction. Thought will come up against the power of negation *as a real point that restricts it*, a point to which I will relate everything. We absolutely must have an obstacle that's indisputable.

For the experiment to be conclusive, the exercise of my negative freedom must be total (the first principle), and I must therefore adopt an attitude of absolute doubt. It is only on the basis of the decision to deny everything that the point of the real can emerge as an obstacle: *from denial as All, I hope to infer the One as real.* So we're dealing with a dialectic of the One and the All: the All of doubt and the One of the obstacle.

Freedom will be brought to bear on the complete doubting of the contingent multiple (the existing world), a denial from which I will expect the One, which will therefore be necessary. This is what Descartes will call, in the very first paragraph, the "immovable point." And he presents his approach with a reference to Archimedes and the legendary tradition according to which Archimedes supposedly said, in essence, that if he were given an immovable point and a lever, he could move the world.

This signifier, "Archimedes," is of the utmost importance, the reasons for which can be found in Galileo, Descartes, and other mathematical thinkers of the time. Four reasons can be given for this.

1. The whole latter part of the sixteenth century and the beginning of the seventeenth were marked by a great revival of interest in mathematics, signaling its rebirth, and in the Greek belief in its paradigmatic nature, in its value as an incentive, as a model, which made it the means of salvation for all rational thought. Archimedes obviously exemplified that trend.

2. Then there was the actual content of Archimedes's work: the calculation of surfaces, the determination of tangents, and so on. This was the most valuable contribution Antiquity could make in this connection.

3. Even more important was the birth of mathematical physics in the seventeenth century. Galileo's idea was that, since the world was written in a mathematical language, theory, too, should be mathematical. Archimedes had touched on this question in the form of static mechanics (the lever, the immovable point).

4. Archimedes is a textbook example of the relationship between a scientist and history because he was an ambiguous, contradictory figure. On the one hand, he was a patriot who helped defend Syracuse against the Romans and used his scientific knowledge to develop war machines. So he was a committed scientist, a man of his time, a man of the world. But, on the other hand, he was also the figure of someone who, in defiance of history, was engrossed in science. Indeed, the legend of his death has it that, absorbed in drawing geometric shapes in the sand, he wouldn't give way to a Roman soldier, who then supposedly killed him. This story really captures the tension felt by the seventeenth-century philosophers in their relationship to history and the state. That relationship was characterized by a double tendency that combined a principle of engagement, including science, with a principle of withdrawal wherein intellectuality was asserted for its own sake. Archimedes combines these two images of modernity.

Descartes's argument will therefore be Archimedean, even in terms of its similes and metaphors.

That said, what is the big difference between Descartes and Archimedes with respect to the method? We should bear in mind that the Greek mathematicians—just think of Euclid—begin with a number of statements (the axioms) that are held to be self-evident. Cartesian freedom, however, cannot be restricted by any statement. If the statements are understood as denoting a relationship or a property, then none can stem the power of doubt. What is primary won't be any particular axiomatic statement but the enunciation itself.

We'll ask: is even belief in mathematical statements suspended? The answer is yes. Descartes suspends belief in them in the First Meditation.

But how does Descartes call them into doubt? Well, he needs a big Other for that, a powerful God who deceives him. The calling into doubt isn't direct, since freedom doesn't mean thinking that $2 + 2 = 4$ is false. It can, however, be done through the mediation of the deceiving big Other: freedom can assume that the fact that I can't doubt that $2 + 2 = 4$ is itself a trick. The mathematical statement is seemingly binding, but I can believe that the impossibility of not believing it is itself an error. So my freedom bears on the subject itself: if, in experiencing that a statement is binding, I can be tricked *as a subject*, my freedom may conclude from this that it is possible to suspend all constraint. To be sure, the mathematical order of reasons constrains freedom. But Descartes reflects on this constraining character so as to allow freedom to circumvent it by denying the absolute subjective value of a constraint. Indeed, God's freedom is not constrained by mathematics. So it may be through deception that a God constrains my own freedom to obey mathematics.

We can refer here to a passage from the First Meditation: "[God may have brought it about that] I go wrong every time I add two and three or count the sides of a square, or in some even simpler matter, if that is imaginable" (2:14, trans. modified). So there is a split in the concept of freedom: to extend my freedom to infinity, the mediation of an even more infinite freedom than my own is required. Something of the "I" always refers to the Other. The principle of the infinity of freedom is itself a split principle: it is only through its splitting that it is constituted as truly absolute and insofar as my freedom can conceive of God's freedom as even more absolute than the system of constraints imposed on it.

My immovable point, my original truth, therefore, cannot be a statement. You can see that the approach is neither Archimedean nor Euclidean since there is neither a primal statement nor an axiom. The point from which this discourse originates isn't a statement; it may be a chimera (says Descartes). The problem for him, then, is what a "discourse that would not be pure semblance" (the title of one of Lacan's seminars) would be. This is a very radical framing of the problem. The totality of the statements might be pure semblance since any statement can be invalidated by the method of doubt. Therefore, the point of the One, my original truth, is prediscursive; it is prior to the general sphere of statements, which is undermined in its entirety by doubt. The point of the One is necessarily of the order of the immediate and does not tolerate the mediation of the statement. The totality of what is mediated, the whole of the statements, may be pure semblance. Only something extradiscursive can act as a limit to the fictional and to meaning. And what is this immediacy? It's the act of fictionalization itself. In Lacanian terminology we'd say: the point that prevents the discourse from being entirely semblance is the process of semblancing. The act by which the All ends up as fiction is the subtractive One of the fictitious.

"Am not I, at least, something?" asks Descartes in the Second Meditation. The problem is what this category of "something" might be. The calling of everything into doubt had posited that there is nothing, that nothing that is sayable exists. It had posited that no "thing" exists. What is thought here as "something," which is, is pure, unqualifiable, unsayable existence, with respect to which no statement is possible. It is the existence of that for which there is nothing. The central statement might be put like this: "I cannot be nothing given that I think there is nothing." It is this "I cannot be nothing" that Descartes calls "something." The "something" that

I am is the only possible point of excess over nothingness, that is, the expression of nothingness.

You could say that "thought" is already much too much; it would give an intellectual quality to this something. Descartes is aware of this. "Thought," as he uses it here, is simply the immediate. It's not the thinking of something as knowledge; it doesn't fill the existential void of the "I am." In the letter he wrote to Father Gibieuf in 1642, Descartes uses the phrase "my own thought or awareness" (3:201). There's no intellectual quality in it, no specifiable operation, but rather a pure immediacy of presence to self, pure awareness. We can also read, in the *Principles of Philosophy* this time: "By the term 'thought,' I understand everything which we are aware of as happening within us, in so far as we have awareness of it" (1:195). Thought is everything that exists in us *subject to immediacy*. Having doubted everything through the operation of freedom, I thus hit a point that acts as a limit. But this point is empty, in the sense that it is unqualifiable, in eclipse behind any possible statement, and thus its only determination is that it exists.

Here we find the Lacanian distinction between statement and enunciation, which, in a way, structural linguistics borrowed from Descartes. I can call into doubt any statement provided that the statement (in the sense of the said) is actually enunciated (in the sense of the saying), provided that there is an enunciation (which, for its part, exists) of this statement. The point of the real is the enunciation. I can say: in statements no truth circulates, but there is the enunciation, I exist, I who doubt, who express doubt. In the enunciation there is nothing, there is vanishing as the pure existence of the subject, unqualifiable, unsayable, which Descartes refers to as "I am, I exist."

Nowhere do we find the dictum "I think, therefore I am," the customary capsule summary of Descartes's thought. But what Descartes does say is that "this proposition" ("I am, I exist"), "every time I utter it," guarantees the truth of the "I am." As long as I utter that I am,

"I am." This proposition is true every time I utter it, but Descartes absolutely does not say that it is true in and of itself. It is only true in the simultaneity with its utterance.

The "I think, therefore I am," was the putting into statement form of what was a truth of enunciation. The enunciation is the preventing of the semblance of the statements. Hence Lacan's assertion that the subject he is speaking about, or the one Freud speaks about, is precisely this empty point where the enunciation is articulated. Lacan repeats that the subject is Descartes's, the subject in eclipse behind any and all statements, the empty point on the basis of which there is a statement, whether it can be called into doubt or not. You can refer to *The Seminar: Book XI* and to the essay "Science and Truth" in *Écrits*, where Lacan has this to say: "I took my lead last year from a certain moment of the subject that I consider to be an essential correlate of science, a historically defined moment, the strict repeatability in experience of which perhaps remains to be determined: the moment Descartes inaugurates that goes by the name of *cogito*. This correlate, as a moment, is the defile of a rejection of all knowledge."[3] Lacan reads Freud's fidelity to Descartes in the rupture between Freud and Jung. Jung wanted to endow the subject with a certain number of substantial depths, origin narratives, constituent myths. But the Cartesian subject, to which Lacan lays claim in the name of Freud, has no depth, and any depth attributed to the subject is spurious. The subject is fleeting and vanishing.

At this point the problems begin. How can this pure existentiality fall under the category of truth? What recovery of truth is possible from the pure "I exist"? And since the destiny of all truth is knowledge, which is set out in statements, the statement will have to be recovered from the enunciation. These are the problems facing Descartes.

Let me ask a first, very simple question: what statement is related to the enunciation as such? If I don't solve this problem, I'll fall into radical skeptical existentialism. Descartes, moreover, mentions such a possibility: the first statement of the enunciation he gives is "I am, I exist." From the standpoint of linguistics, it is enunciative, even performative, which is to say that its meaning is intrinsically bound up with its utterance and it cannot be assessed apart from its utterance. I refer you to J. L. Austin's book *How to Do Things with Words* on this issue. It's precisely because it's "performative" that Descartes is careful to say that the statement is true at the time it is uttered. It's a meaningless statement apart from its position in reality. But then in what sense can such a statement be said to be true? I mean obviously true, in the absence of truth criteria, of external guarantees of its truth. The answer is necessarily this: *The point of truth is of the order of the event.* When there is the effective event of its utterance, the statement "I am" produces an intersection of the real and the enunciation. It is a matter here of truth as event, hence strictly punctual, in the empty form of a *point of truth.*

So let me rephrase the problem. How can truth as event tolerate truth circulating in discourse? How can truth as event sanction truth as discursive circulation (since there needs to be an order of reasons)? Descartes immediately turns to this problem in the rest of the text: "But I do not yet have a sufficient understanding of what I am, even as I am certain that I am" (2:17, trans. modified). The "what" I am is the open question of a statement for the "I am." Knowledge is dead because my infinite freedom has invalidated it; the "I am" is embedded within this death, the enunciative bedrock of this death. The "what" is the recovery of the statement, that is, the revival of dead knowledge

So, based on the truth-event of the "I am," I will have to distribute truth to statements of the "what I am" type. It is therefore the problem of connecting subjectivation with the subjective process.[4] How can pure, empty subjectivation be given substance or qualities such that something can be said about it? This is the most dangerous step for any doctrine of the subject. It will take Descartes no less than the whole rest of the *Meditations* to answer this tricky question.

In a very general way, the question is what the enunciation can found in terms of the statement or, even more generally, what an event can found in terms of being. Between the "I am" and the "what I am" there is the whole relationship between truth as event and truth as statement, between the thing that happens and the thing that I speak about insofar as it is. The underlying conflict will be between being and event, and for Descartes it's the conflict between "I [am]" and "what I [am]."

Here, in advance, is what our own framework will be.

1. Being qua being, that is, understood in terms of what can be said about being, is in my view said by mathematics, which is the historically constituted system of ontology. The problem for Descartes is that he rejects mathematics at the beginning, does not begin with it, does not assume its axioms, does not begin with ontology. Descartes's modernity lies in his introducing the evental radicality of the enunciation into philosophy. But it is part of the essence of the Cartesian method not to begin with ontology. And this is very difficult, indeed problematic. I see a sign of it in the fact that to reject mathematics he needs a fiction as cumbersome and dubious as that of a deceiving God.

2. The event is not of the order of being as such; it is neither mathematical nor mathematizable. It is a specific category to which historicity, which has no being (history does not exist), is attached. Ontology says nothing about the event.

3. There are disciplines of thought and practice that deal very precisely with what an event is in terms of the being that it is not. On what being is the fact that there is this event based? What is the place, the destiny of being, of this event? They are disciplines whose content is the dialectic of an event with being: the nonmathematical rigorous sciences, art, and politics (including ethics). We will call

these three disciplines (sciences, art, politics) "discursive systems of the event." As for philosophy, it refers to the general dialectic of being and event as the doctrine of the Subject. It has, as a conditioning practice, as a referent, all the foregoing, i.e., mathematics (ontology) and the three types of discursive systems.

That will be our general framework.

We're now going to look at the approach taken by Descartes to move from the performative statement "I am" to that embryonic knowledge, "what I am." This is the first step in the order of reasons. It's a very unusual approach. We'll see how he manages to reconstruct knowledge from its void, from its vanishing point—to reconstruct plenitude from absence.

For this, as I mentioned, Descartes actually needs a second immovable point: the big Other, which is to say, God. He needs a second existence. This is only natural since, for meaning to emerge, the Two is needed; the One isn't enough. Meaning always involves betweenness. And here we need something actually in between, that is, a second existence. Descartes needs an Other about whom there's a nonperformative judgment: God exists. The statement cannot be that of an "I"; rather, it must be ex-centered in relation to the "I." A positing of the infinite, a predicative positing, is required: the infinite exists. To move from the absolute finitude of the "I am" to a description of this point, it is imperative that the infinite exist. Clearly, this is an extraordinary and yet perfectly rational leap: if finitude provided for it, we'd have a seamless transition from one to the other.

The same problem can be found in set theory. We've got two axioms, the empty set and the infinite set. Both are necessary. It's very Cartesian. Descartes does the same thing: he posits the void, this unqualifiable "I," immediate existentiality, and he posits the

infinite, thanks to which he has a theoretical space that can be constructed, hence an order of reasons. If you assume that the origin
is the empty set, the pure point of existence, the only way out is
through the infinite.

What, then, is the antidialectical side of Descartes? Well, it's that
he tries to infer the second immovable point from the first, that
he believes he can infer the "God exists" from the "I am" and thus
do away with the inaugural nature of the Two. Descartes refuses
to accept the axiom of dialectical thought, which is that the Two
always precedes the One. We've got to admit that, here, Descartes
fails with respect to any real logic of the subject.

Next time, using another text, we'll see how, through this very
failure, he nonetheless touches a real again, albeit under the sway of
misrecognition.

Session 2

December 6, 1983

I want you to have a clear understanding of my thesis regarding the revolutionary dimension of Descartes. It's not because he speaks about the subject. For, as we'll see with Plato, in philosophy, even when there is apparently nothing remotely resembling a theory of consciousness, a theory of the subject—as is obvious in Greek philosophy, for instance—this absence can be retrospectively understood as indicating the site of such a process or of its operators. I am putting forward the radical thesis that in a certain way the subject has always been philosophy's object.

However, in its explicit form, in the emergence of what might be called the subject point as originary, there is without question a Cartesian revolution, a Cartesian inauguration, the opening of a new age. And that's why I am beginning with him. The path from Descartes to Lacan won't be straightforward because there will be some backtracking starting from this point, in particular to illustrate what I said, namely that the operators of the subject can be seen, even in the philosophies where the question of the subject has not been formulated as such.

That said, where were we? We were considering a very difficult problem, namely, how, from the empty point of enunciative truth (the "I am" that's identical to the time of its utterance), can we reconstruct the truth of at least some statements, subjected to the order of reasons? To put it another way: how can we recover the possibility of knowledge from a fleeting certainty? If we don't, we'll lapse into what might be called an existential skepticism. There would be pure existentiality (the enunciation) but no statement. It would be impossible to go beyond the "I am," the empty real point of the enunciation since the statements remain suspended by their having been called into doubt. Yet, since Descartes is in no way a skeptic, his programmatic task, starting with the cogito, is the reconstruction of knowledge, but a knowledge in truth, in the sense that "in truth" would mean a knowledge henceforth entirely in the element of truth. It must be a certain knowledge—"certainty" here meaning the element of truth in which knowledge will be reconstructed—a knowledge this time inaccessible to doubt.

Last time I said that the first step in this reconstruction of knowledge in Descartes's project was the move from the "I am" to the "what I am." If I'm capable of moving from "I am" to "what I am" without losing the element of truth, I will have taken the first step, which, as everyone knows, is the hardest. Only, how hard *is* this first step? Very hard—it's nothing short of God. I need God for this first step, so it's the hardest step of all. This means that I need a big Other that will be the place of the guarantee in truth of knowledge. I need, as we anticipated last time, a second existence.

Let's summarize the operation. I move from the empty existence of the pure "I am," without any content or determinations, to "what I am," the first step in my reconstruction of knowledge, through the mediation of a second existence, in the position of the big Other, which is God's position.

—⊗⊗⊗—

Someone in the audience: *But the sentence "I who doubt, who therefore think, I am" is already true. So I already have a true knowledge, the knowledge of this real fact that I am, that I exist.*

If the sentence is true only at the moment I utter it, no sooner has it ceased to be uttered than it is divested of its truth, so obviously no segmentation of knowledge is required as far as it is concerned. I had stressed the fact that Descartes asserts very rigorously, and even at great peril, that the "I am" is true only at the time of and so long as there is the enunciation. Thus, no sooner has he said "I am" than truth vanishes. Here again we naturally find the characteristics—which we'll come back to—of the eclipse of the subject since Descartes says that the truth of that "I am" lasts no longer than that of the saying "I am." So it can't be inscribed in knowledge.

The same person as before: *But Descartes is already in the element of truth, since he knows that he is thinking.*

As we'll see in a moment, what Descartes means by "thought," which will be partly the determination of the "what I am," may be quite circular compared with the "I am."

But let's continue along our arduous path. We saw that the constraint of mathematical statements—which are the most certain of statements, those it is difficult to say are pure semblance—this constraint, then, might stem not from the statement itself but from a different freedom, a different existence, which would try to deceive me. I can't rule out this possibility. It's why I can ultimately doubt mathematical truths, even though, in a certain sense, I can't doubt them.

The "I am," on the other hand, does not warrant the same concern, for, even assuming that a God is deceiving me, the "I am" is indispensable even for supporting the hypothesis that "I" am being deceived. The subject as pure point of existence may also be the subject of an error, but the subject of an error must exist just as much as a subject of truth.

By contrast, I could only doubt mathematical truths under the assumption of another existence, that of a deceiving God, the mastermind behind the spurious "truth" of these truths. My project, to move from the certainty of the "I am" to knowledge (for example, the knowledge of "what I am") or to mathematical truths, is therefore very clear: it entails first demonstrating that a God exists, and, second, *that he is not a deceiver.*

In modern terms we'd say that Descartes's project is as follows: to establish a place of truth in language. For if there is a guarantee, a place of truth with regard to language, then the statements that constrain me cannot deceive me. If, on the other hand, God is a deceiver, that means in a certain sense that language may be thoroughly deceptive, that I have no identifiable point of truth in the system of language. God is thus the ultimate guarantee of speech; he is the given word, which means that, since by the statement 2 + 2 = 4 I am forced to believe that this statement is true, I can trust this constraint. Language, inasmuch as it constrains me as to truth, is guaranteed.

Thus, Descartes's fundamental approach will be to guarantee by God the self-evident statements like 2 + 2 = 4, along with all those of the same type, and, more generally, by the existence of the big Other, to establish a transcendent place of truth of language, and in particular a guarantee for answers, in keeping with the order of reasons, to the big question, "what I am."

As regards this approach, I'd now like to say a little about my own point of view.

Descartes's problematic is basically that of the guarantee of truth. Guaranteeing truth requires validation by a second existence. There has to be the "I am," and then the big Other as transcendent existence, in order to then return to the truth of the statements that constrain the "I," to move from the "I am" to the "what I am." In other words, what Descartes is committed to is finding a foundation for the statement "there is truth."

Now *my* position on this issue is that the assumption "there is truth" is absolutely unfoundable. More specifically, truth is only the "there is." This doesn't mean that it therefore doesn't have its knowledge procedures, but the fact that there is truth is always an unfoundable assumption. What's involved is of the order of the event: some truth occurs, or has occurred. The undeniable fact is this, but of course it's not a foundation; it's an event. I think there's even a historical absoluteness to this event, as a historial event, which was subsequently repeated, extended, etc., and which, for me, occurred at the dawn of mathematics in Greece. The dawn of mathematics in Greece was the inauguration of truth as event. It is the originary evental figure of the "there is truth," which is also without foundation. It was a primordial chance occurrence. I am in profound agreement about this with Spinoza, who, in the appendix to Book I of the *Ethics*, says that it is highly likely that if mathematics had never existed, humanity would never have been in the element of truth.

Spinoza has a very different position from Descartes on the question we're considering here, a position that, in its own way, is evental. In his *Treatise on the Emendation of the Intellect*, Spinoza says "we have a true idea,"[1] and that's all. This means that there's no problematic of the guarantee of truth, no foundational problematic of the question of the guarantee of truth. We have a true idea: this is a situation, not a foundation. Spinoza ushers into the history of philosophy what I call the evental figure of the problem of truth, namely that the problem of truth ultimately results in a "there is." Truths have occurred, and we can't go back prior to that time. On this basis, Spinoza develops an entirely different approach from Descartes's, an approach consisting in determining the conditions under which we are in some way in fidelity with this "there is truth." He will study the system of effects of truth rather than the question of its guarantee.

For me, the question of the subject is not the question of the guarantee of truth. On the contrary, the question of the subject results from the fact that there is truth in the form of the event, or, to put it a different way, the nature of the process of the subject is consistent with the evental figure of truth. It is therefore a reversal of perspective compared with Descartes or Kant. The question of the nature of the subject process results from the eventality of truth. It's not the other way around, which involves positing a transcendental or divine subject as the point of foundation and guarantee of truth.

Someone in the audience: *But then does that mean that, after Spinoza, mathematics is the only place where truth finds its guarantee? Is mathematics, in fact, what says "there is truth"?*

The answer would be a long one, and it's covered in Saturday's session. I don't intend to deal with this issue for the time being because we'd have to clarify what is meant by mathematics and that's not exactly our subject here. To answer somewhat indirectly, I would say that there are four stages in the history of the question "there is truth." First, the Greek age, in the form of the inception of mathematics, so strongly asserted by Plato. Next came the age of Descartes, when, owing to the Galilean Revolution, there was the foundational act of modern science, the horizon of the first modern theory of the subject, in which Descartes played the main part. The third age was that of the French Revolution and Hegel, and even of a significant facet of Marx's work. This age marked the inception of the historical figure of the question, that is, of an explicit link between "there are truths" and "truths emerge historically." Today we're in the fourth age, when the question being debated is of a political figure of truth, of politics as a *sui generis* possibility of the "there is truth," a possibility that is overwhelmingly evident in the form of its negation: "Politics is nothing but lies." So there's no temporal linkage between truth and mathematics. My position is simple: mathematics yields the truth of being qua being. But there "exist" plenty of things that can't be reduced to being qua being!

Let's get back to Descartes. Clearly, for him, the subject, the "I am," is not in itself a guarantee. The Cartesian subject is not the guarantee of truth. It is the first point of the real, but it does not go beyond itself. It does not form the basis for a guarantee of truth; rather, the problematic of the guarantee is completely maintained, constituted, and reinforced in the place of the Other. Descartes needs a big Other to seal the great pact of truth with the seal of a divine transcendence. His fundamental statement is that nothing can be said in truth if God does not exist.

This is quite a remarkable problematic, since, as a rule, the problematic of the existence of God depends on the existence of the world, of humanity, or, in other words, the problematic is the one that moves from existence to existence. God exists because the world exists. The existence of God is inferred from any existent whatsoever. For Aristotle, for example, the existence of movement makes a primary unmoved mover, a divine mover, necessary. This is not the case with Descartes: for him, the existence of something rather than nothing is beyond all doubt. Indeed, from an evental point of view, the "I am" is beyond all doubt and does not need the divine guarantee. But neither is it, as such, proof that God exists. As a result, it is truth, not existence, that is dependent on God. So there's a break between Descartes and the previous framework of the problem of God, which was either physical or spiritual: the world, in the first case, or my salvation, in the second case, requires God. The Cartesian point of view is, shall we say, scientific: it is the problem of the truth of statements, especially mathematical ones, that requires God. God therefore exists fundamentally because mathematics is true, not because I have reason not to believe it to be true (since indeed, I *don't* have any such reason), but rather because the only reason I could have for not believing it to be true would be if there were no God, or if God were a deceiver.

Someone in the audience: *I get the feeling that it's mainly physics.*

Tendentially, of course, it's physics, but the first step is based on the mathematical statements themselves, because they can't be directly doubted. They can be indirectly doubted, but this indirection depends on God. There is therefore an implication and an internal torsion in Descartes between mathematical truth and the existence of God that is organic. On a first level, mathematical statements need the divine guarantee, since I must be sure that the constraint these statements impose on my mind is not false, and I have no way of knowing this other than by knowing that God exists, a real, "veridical" God, as Descartes puts it. Subsequently, this will of course guarantee the physical statements, which are necessarily mathematized.

———— ∞∞ ————

Basically, when Descartes says that mathematical statements constrain me, he means that these statements have a consistency that I can't reject, but he distinguishes the question of consistency from that of truth. What constrains us is that it's consistent (if I know what 2 is, what + or = is, then I'll necessarily get 4), but the constraint itself, if it's not guaranteed, may be deceptive. So for Descartes the crux of the matter is that I have to guarantee mathematical statements as true statements, because consistency is not sufficient. Some formalist thinkers, beginning even, in a sense, with Leibniz, would later say: there is no truth in mathematics other than consistency. The Cartesian position is absolutely not formalist; on the contrary, it requires a guarantee of content: it must be really true. Hence my need of divine existentiality, that is, of a place of truth in language. There's nothing to be done about it: I need a big Other who exists.

Descartes is absolutely categorical about the fact that if God does not exist, then nothing can be said in truth. Let me read you an excerpt about this, from the Third Meditation:

> And since I have no cause to think that there is a deceiving God, and I do not yet even know for sure whether there is a God at all, any reason for doubt which depends simply on this supposition is a very slight and, so to speak, metaphysical one. But in order to remove even this slight reason for doubt, as soon as the opportunity arises I must examine whether there is a God, and, if there is, whether he can be a deceiver. For if I do not know this, it seems that I can never quite be certain about anything else. (3:25)

That's very clear. But what's the crux of this process? It's that, in order to say that "God exists" is a statement, God's existence must be stated in one way or another, and, what's more, in keeping with the order of reasons, I must link the statement "God exists" to my previous statements, and this alone will be regarded as a proof.

Just as an aside, let me tell you what I think about this: there's not the slightest proof of God's existence in Descartes. You suspected as much, I imagine: if there were a proof of God's existence in Descartes, we'd know about it! There is actually the positing of God's existence, and, in fact, it's the implicitly dialectical form of Descartes's thought that leads him to posit from the outset that there are two existences. Actually, his true point of departure is to posit the finite and the infinite, the "I" and the other, simultaneously. In this respect he's right, in a way, because the subject can never be thought without its place, the "I" can never be thought without the other. He is thus quite right to posit both the radicality of the "I am" and the big Other, because the complete dialectical thinking of the subject requires it to have its place, and because its place always preexists it in a certain way while at the same time being coextensive with it. And if Descartes—for entirely understandable reasons—feels like calling this place "God," it won't be an important quibble. After all, there's only a difference of one letter between *Dieu* [God] and *lieu* [place]! We won't be fool enough to pick an anticlerical argument with Descartes. The philosophical signifiers must be interpreted in the context of an age when everyone called the place of truths God. And this was true even of someone as staunchly atheological as Spinoza, who in no way believed in the existence of God as a separate transcendence but who nevertheless called substance, or Nature, God.

Our problem cannot be that there's a primacy of the Two over the One in Descartes, that the "I am" should be considered as a first type of existence and God as the second type. That's of course necessary.

I too believe that the existence of truths is thinkable only in the register of the Two: *one* existence is actually a *non*existence.

Yet there's a philosopher who says the exact opposite: Leibniz. "What is not *one* being is not a *being*."[2] Leibniz links the existent to the One. He's right, too, though for different reasons. Leibniz says: what is, is One. As for me, I follow Descartes in saying that in order to state that something is, there has to be the Two, that in order for there to be One being there have to be Two beings.

These are very serious questions, but they're not our immediate concern. What I just wanted to stress is that, in this fundamental dispute, the Cartesian position can't be discredited on the grounds that its initial assumption is actually that there are two completely asymmetrical existents, intertwined with each other. The problem is that Descartes attempts to infer one from the other. He seeks a linear sequence of inference that makes it possible to do away with the Two, by means of what to my mind is a sham contrivance. In the order of reasons, Descartes claims, it's possible to infer the statement of the second existence from the statement of the first. From the statement of an enunciation ("I am") he says he can infer the objective statement, the scientific statement, "God exists." From this all the rest can be quite easily inferred: the guarantee of mathematical, physical, etc. truths. There is a Cartesian antidialecticity about this that's an obsession with the linear in thought, a mathematical appearance, the idea that philosophical statements form a single chain.

This, in my opinion, explains why *the Two in Descartes is represented by two existences*—the existence of the "I" and the existence of God. In a nutshell, there is a unity of proof and a duality of existence for him. There is the One of reasons, which infers everything from one point, and the fundamental duality of existence, that is, the finite existence of the "I" and the infinite existence of God, which are incommensurable with each other albeit interrelated.

My own thinking is as follows: To the extent that I think that there is the Two, I think that there is a big Other, but this big Other isn't an existent. It's not a subject. And this is why, in this respect, I agree both with Descartes when he claims that there is the Two and with Leibniz when I grant him, in a certain sense, that what is not *one* being is not a *being*, that is, that what is not *one* subject is not a *subject*. This is perfectly true. But at the same time there is only a subject if there is the Other. And there is no reason to go below the Two, i.e., the subject and its other.

The point of difficulty for Descartes is that the guarantee must be deducible from the original existential certainty. The statement "God exists" must be inferred from the statement "I exist" if you want to save the One of the order of reasons and consequently conceal the fact that there is organically the Two. Except you can easily see how it all holds together: if I posit at the outset that there is the Two, then that means that I don't know how, that I'm unable, to found truth. This is incidentally my own thesis: in my view, truth cannot be founded. Conversely, if you want to found truth, you'll need *one* truth of the reasons. The two things are completely related. So if Descartes posits the unity of the reasons, it's not because of any aberration; it's because he's convinced that he can, that he must, found truth. Of course, if you give up the idea of founding truth, if you say that truth is unfoundable, well, then, you're giving up the One of the reasons and taking off into the Two; you're dealing with the Two as originary element. This is why I would say that the Cartesian operation is really a suturing operation. Descartes will suture the Two to the One of the order of reasons; he'll stitch together these two existences—the "I's" existence and God's existence—through the proof sequence. As far as I am concerned, I assume that there's no suture, that the subject is never sutured to its place, and that there is a plane of irreducible heterogeneity, whereas Descartes is after the homogeneity of the reasons, hence suturing. The proof of God's existence is the suturing of two existences, but this suturing is imaginary. Therefore, it will come as no surprise that this proof proves nothing: it's the suturing mechanism, an essential philosophical mechanism for Descartes, while at the same time an entirely useless one.

What's interesting is not whether the proof is true or not. Would that mean that the proof is uninteresting? Not at all. The proof is very interesting because it will allow us to define what suturing is, namely, an operation aimed at thinking the Two as One.

Thinking the Two as One is something that's done all the time. There's an enormous number of people who, regarding anything at all, actually re-prove the existence of something like God, i.e., a comforting imaginary suture, by eliminating the irreducible duality (of class, of the splitting of the subject, etc.). You see this constantly in parliamentary political discourse, in journalism, in family morality, in anything at all. And the mechanisms at work are very comparable to the ones in the Cartesian proof of God's existence. Here, with Descartes, we find, in a form of philosophical purity, a gap-bridging principle that is everywhere at work in imaginary mechanisms, and especially in the social, political, and theoretical imaginary. So, quite apart from the existence of God, the Cartesian proof is very interesting: it's a primal, archetypal suturing operation that eliminates the gap, splitting, dialectics. This elimination is clearly at work in the Cartesian proofs of God's existence, hence the importance of examining them. It's a very complicated operation whose mechanisms interest us because, as imaginary mechanisms, they are part of the theory of the subject. This is why the text we'll begin with next time is a compilation, which could be called synthetic, of the proof of the existence of God.

Let me explain where this fits in. When the *Meditations on First Philosophy* was published, it was accompanied by Descartes's replies to objections that had been made to him. There were six objections, six authors, people who had seen copies of the text before its publication. This was in the great scholastic tradition of the *disputatio*, that is, the exposition of your own thought through the refutation of objections either that other people have made to you or that you've made to yourself. We thus have the example of Saint Thomas Aquinas. So the objections and replies are part of the *Meditations*, and we're now going to see who the six objectors are.

1. The first set of objections came from a Dutch theologian, a certain Caterus, someone who was no doubt rescued from the depths of historical oblivion only because of his objections to Descartes. He was the perfect representative of the orthodox philosophical point of view, that is, his objections came from Saint Thomas Aquinas and Aristotle. He was otherwise quite civil and didn't understand much. He tried to make things fit his own frame of reference. He was light-years away from appreciating the importance of the *Meditations*. His objections allowed Descartes to clarify his break with the dominant philosophical system. For us moderns, this refusal of Descartes's to situate himself in the history of philosophy is a very interesting issue. To be sure, he proceeded by way of a radical break, but he didn't want to situate his argument in any history. There was to be no identifiable inscription in the history of philosophy: it wasn't a break in thinking but a break in actuality. Descartes would have nothing to do with the other philosophers, especially those of the past. This is what he wrote:

> At this point my critic has, through his excessive desire to be kind to me, put me in an unfortunate position. For in comparing my argument with one taken from St. Thomas and Aristotle, he seems to be demanding an explanation for the fact that, after starting on the

same road as they do, I have not kept to it in all respects. However, I hope he will allow me to avoid commenting on what others have said, and simply give an account of what I have written myself. (2:77)

This passage is interesting for a number of reasons. To begin with, note the extreme cautiousness of Descartes, who will be careful not to speak ill of Saint Thomas Aquinas or Aristotle. That's a tactical point. At the same time, this clearly indicates his inaugural position, i.e., his position on the brink of a rupture. As this rupture produces its effects, philosophy will increasingly refer to its own becoming. Henceforth, and particularly after Hegel, philosophies will be under the obligation to situate themselves in relation to the others, to indicate themselves to what extent they are breaking with them and what they are contributing that is new. But the Cartesian novelty, which is tremendous, which is a sort of shifting of the ground, doesn't situate itself.

At the other end of this trajectory of modern philosophy we'll find the opposite: philosophy is almost nothing but its historical position. It's nothing but a turning back (in the Heideggerian sense) to its historicity. Between the two we've got Hegel, who views philosophy as coextensive with its own history, as the historical becoming of itself. So there's a first, practical rupture, indifferent to History, and, at the far end, almost nothing remains but philosophy's reflection on its own history. It could be shown that the same is true for art. There is a gradual saturation by the historical consciousness of the process itself, which ends up being completely swallowed up or bogged down in the retrospection of its becoming and no longer capable of anything but a commentary on itself in the depths of time. In Descartes—and this is his originality—there is no historical reference system.

⁂

2. The second set of objections were those of Father Mersenne, a figure who could be considered the philosophical postal service of the
seventeeth century! Since journals didn't exist, Father Mersenne, a
formidable publicist of the day, ensured the circulation of ideas. He
was really a courier of philosophical modernism. His objections were
probably not all his own—far from it: they were things he'd heard
and formulated. There was an at once affable yet rather confused
aspect to these objections. Descartes replied very courteously to
him. It was these objections that would lead him to the synthetic—
or geometric, in the parlance of the day—type of presentation of his
proof of God's existence.

———

3. The third set of objections were Hobbes's. Hobbes was one of the
chief founders of modern political philosophy. He was a theorist of
the highest caliber. Significantly, his fundamental object—the foundations of politics and society—was entirely foreign to Descartes's concerns. We're dealing with a principle of fundamental heterogeneity
here. It's the face-off between Descartes and what was to be the other
great philosophical school, that of Hobbes, Locke, and Hume, which
would found what is traditionally called empiricism. The debate was
very acrimonious, very clearly defined, and Descartes showed considerable ill humor. With this began something that would dominate the
seventeenth–eighteenth century period: the debate between continental rationalism and British empiricism. This was its original form,
with historical statements of the utmost importance.

———

4. The fourth set of objections came from Arnauld, who was associated with the Jansenists. In a way, these objections constituted the
link, even if indirect, between Descartes and Pascal. It was a very
antagonistic link, a mediation or marker of which is found here.

Descartes was faced with what would become the Jansenist theological movement, of which Pascal was to be both the theorist and the militant polemicist, the standard-bearer. You no doubt know Pascal's verdict that Descartes was both "useless and uncertain."[3] He was a great adversarial figure.

I will come back to the notion of "classical thought." It's a conjunctural notion, inasmuch as it lies at the heart of André Glucksmann's latest book (*La Force du vertige*, 1983), which advocates a return to classical thought. Glucksmann's reduction of the thought of the classical age to Pascal does away with the fact that there was a crucial conflict between Pascal and Descartes. Yet this conflict, in my opinion, was actually constitutive of the classical age, which was under the sway of the Two, not the One. One of the places where this conflict had not yet come to light but to which its origin can be traced was in fact the debate between Descartes and Arnauld, that is, the fourth set of objections and replies. This was a marker, an important component in the establishment of the Pascal/Descartes debate as the pivotal moment of the classical age of philosophy.

—⊶⊷—

5. The fifth set of objections came from Gassendi. Gassendi was a proponent of atomism, and his worldview was taken from the Greek atomists, Lucretius, Epicurus, Democritus. Gassendi was one of the founders of the eighteenth-century French materialist current, along with Helvétius, d'Holbach, La Mettrie, et al. His text is pretty funny because he makes huge objections and offers us seventy pages of charming materialist coarseness. Descartes found Gassendi's materialism very vulgar and let him know as much rather forcefully. The debate was interesting because it was a debate between Descartes and what would become the materialist tendency of French thought. And yet in the eighteenth century many of these materialists adhered to the Cartesian conception that everything that exists

consists of extension and motion. So these were very complicated conceptual entanglements. There was doubtless a vehement polemic between Gassendi and Descartes, but it was also the very beginning of a certain ambiguity: whole swathes of Descartes's thought would become part of post-Gassendi materialism. Descartes was unwittingly dealing with one of his potential heirs, although it was the one he thought was stupid and vulgar.

—⚬⚬⚬—

6. The sixth set of objections were from a group of theologians and mathematicians, probably from the Sorbonne. Their issue was the compatibility of Cartesianism with dogma and with mathematics as it was being taught. The question was how what Descartes was expounding fit in with the Church and the University. Descartes replied rather calmly, since on matters of dogma he was both very cautious and very uncomfortable. His reply was therefore detailed and courteous.

—⚬⚬⚬—

These objections offer us an almost exhaustive panorama of the historical context and of the debates of the time. That's why they must be read.

Let's go back to the second set of objections. At the end, Mersenne, who must have heard people who were unconvinced, says to Descartes: "Your text is hard to follow." So he asks him to put it in the form of a demonstration, in a Euclidean order. Now, one of the great originalities of Descartes's text, as compared with the scholastic arguments of the time, was its form. The *Meditations* is not only remarkable for its order but also for a sort of subjective atmosphere that makes it resemble meditations in the sense of the elevation of the soul. Descartes borrowed from the form of religious meditation a subjective element suited to his purpose, which was to make everything originate in the "I am," and for this there had to be a textual existentiality, a subjective prose. The first two Meditations are very steeped in this personal atmosphere, which must have shocked readers trained in Sorbonne scholasticism because they would have seen in it a lack of philosophical seriousness. Mersenne therefore suggested replying to these anxious people using the "method of the geometers." Descartes replied, complying. He prefaced this presentation with a long introduction in which he explained his way of writing philosophy. He distinguished between the "order" and the "manner of demonstration." "The order consists simply in the following. The items which are put forward first must be known entirely without the aid of what comes later; and the remaining items must be arranged in such a way that their demonstration depends solely on what has gone before" (2:110). This is what I called the chain effect, or linearity. There's no principle of double beginning or of disruption. The "manner of demonstration" concerns the means of the order: *how* does one move from one point to another, in the order? For Descartes, there are two ways of proceeding: by analysis and by synthesis. Analysis "shows the true way by means of which the thing in question was found methodically" (2:110): it's the actual process of the demonstration; it is the real process of truth.

> Synthesis, by contrast, employs a directly opposite method. . . . It demonstrates the conclusion clearly and employs a long series of definitions, postulates, axioms, theorems and problems, so that if anyone denies one of the conclusions it can be shown at once that it is contained in what has gone before, and hence the reader, however argumentative or stubborn he may be, is compelled to give his assent. However, this method is not as satisfying as the method of analysis, nor does it engage the minds of those who are eager to learn, since it does not show how the thing in question was discovered. (2:110–111)

So synthesis is an operation of conceptual arrangement that compels the other person's assent, prevents or prohibits any objection, and yet doesn't necessarily follow the path of the discovery of the thing in question. The materials can be rearranged in such a way as to achieve a convincing synthetic demonstration, but it won't necessarily be the actual path that thought followed to find the thing in question. This, says Descartes, is why synthesis is not very useful for those who are eager to learn, that is, for those who are eager to reinvent themselves. They are shown an argumentative façade behind which the history of the process has faded away or been erased.

This is the same distinction as the one Marx makes between the method of inquiry and the method of exposition, a Marxist distinction that Althusser discussed. Marx notes that, in *Capital*, he followed a convincing, demonstrative method of exposition but one that wasn't necessarily the actual process by which the thing in question was discovered. And Descartes, for his part, explains why he is not very much in favor of a synthetic method, since it doesn't convey the actual process of truth but instead reconstructs it in a figure of knowledge. Underlying the analysis/synthesis distinction is the truth/knowledge distinction. Analysis is closer to truth, synthesis to knowledge, insofar as it is the putting into knowledge of something whose truth process is hidden, concealed. For Descartes, any systematically presented knowledge partly conceals the processes of its truth. He thus favors an analytic rather than a synthetic prose. This also has the important consequence that, for him, it is impossible for mathematics, as was later maintained, to be hypothetico-deductive, for its essence to be to posit axioms and then, by following rules, to draw a number of conclusions from them. In his view, that's still a method of exposition, but it's never the truth of the matter. Mathematics isn't axiomatic; it isn't based on hypotheses, axioms, postulates, and ultimately demonstrations. It's an illusion of exposition, a strategy to compel assent.

With only a little exaggeration, it might be said that for Descartes the axiomatic method is a demagoguery of knowledge, something that wrests assent by external means and does not touch the essence of truth. The true mathematical exposition is analysis, the method that follows the process of discovery. There is a very rich Cartesian awareness of the fact that if mathematical truths have a being, if they touch a real, if they are not empty forms, then only the recovery of the process of discovery makes it possible to touch this real. I would translate this by saying that, for Descartes, there is the mathematical event and not just an axiomatics. If you want to touch the real, you'll have to create, or re-create, the process of this event. The axiomatic reconstruction of the thing in question conceals this evental structure. Descartes is keenly aware of this. In this he is at once an antiformalist and a forerunner of the modern breakthrough on the question of truth.

Having said all this, Descartes will set his arguments out in synthetic form, since, as Mersenne tells him, he needs to compel the assent of the Sorbonne people. The excerpt, which we'll examine next time, presents one of his proofs of God's existence. We should bear in mind that there are not one but three proofs of God's existence in Descartes's work. The root of this mystery, as I had occasion to suggest, is that there is none. That there are three of them is due to the fact that there is one main one, presupposed by the others, and it's the one I'll give. It's the synthetic presentation of the first proof of God's existence, the one that will infer it from only the assumption of the existence of the "I am." It will proceed by definitions, axioms, and a theorem. I will undertake a detailed, critical commentary on its three movements in order to identify what is said in them about the suturing operations, the suturing whereby the Two is concealed within the One.

Session 3

December 13, 1983

Where did we leave off? Descartes guided us to the point where we're in a position to grasp the "I am." But what he wants, and what we want, too, is to reclaim reality, the world, which will be given in the "what (I am)." For now, in fact, the "I" is empty; it is a pure point of the real, without any qualities. It will be necessary to move to the "what" as a substantial principle, i.e., to say what the "I" is. So at this point a hurdle needs to be overcome, the hurdle that separates the "I" from its order and makes truth possible. What acts as a suture for this move is God. Using the suture of the divine guarantee, I will be able to unseparate the enunciation and the statement. As a result, the whole symbolic order will open up as the place of the Other and the guarantee.

I had said that a suturing operation was involved, meaning something that bridges the gap, closes it up, joins it together, something that will ensure that there is a unity of plan, of the demonstrative plan, between the order of the "I" and the order of the world. In Descartes, God is far more the concept of suture than a religious concept. We'll also ask why, conversely, the suture is God and why it must be infinite. Why is there this presumption of the infinite? Couldn't he have done without the infinite?

To address these questions, we'll examine the proof of God's existence using the passage below. I mentioned it last time and said it was a compilation based on a sort of appendix to the "Second Set of Replies," the replies to Father Mersenne. The general title of this appendix is "Arguments Proving the Existence of God and the Distinction Between the Soul and the Body," with the subtitle "Arranged in Geometrical Fashion."

DEFINITIONS

I.   *Thought.* I use this term to include everything that is within us in such a way that we are immediately aware of it. . . .

II. *Idea.* I understand this term to mean the form of any given thought, immediate perception of which makes me aware of the thought. . . .

III. *Objective reality of an idea.* By this I mean the being of the thing which is represented by an idea, in so far as this exists in the idea. . . .

IV. Whatever exists in the objects of our ideas in a way which exactly corresponds to our perception of it is said to exist *formally* in those objects. Something is said to exist *eminently* in an object when, although it does not exactly correspond to our perception of it, its greatness is such that it can fill the role of that which does so correspond. . . .

V.   . . . The only idea we have of a substance itself, in the strict sense, is that it is the thing in which whatever we perceive (or whatever has objective being in one of our ideas) exists, either formally or eminently. For we know by the natural light that a real attribute cannot belong to nothing.

. . .

VIII. The substance which we understand to be supremely perfect, and in which we conceive absolutely nothing that implies any defect or limitation in that perfection, is called God.

. . .

AXIOMS OR COMMON NOTIONS

I. Concerning every existing thing it is possible to ask what is the cause of its existence. . . .

. . .

III. It is impossible that *nothing*, a non-existing thing, should be the cause of the existence of anything, or of any actual perfection in anything.

IV. Whatever reality or perfection there is in a thing is present either formally or eminently in its first and adequate cause.

V. It follows from this that the objective reality of our ideas needs a cause which contains this reality not merely objectively but formally or eminently. . . .

VI. There are various degrees of reality or being: a substance has more reality than an accident or a mode; an infinite substance has more reality than a finite substance. Hence there is more objective reality in the idea of a substance than in the idea of an accident; and there is more objective reality in the idea of an infinite substance than in the idea of a finite substance.

. . .

PROPOSITION II

The existence of God can be demonstrated a posteriori merely from the fact that we have an idea of God within us.

DEMONSTRATION

The objective reality of any of our ideas requires a cause which contains the very same reality not merely objectively but formally or eminently (Axiom V). But we have an idea of God (Def. II and VIII), and the objective reality of this idea is not contained in us either formally or eminently (Axiom VI); moreover it cannot be contained in any other being except God himself (Def. VIII). Therefore this idea of God, which is in us, must have God as its cause; and hence God exists (Axiom III). (2:113–117)

In this passage the proof is synthetic. It's given in an order of exposition rather than in the order of discovery, and so it is to some extent a retrospective proof: I mean that the proof first had to be found so that it could be set out as is the case here. The order of exposition involved is taken from mathematics, specifically from Euclid's *Elements*. In that great treatise of Greek mathematics there's a classification of statements into four types. In Descartes's text there are three: definitions, axioms, and theorems. Here is the meaning of the terms used by Euclid:

1. *Definition.* This is the act of positing a concept. The definition gives the meaning of a word without assuming existence. Its criterion is solely transmissibility; it has no other aim and does not claim to concern being. Its criterion is formal coherence, meaning. The negative aspect is that there's no predication of existence.

2. *Common notions or axioms.* How can they be identified in relation to what's been said about Descartes? They are constraining statements, relationships among concepts. These notions are "common" insofar as any mind whatsoever is forced to admit this type of statement. They can only be suspended by means of the so-called "deceiving God." Axioms compel the assent of my mind naturally (nature has no deceiving God).

3. *Postulates.* They are absent from Descartes's work.[1] The Greeks single them out because they are not constraining: they are plausible but not constraining statements. You are asked to accept them; it's a contract. There are no postulates in the

Cartesian proof: since every statement is to be guaranteed, you won't be asked to "accept" certain ones.

4. *Propositions or theorems.* They are what can be deduced from common notions and definitions by means of deductive chains, which are themselves constraining. They are secondary constraints.

Using definitions, axioms, and propositions, Descartes will situate himself in the world of constraint. How can proofs be put to use when one is in the element of doubt and the element of doubt has affected even what is constraining, using the "deceiving God"? What is the proof? The proof suspends the "deceiving God" long enough to show that he is nonexistent. You comply with your constraint and the imaginary term (that conceptual demon, the "deceiving God") is no longer in play. The proof unfolds in the element of constrained freedom but not in the element of absolute freedom—which exists only when I hypothesize that I am being deceived by that demon. If Descartes asks us not to doubt everything and to accept constraining chains, it's because he has rejected the hypothesis that constraint itself can be deceptive. He removes the evil God just long enough to show that he was right to remove him, since the good God exists.

Basically, the crux of the proof is the removal of the evil God. It is a *reductio ad absurdum* argument: an initial hypothesis is suspended long enough to prove that it was unwarranted. At no time does the evil God have any substantial effect; he appears only to disappear. Yet the interplay between the two Gods is intricate: to prove the existence of the true one you need the evil one, for the sole purpose of denying his existence. Once he has disappeared, the problem will be how to justify his disappearance.

This proof process is a process of torsion that we'll find throughout. To initiate the suture—the proof of God's existence—I need the hypothesis of the evil God (in the imaginary position). But to unfold the proof I need the disappearance of this imaginary position, because that alone allows there to be a proof, hence a constraint. In fact, the evil God had cast doubt on the constraints. The imaginary operator is a vanishing term in the setup. When the assumption of its existence is eliminated, the constraint returns, and so the proof is possible. Thus, proving God, the guarantee of truth, is intrinsically based both on the evil God and on his disappearance. In other words, God is proved through the causality of the absence of the demon (the false, deceiving God), since the demon is that whose absence is required for establishing the existence of the true God.

Descartes evinces a certain palpable discomfort about this: to demonstrate God's existence, it's absolutely necessary to say that nothingness (and the "deceiving God" is nothingness) has no properties and that it has nevertheless been given one: to be included, by its absence, in the demonstrative chain.

<hr/>

But let's get back to the text. As you can see, it begins with a number of definitions.

1. The first definition pertains to thought. Here once again we find that, for Descartes, thought means the immediate dimension of the "I." So, in order to understand Descartes's meaning, we need to deintellectualize the word *thought*: Descartes doesn't mean the operations of cognition by it. Immediate perception, vision, are thoughts for him. When he says that the "I" is a thinking thing, he's referring to the immediate operation whereby the "I" is perceptible as "I." This is why "I think" and "I am" are interchangeable statements.

2. For Descartes, the idea is the atom of thought, an isolatable form of the "I am" insofar as I think. The only mediation here is to say that the "I am" is the place of a multiple. It is each "one" of this

multiple that he calls an idea. The idea is the point for which thought is the general term. It is the punctuality of thought, and the question of the idea is the question of the multiple, of the "I" as the place of the multiple. The very being of thought is the multiple of ideas.

3. This third definition is the crux of the matter. It is in a certain sense at the heart of the proof of God's existence. The first hypothesis: for Descartes, every idea is the idea of something, every idea is representational. We could say that the objective reality of the idea is the being of this something. Yet it's not the being of the thing that is represented by an idea, since the definition says: "in so far as this exists in the idea" (2:113–114). This objective reality is in actual fact subjective. The nodal point is that the idea is linked to a particular being, and this being is present in the idea itself. So the concept of representation must be eliminated. And yet, to a certain extent, Descartes has a representational view of things. Let me give you an example. I have the idea of a horse; the horse is not in the idea—it's not objective reality—and yet something related to what a horse is is nevertheless, as "objective reality," in the idea.

I would propose the following interpretation: the objective reality of an idea is how I think its difference from another idea. It is the idea's differential. For Descartes, the differential of the idea is a differential of being of the idea itself. Ideas are differentiated from one other according to a sort of weight of being of their own, in the simplest case when they are representational, but also when they're not. For Descartes, an idea can be an intention. An intention will have a certain weight of being; it can be weak or strong, finite or infinite. The ontology of the idea, which justifies our speaking of its objective reality, is simply what differentiates one idea from another *in its relationship to being*. It is differentiated not just by its name but by what may be called its weight of being.

The proof of God's existence is contained in this point inasmuch as the notion of "the objective reality of the idea" is already ontological. It introduces being into the "I," which was not the case either for "thought" or "idea." The multiple of ideas is a multiple of being, which is related to something very profound, namely, the thinking of difference. We'll have occasion to come back to this. For the classical philosophers, all difference must be a difference of being. The multiple of ideas is only thinkable as a difference of being. So for Descartes this paves the way for a hierarchy of ideas, which can be classified according to their weight of being.

Descartes could be said to still be a classical philosopher since multiplicity is necessarily ordered, since it's a form of the concept of order. It is their objective reality that orders ideas. God, who will be the highest idea in the hierarchy, begins to emerge. So it will be concluded that he exists. The summit of the hierarchy of ideas will take us into the Other; it's what will touch the Other. At its core, Descartes's proof of God's existence is always an ontological argument–type proof, a proof organized entirely around an ordered vision of the multiplicity constituted by the "I," which is the multiplicity of ideas.

The debate involved is as follows: can there be a nonhierarchical thinking of the multiple or not? This is a crucial question, including in politics, and one that has not yet been settled because the idea that the thinking of the multiple is hierarchical is a very deep-seated idea that's difficult to uproot. This leads to a further question: can difference be thought otherwise than in terms of being? We would thus have, on the one hand, a nonhierarchical thinking of the multiple and, on the other, a nonontological thinking of difference. This is a very topical issue. People say, for example: "We should accept our differences." Yes, but what differences do they mean? It's not a matter of accepting a difference when it comes to religion any more than when it comes to "race" or other pseudo-terms of difference. The basic question is: "What difference are you talking about?" Racists are big fans of difference—just think about segregation or apartheid. They're all for taking the greatest account of it. That's why the foundation of the thinking of the multiple is a crucial problem in contemporary thought. Is there a nonontological conception of difference? And once that's been established, what doctrine of the multiple will be inferred from it? For Descartes, the multiple of ideas is only representable in a figure of order, and the thinking of difference is necessarily a thinking of order. The differential marking of ideas occurs in an ontological logic aimed at the hierarchization that orders everything from the finite to the infinite.

4. In the fourth definition we find distinctions borrowed from scholasticism. They are definitions in the strict sense of the term. A thing is formally contained in an idea; that is to say, a property is a formal property of an idea when it is really contained in it. For example, the fact that the sum of the angles of a triangle equals 180 degrees is formally contained in the triangle. There is empirical exhaustion: no remainder, no indecision or uncertainty. The property is completely assimilable to the essence of the triangle as I have its idea. It is therefore a verifiable property of this idea and is such that I have its idea. When I have an idea about an idea, it is in it "formally" if it is in it exactly as I have its idea, and it is in it "eminently" if it is not in it exactly as I have its idea. When I say "God is good," the idea of goodness is contained in the idea of God. That's true, but the idea I have of goodness is incommensurable with the idea of divine goodness. There is something extra. Thus, it is in it eminently. In this algebra of adequation of ideas, "eminently" means excess. Goodness is in God, but eminently, which is to say that the idea of goodness, as soon as it's a question of God, exceeds the idea I have of it. In this definition there emerges the idea of excess, namely, that there are not only ideas, or ideas of ideas, but that an idea may be either adequate or limited by things that exceed it. Another important example is given us by "God is infinite." There, too, the "infinite" is in the idea of God eminently because the idea I have of the infinite is exceeded on all sides by divine infinity.

5. Given an idea—that's still all there is for the time being—
I will call substance what is assumed to be a real existent, so to
speak, a bearer of the idea. If I have an idea of the infinite, I will
call "infinite substance" an existent that has the property of being
infinite. Descartes defines substance but does not say whether any
exists: he defines its concept. If I have an idea of largeness, a large
substance will be an existent with the property represented in the
idea of being large. Substance is simply the existentiality of a property, existentiality as an idea and not just as existence. Substance
is the ontological index of a property. It is merely the assumption
that a given thing is really the property of something that exists.
If there is an existent that is infinite, this existent will be the substance whose property is infinity. Substance is therefore pure existentiality. There are properties, and then there is substance, about
which it can be said that it possesses this or that property. So substance is not a property; it is not definable in itself; it is always
related to a property. There is no specific concept of substance in
Descartes. This is a fundamental difference with Aristotle, who,
on the contrary, has a specific concept of substance as a category
of being.

For Descartes there is no concept of being qua being, of existence
qua existence. It's an empty index, merely the basis for a property,
but there is no thinking of it per se. There is a Cartesian desubstantialization of being: being has no substance other than to be and to
have properties. As such, it has no substance. The concept of being
in Descartes is therefore an absolutely empty, absolutely tautologi-
cal concept, referring only to itself.

Heidegger says that the great question of philosophy is: How
does it stand with being qua being? What is ontology? Well, Descartes's answer invalidates the question, because there's no substan-
tive answer conceivable: being qua being is interchangeable with the
void. There are only properties with an index of existence.

Descartes paved the way for a radical critique of ontology, regarded as an absolutely pointless project. This was a tradition that continued up through Sartre, who was thoroughly Cartesian in this respect. At the beginning of *Being and Nothingness* is a passage about being-in-itself dominated by the idea that being is unattributable. (The same thing is found in literary form in *Nausea*: the meditation before a chestnut tree root.) As soon as you try to think being-in-itself, all you find is absolute indeterminacy, something Sartre translates by saying that being is always in excess, in excess over any possible determination. With Descartes, then, begins the great modern trial of ontology.

I have two statements critical of this trial: (1) Being serves as a basis for the pure determination of the One and the multiple, which is indeed a rational ontological dimension. But (2), this does not constitute being in the realm of presence or of experience. For me, there is no intimate, poetic, or theological experience of presence, of the proximity of being qua being. Now, how are these two statements connected to each other? Well, my thesis is that the thinking of being qua being is strictly mathematical.

Someone in the audience: *How is that different from Hegel?*

Hegel, by contrast, thinks that being is the basis of the totality of determinations. To him, the One and the multiple are the weakest determinations, those of being's immediacy. Being is self-determining. This is a very unusual solution. Being is the basis of the totality of determinations because it is self-determining; self-determination is precisely the history of both being and the spirit, a joint and single history. This is not at all my overview. Mine, on the contrary, is that ontology is an utterly unique discipline. Specifically, I in no way hold that ontology founds or organizes the other donations of meaning. What belongs to the realm of presence is not ontological. Fundamentally, being is unpresented, unrepresented. What kind of thinking eliminates its object and unfolds in a pure dialectics of the One and the multiple? It's mathematics. Mathematical discursivity doesn't present anything: that's its fundamental characteristic. It was very wrong to speak of "mathematical objects." There are no mathematical objects: the whole history of mathematics is the history of the gradual elimination of these so-called objects. What's more, at the absolute basis of the architectonics of mathematics is the empty set, the very thing that doesn't present anything. It will be shown how it is only by building on the empty set that mathematics is mathematical, that is, ontological. That's how it's tied to nonpresence, and nonpresence alone is the place where being qua being occurs.

Was Descartes completely unfamiliar with such thinking? No. He's the absolute source of all modernity, so he couldn't be unfamiliar with it. He touched on it through his conception of the body. For him, the realm of being is split between soul and body. That's what Cartesian dualism is. When he talks about extended substance, about the extended existent as such, he says that knowledge of the extended existent is mathematics, i.e., that the being itself of mathematics, the corporeal being, operates solely by figures and movements. It is thus essentially geometrical. For Descartes, mathematics is not an organon or an instrument for knowing extended being. It is adequate to that being itself; there is a scalar plan of being. In the mathematicophysical part of Descartes's oeuvre there is an intuition similar to the idea that mathematics is actually the system of ontology. This intuition that mathematics is ontology has a long philosophical history stretching from the Pythagoreans . . . to me!

I am not saying simply that the universe can be thought through mathematics, which is a very common claim; I'm saying that mathematics is the thinking of being qua being, something the Pythagoreans would never have said. Indeed, they said that arithmetic lets you create an ontological schema based on the interpretation of the idea that the universe is made up of numbers. What I'm saying is that the development of mathematical discursivity is simply the development of the thinking of being qua being, its historical development. There must not be any intuition of objects, or else we'd ultimately be dealing with representation, not with the description of being qua being. Being must be unrepresented, and it is only so in mathematical discursivity, which is ultimately based on the absolute purity of the empty set, on the absolute absence of any determination. Ontology is what creates determinations from nondetermination, what is constructed from indeterminacy (the empty set) and organizes this indeterminacy itself in the network of the One and the multiple. So there is a determination of indeterminacy, and this doesn't produce any object or any presence. In speaking about nothing, ontology speaks about being qua being.

We're skipping ahead now to the eighth definition. God is the idea of a substance that would be capable of being the basis of the property of being perfect, the idea of the substance to which the idea of perfection would apply. So Descartes assumes that we have an idea of perfection. The idea of God is a combination of the idea of substance and the idea of perfection, a composite idea.

With the idea of perfection, we already have a suturing operator. Descartes attempts to define perfection negatively by the absence of defect—specifically, by the absence of limitation. It's the idea of what has no limit, hence the idea of the infinite. God is substance plus the infinite, an idea taken negatively here, in the sense of something that has no limits of any kind. Perfection and limitlessness are very similar.

The nodal point is that we have an idea of the infinite, that is, that one of the modes of existence of the "I am," which is the multiple of ideas, is the idea of the infinite. Later, we'll ask what the objective reality of this idea of the infinite is, and we'll find that since the "I" is too cramped to contain it, it has to break apart and open up to a second existence, to the big Other, which is God.

God is the combination of three ideas: negation (which results in the nonfinite); limitation (the finiteness of the "I"); and substance (actual existence, outside of the "I"). Or to put it another way: negation, finite, substance. But do we have an idea of the finite? It's indispensable if the idea of the infinite is the negation of the idea of the finite. This will be the final debate. Descartes thinks it's self-evident that we have an idea of the finite, which allows the infinite to be the combination of negation and the finite, a combination that, being incommensurable with the finiteness of the "I," must exist materially outside of it.

I myself believe it's the opposite: that we first have the idea of the infinite and what's complicated is the idea of the finite. The idea of negation is self-evident. It's been used right from the start, since doubt contains the idea of negation. It's the initial action. For Descartes, the absolutely initial idea is that of negation, in which respect he is also the forerunner of Hegel's dialectic.

I begin with the inaugural idea, negation, since the idea of the finite has not yet made its appearance. Where will it come from?

We shift to the axioms here. First, a point of introduction: the axioms are statements that are a constraint for my negative freedom. When it comes to the axioms, we're outside the sphere of radical doubt and have put the "deceiving God" into eclipse. We're in the element of the "I am," and we have a kind of certainty. There are the axioms, since there is already the truth of the enunciation. They are only operative because there is already a truth and because the imaginary principle of the second God is in eclipse.

The type of constraint imposed by these statements needs to be tested. According to Axiom III, it is impossible for nothing to be the cause of the existence of anything, and according to Axiom V, the objective reality of our ideas also requires a cause. This is the axiom that will contain the proof.

What is impossible in Descartes's thesis is that the "I am" might be said to be nonfinite. Descartes assumes the finiteness of the "I am," which is not self-evident, even for him, since it's the mere punctuality of the enunciation. So we need to ask how Descartes can conceive of the infinite positively and not just as the negation of a problematic finite. But here we run into a major problem, which is that there is actually no truly rational concept of the infinite in Descartes. What is impossible at any rate for him is that the infinite can be simply a mark of excess, the almost nonexistent indicator of a limit, a kind of purified One—or, to put it another way, that there may be nothing in the idea of the infinite but the demarcation of the totality of our ideas, that it is the concept of the All.

This absence of any really positive, nontranscendent idea of the infinite, either as One in the form of a limit or as All in the form of an effectively infinite multiple, indicates that the Cartesian proof of God's existence is consistent with the fact that Descartes was not the inventor of differential and integral calculus in mathematics. He remains within the bounds of Cartesian mathematics: neither the thinking of the differential (the vanishing punctual One as limit) nor that of the integral (the totality of a surface). In other words, there is really no mathematics of the infinite in Descartes, and that's why there is only a theology of it. Since the infinite is conceived neither as One nor as All, it follows that there is only one existing concept of it, the determination of a singular being, whatever it is called ("God," for example). The incommensurability of the infinite with the "I am" is the absence of this new mathematics. Once differential and integral calculus was introduced, no longer would anyone think that the idea of the infinite was incommensurable with the "I," since under the pure constraint of mathematics the subject would be able to give algorithms of the infinite. Indeed, a mathematical concept of the infinite would be available, even if it wasn't until Cantor that this concept was decisively clarified. There is only an existential conception of the infinite in Descartes, which places him at a pivotal point between scholasticism and full modernity.

Strictly speaking, the infinite is a mathematical concept, and Cartesian mathematics, by leaving it out of account, comes up against its limit, its boundary. Does this mean that the category of the infinite is not relevant to the subject? Quite the contrary.

As for myself, I will argue that the subject is infinite in a fourfold sense:

--By way of anxiety, as an eclipse
--By way of courage, as the empty set
--By way of the superego, as the All
--By way of justice, as consistency[2]

There are, in my view, four concepts of the infinite, which are related to the four cardinal determinations of the subject. It remains to prove these theses. For that, we'll need texts other than those of Descartes, whose stumbling block is precisely the question of the finiteness, or noninfiniteness, of the Subject.

Session 4

December 20, 1983

L
ast time, we were examining the section in the "Reply to the Second Set of Objections" devoted to providing a "synthetic" proof of the existence of God, that is to say, a proof modeled on Euclid's *Elements*. Such proofs begin with incontrovertible statements called "definitions" and "axioms."

We had examined the definitions. But let's go back for a moment to the axioms. For Descartes, in his trajectory, the axioms—which he also refers to as "common notions"—are statements that compel my assent. They are statements whose truth, at the time they are uttered, I am unable to deny. This means that no axiom, no "common notion," can be of the type "such and such a thing exists." Indeed, to be valid, any statement of that sort requires something more than just the constraint of coherence to which my critical freedom submits. When it comes to existence, a verification or a proof is required. But an axiom is precisely something whose self-evidence requires neither verification nor proof.

This leads us to a brief reflection on the status of existence in relation to discourse. How can discourse bring about assertions of existence? Under what conditions, with what status, can a statement be truly an existence statement? At this point, we have two types of admissible statements that are existence statements, asserting that "this exists." On the one hand there's the "I am," which is barely a statement; it's more of an enunciation, a simple positing of the "I," although it's existential: at the time I utter the "I am," I am. And on the other hand, there's the existence that results from a proof, God's existence. It can be formulated as follows: either existence is immediate or it is proved. There is no other discursive status of existence possible. In other words, where discourse is concerned, existence is in the position either of a starting point or an end result. From one to the other, from the immediate to the result, the intermediate statements contain no presupposition, no positing of existence. This means that existence is not an object of experience. Descartes is profoundly antiempiricist: existence is in no way a complex given of which there is supposedly experience. There is no evidence of existence, of things in the world, and so on. There is ultimately no experience other than the "I am," which is in a sense an empty experience. God himself is not experienced but proved. So it's fair to say that for Descartes, existence is a phenomenon of discourse rather than of experience. To assert existence is either a matter of the enunciation—this is the case of the "I"—or of a deductive procedure, to which no experience corresponds. We might almost say that for Descartes existence is a category of discourse.

In this way, Descartes initiated a radical antiempiricist tradition. If empiricism is defined as a philosophical current that considers that existence is merely a category of experience and that only what is experienced exists, it could be said that we are dealing here with an absolutely antiempiricist current, which holds that all experience is open to question, even as regards existence, and in which what exists is tied to discourse, either in the position of the subject of discourse—the enunciation—or as the result of a controlled discursive procedure—the proof.

This raises the following question, a general question of the utmost interest. What is the actual field of philosophical assignation of the category of existence? I think it's fair to say that there are actually two fundamental philosophical traditions: one whose horizon is discourse, and another whose horizon is experience. The status of objects is immaterial, and we will say neither that the former is idealist and the latter materialist, nor that the former is theological and the latter atheistic. Remember that in the mystical tradition God's existence is experienced, and there is therefore a kind of mystical empiricism. Enlightenment philosophy will itself be divided. It will accept Locke's and Hume's idea that existence is a category of experience, but it will retain Descartes's idea of a possible mechanical and deductive discursive chain, the ideal of a *mathesis universalis*.

Regarding the discursive current as conceived of by Descartes, it can be said that it treats existence as a philosophical category.

Someone in the audience: *Are we dealing with the purely speculative?*

You could say that, except that there is the existential radicality of the "I am," the originary point where discourse intersects with an existential principle. To be sure, the "I am" is linked to discourse, but as a condition of discourse itself. Indeed, the discourse of absolute doubt must exist for the "I" to rise to the certainty of existing. But the enunciation, which founds the certainty of the "I am," is in fact the actual existence of discourse, and the "I am," the pure empty point without content, constitutes the existence of discourse itself. So there's an initial linkage between existence and discourse, which precludes positing a statement such as "There is only discourse."

The most debated problem in the commentary on Descartes is whether the "I am" is an experience. I would say that what precludes the "I am" from being an experience is that the "I" is not an object. For there to be an experience, there must be an experience of an existing object, and empiricism goes hand in hand with the experienced object. However, the "I" is not an object. It is important here not to conflate the "I" [le je] and the self [le moi]. If the "I am" is a "self am," we could say that the cogito is the experience of the self. But in reality the "I am" is not the experience of a singular self, of a particular object. So it's wrong to say that the "I am" is an experience; it's not the experience of anything. The cogito as "experience" is simply the indisputable event of the radical conditions of discourse. And these conditions only give us an empty and vanishing point in which no object can be found.

Strictly speaking, I would say that it is possible to argue that Descartes remains committed to a radical antiempiricism in which existence is dependent on discourse, provided that "discourse" also means the being of discourse. But the being of discourse, which is the eclipse of the subject, is in no way an object of experience. As for the second existent, God, there is no experience of him; there is no Cartesian mysticism. God is not experienced but concluded.

⸻

We now return to the axioms that Descartes also calls "common notions."

Axiom I. Concerning every existing thing it is possible to ask what is the cause of its existence.

This first axiom formulates the requirement always to ask what is the cause of a certain thing's existence. It is about existence that the question of the cause must be asked. This formulation is known in the history of philosophy as the "principle of sufficient reason." It's a great fundamental principle of classical rationalism. It is even the very hallmark of it, you might say, since it radically eliminates any suspicion of absurdity in the modern sense (Camus, Sartre). The idea that the existent cannot exist without a cause, which means that we should ask what is the cause of the existence of any existent whatsoever, is for Descartes an axiom, not a statement open to question or requiring a proof. This is the affirmative heart, as it were, of classical reason as regards the existent.

This first axiom indicates Descartes's inclusion in the Age of Classical Reason, by way of what is for him the self-evidence of the principle of sufficient reason. How will this be connected with a proof of God's existence? Here, the cosmological argument—the allegedly existing world must have a cause, which is God—which is the most traditional argument, is clearly based on the principle of sufficient reason.

But it is completely rejected by Descartes, because the existence of the world is the least certain thing there is. The use of the principle of sufficient reason will take a very different path.

But let's continue our examination of the axioms.

Axiom III. It is impossible that *nothing*, a non-existing thing, should be the cause of the existence of anything, or of any actual perfection in anything.

This axiom posits that every existing thing must have a cause and that this cause itself must be existing. So a judgment must be made about the cause of an existing thing, not just ideally but really, since the cause must itself exist. As you can see, through causality the existent is linked to the existent, and we are dealing with a chain principle. Causality is the endless concatenation of existents.

Just as an aside, here we could make the objection to Descartes that is often made to him: what about God, with respect to the principle of sufficient reason? If we assume that God exists, don't we need to ask about the cause of his existence and what it might be? Descartes makes this objection to himself, and his answer is that, since the principle of sufficient reason is absolutely universal, we must ask with respect to God, too, the reason he exists. But there is only one answer possible: God is the cause of himself (*causa sui*, Spinoza will say). This a fundamental difference with Aristotle. Indeed, when Aristotle asks himself about the ultimate cause of motion, he answers that there must be a prime mover, which is a sort of cosmological proof of the existence of God. However, this prime mover is unmoved. The category of motion doesn't apply to God: God is not the cause of his own motion; he is unmoved. For Descartes, as for the classical thinkers of the seventeenth century, the principle of causality leads back to God. God is not an existent "without a cause" who is also the cause of all things. God is himself caused, of course by himself. The category of causality, for the classical metaphysicians, is relevant to God, whereas, for Aristotle, that of motion wasn't.

We should note, moreover, that the category of "cause of itself" is not reserved exclusively for God. Indeed, the existence in man of an absolute negative freedom means that, in a sense, man himself is *causa sui*. The universalism of classical reason therefore ends up submitting God to a number of rational categories, and this means he is never in a position of absolute exception—except, perhaps, as regards the infinite.

Someone in the audience: *Isn't it God's freedom, or indeed man's, that introduces motion into the world? Also, what role does the pineal gland play?*

Let's begin with the famous pineal gland. Its function is to define the material boundary between necessity and freedom, between the body and the soul. Cartesian dualism is absolute: provided you have an action inscribed in the material world, in extension, you can always trace it back through the system of its causes and you'll never have an ex nihilo creation. Free thought, on the other hand, seems to make the soul the cause of itself. The pineal gland is an utterly enigmatic mediation between these two registers. It's a metaphor of the point where the free determination of the soul intersects with the constrained determination of the body. That said, Descartes does not explain it convincingly; he just gives a name to this mediation between absolute freedom and total necessity.

To assert that God is the cause of himself actually paves the way for a far-reaching transformation of God. This can be seen in the consequences Spinoza draws from it. For if God is the cause of himself, there is no longer any reason to keep him in a position of transcendence. If the causal principle is absolute, if God is not its limit, then that means that the gulf supposedly separating God from the world is by contrast not absolute. And if it's not absolute, Spinoza concludes, then it is nil. Spinoza resolutely draws the consequences, saying that since the principle of causality extends to God, God must be posited in a position of immanence. This is the equation *Deus sive Natura*, "God, or in other words, Nature."

So Descartes paves the way, via the principle of sufficient reason, for a kind of nonthinking of the radical disjunction between God and the world, between Heaven and earth. This will be one of the fundamental pieces of supporting evidence in Pascal's case against Descartes. In Pascal's view, the Cartesian God is nothing but an ephemeral machinery of physical causality and therefore a radical debasement of the divine figure. In the view of Pascal, for whom God's essence is his absolute transcendence, there is only a hair's breadth of difference between the "God" of the principle of sufficient reason—the God of Descartes, Spinoza, and Leibniz—and atheism.

It is indeed true that to say "God is the cause of himself" is to slyly introduce difference into God, because you're forced to posit a causing God and a caused God. There is "naturing" nature and "natured" nature, Spinoza will say more radically. With Descartes, divine simplicity is undermined because a split is introduced into the concept of its existence.

―――∞――

Someone in the audience: *But when exactly does Descartes need to submit God to the principle of sufficient reason?*

―――∞――

In a way, eliminating the hypothesis of the deceiving God already submits God to the principle of reason. The fact that we are necessarily oriented toward a nondeceiving God means that there's a presumed homogeneity between God, and, broadly speaking, all the principles of reason. In particular, God is homogeneous with the principle of sufficient reason. If he weren't, we might still believe he is deceiving us.

It's important to understand that the hypothesis of a deceiving God gives rise to that of an inscrutable God. There is an undeniable link between the two. Because how can we understand why a God should want to routinely deceive us? To eliminate the hypothesis and introduce the idea that God is necessarily comprehensible, Descartes takes all sorts of precautions, of course, but ultimately he needs what could be called the rationality of God.

Here again we find, in the assessment of Descartes, the Pascal/ Spinoza opposition. Pascal's major point of reference is the divine mystery, divine existentiality as *super*-experience, whereas Spinoza will say that God is entirely comprehensible. As for Descartes, he didn't go that far. As a proponent of moderation in religious matters, he maintained the idea of a precarious transcendence.

It's important to understand that this division runs through classical thought, even through theater. It can be found in the opposition between Corneille and Racine, with Corneille on Descartes's side and Racine on Pascal's.

<hr>

Someone else in the audience: *But does something false have a sufficient reason? If so, then there should also be a sufficient reason why someone asserts the existence of a deceiving God, for example. After all, our absolute freedom can give being to what is false. Even doubt, which is negative, must have a reason, mustn't it?*

<hr>

Error and doubt aren't the same. For Descartes, a false statement has no being, so it does not come under the principle of sufficient reason. The being of the statement is the objective reality of the idea. But a false statement is a statement in which the ideas linked together within it no longer have an objective reason, and thus error, having no being, doesn't come under the principle of sufficient reason. Furthermore, as we saw in connection with mathematical statements, my negative freedom isn't so great that it can deny true statements. So it is not, strictly speaking, at the root of error either. The negative capacity of freedom is not a capacity for error; it's a capacity for doubt, because doubt is a matter of will, not of knowledge. As for the deceiving God, Descartes doesn't say that he doesn't exist (he couldn't say that). What happens is that, since his existential status is pure eclipse, he only appears in order to disappear. Thus, by virtue of Axiom III, he is not the cause of anything, because it is impossible that nothing should be the cause of anything. Descartes requires a fullness of existence for every cause.

<hr>

But let's get back to our Axiom III. Since the principle of sufficient reason requires us to go back from the existent to the existent as a cause, what is eliminated in this way is, for us moderns, any hypothesis pertaining to the causality of lack. A nonexistent object cannot be the cause of an existing object. Everything that exists can be attributed to something existent; there is nothing that cannot be. The idea that disappearance can be causal is ruled out by this axiom.

Hence the debate on the subject of difference. For Descartes, every difference is a difference of being, in particular every causal difference. There's a causing existent and another, different one (except in the case of God) that is caused. However, I think that a theory of nonontological difference can only be grounded in the logic of the causality of lack. Descartes doesn't allow us to think that two things can differ by what vanishes, that is, by the effect of a disappearance, by their shared inexistent. In my opinion, it is, however, only by accepting this causality of lack or disappearance that we can think difference otherwise than in terms of a difference of being, i.e., think *a nonidentitarian difference*. I refer you on this subject to what I have to say about Greek atomism in *Theory of the Subject*.

We've already encountered this point of debate with Descartes in connection with the reality of ideas. If you try to think the difference between ideas on the basis of the difference of being, you find as regards this issue the ineffectiveness of nothingness, meaning that you can't think a difference other than identitarian, and therefore ontological. This paves the way—which will be used with Axioms IV and V—for a figure of order, a hierarchical figure of the multiple, which is fundamentally opposed to the atomistic thinking of the multiple, which is egalitarian. Atoms are hierarchically indistinguishable, of equal value as far as being is concerned, and what differentiates them causally is a disappearance, the *clinamen*. Descartes is opposed to this view of things, and if I wanted to accuse him in some way of idealism, it wouldn't be in connection with the question of God but with this precise issue. I'd say he is an idealist, first, in that he has no theory of the multiple other than one that's of an ontological nature and is grafted onto the difference of being and, second, in that he ultimately has a hierarchical vision, which does away with the causality of lack. I don't think it's possible to completely establish a materialist vision of things when that's been eliminated.

Let's see what comes next:

Axiom IV. Whatever reality or perfection there is in a thing is present either formally or eminently in its first and adequate cause.

Axiom V. It follows from this that the objective reality of our ideas needs a cause which contains this reality not merely objectively but formally or eminently.

With Axioms IV and V, we move from "the cause of what exists must itself exist" to "there must of course be the same weight of being in both existences, that of the cause and that of what is caused by it, otherwise there would be a causality of lack." Indeed, if there's more being in the effect than in the cause, there is a production of being from nothing, which, for Descartes, is not possible. Rejecting the causality of lack leads necessarily to a transitivity of being: at least as much being must be found in the cause as in the effect, since nothing can be lost or come from a loss. What Axiom IV says— that there is as much being in the cause as in the effect—Axiom V applies to ideas. The objective reality of the idea is its differential of being, and only the existent of the idea differentiates it as such from another idea since there is no causality of lack.

It is here that we find a point of suture. The whole proof of the existence of God is based on this. Let's review its scheme: the idea of God, as the idea of the infinite, must not be able to find its cause in ourselves, who are finite. But where is the suture? In the fact that *Descartes assumes that the cause of the objective reality of the idea cannot itself be an idea's objective reality.* Let me remind you that "objectively contained," for Descartes, means "contained as an idea." The objective reality of an idea is not what it represents but its differential of being, what makes it this particular idea, what differentiates it from another one. Descartes says: the cause of this objective reality of an idea must be contained in something that exists—which is perfectly natural, given the principle of sufficient reason. But he adds: something that exists either "formally" or "eminently." Consequently, the cause of the objective reality of an idea cannot be the objective reality of another idea.

Why this is so is, in my opinion, Descartes's blind spot. Why should it be impossible to imagine that the cause of the objective reality of one idea might be the objective reality of another idea? I've never found an answer to this question. Berkeley got around it by saying that the cause of our ideas could very well be other ideas, which is why he can be considered the third radical descendent of Descartes, after Spinoza and after Pascal. There is no immediately obvious reason why an idea's differential of being cannot be related to another idea's differential of being. I, for one, even if I adopt classical reason again, don't feel constrained by Axiom V. Why must it be "formally or eminently," i.e., according to a different ontological status, that the cause of the objective reality of an idea exists? Yet it is this very point that will free us from the confines of the "I am." If objective reality could be the product of the objective reality of other ideas it would be unnecessary for there to be another distinct existent; that of the "I am" could suffice.

To try to extricate himself from this tricky situation, Descartes will say that he's talking about a very specific idea, the idea of the infinite, and that, quite obviously, you can't find the objective reality of the idea of the infinite in ideas. Therefore, Descartes will proceed in two steps. The first, which is contained in Axiom V, is to eliminate the hypothesis that the objective reality of an idea can be caused purely by an objective reality. The second has to do with the specific idea of the infinite, to which Descartes will try to give a special status in order to justify this axiom, which is certainly not justifiable, even under the systems of evidence or constraints associated with the Classical Age. We should note in passing that this probably explains why the Cartesian proof of God's existence didn't meet with great success.

> Axiom VI. There are various degrees of reality or being: a substance has more reality than an accident or a mode; an infinite substance has more reality than a finite substance. Hence there is more objective reality in the idea of a substance than in the idea of an accident; and there is more objective reality in the idea of an infinite substance than in the idea of a finite substance.

This axiom recapitulates the hierarchical vision of the multiple, which, it must be said, is what is most archaic in Descartes, most Aristotelian, most Thomistic. This vision is introduced gradually, starting from the elimination of the causality of lack. It is then developed in Axiom IV, applied to the reality of ideas in Axiom V, and, finally, fully explained in Axiom VI with the assertion that "there are various degrees of reality or being." Existents are hierarchically ordered in terms of being, and ideas in terms of objective reality.

In summary, Descartes's axioms are actually a hierarchical construction. It's the construction of a figure of order of the multiple, admittedly still within the space of the "I am" since the existence of anything else has not yet been posited but which nevertheless, via ideas and their objective reality, concerns being. The distinctive work of Descartes consists in the fact that, instead of constructing this hierarchy from the experience of the world—which would correspond to a cosmological vision—he gives us a conceptual vision of it, since it's the difference between ideas that is hierarchized. It should moreover be emphasized that he never restored the cosmological hierarchy, which is why he remains a modern thinker of the first rank.

Indeed, the physical world of Descartes is not a world of hierarchically ordered substances but a world in which there are only figures and movements, a desubstantialized and dehierarchized world. *That's* the Cartesian revolution, an admittedly incomplete revolution in that the cosmological dehierarchization is supplemented by the retention of a hierarchy of ideas. This revolution is ultimately a sort of historical compromise between the desubstantialization and the dehierarchization of the vision of the world, on the one hand, and a certain type of retention of the hierarchical principle, on the other. The main idea, to go deeper, the idea that is the crux of the matter and that is missing in Descartes, is the causality of lack—that is, the possible causal reality of lack, absence, or disappearance. Only these notions fully allow for the introduction of the category of event and, with it, the possibility for truly revolutionary ruptures. The reason there's a Cartesian compromise—and therefore also two opposing Cartesian traditions, mechanistic materialism and absolute freedom—is that Descartes never abandons a strictly ontological conception of the difference between ideas.

In my view, for achieving a nonhierarchical thinking of the multiple (which, if you will, is the ontological question of communism), the causality of lack is certainly an indispensable instrument. In this connection, there's a first, fundamental upheaval in Descartes: even if he doesn't conceptualize it, the causality of lack is at work, not as regards ideas but as regards the world. Descartes's completely geometrized cosmology effects a real dehierarchization of the figure of the physical world. It's no longer a cosmos. At the same time, this very profound undermining of the hierarchical vision is accompanied by the retention of what is the basis of every identity-based hierarchy (such as racism, nationalism, anti-Semitism, etc.): the ontological theory of difference. In Descartes, it is reduced to the ideas, which are themselves contained in the space of the "I am." This is the Cartesian compromise between dehierarchization and hierarchy.

Actually, the true heart of the question is the thinking of the multiple that is started from, and this is bound up with the question of the designation and location of the causality of lack. It's a question of which concept we have of difference. If Descartes's physics is bizarre, like a sort of romance of physics, it's because the Cartesian concept of difference is not equal to his task of undermining the traditional hierarchies that have come down from Aristotle. Descartes lags behind his own desire to dehierarchize the multiple.

<hr />

We can now turn to the actual demonstration. As we shall see, the "proof" of God's existence stems from the fact that we have an idea of God within us. If I want to prove the big Other from the "I," the only option is to begin with the idea of the big Other. It's an absurd, and noble, undertaking, as well as a highly significant aberration, a profound Cartesian symptom. It's completely wrong to say that Descartes "found" a proof of God's existence. In reality, he was forced to prove God this way and not otherwise. God's existence absolutely had to be inferred from the idea of God within us. Situating himself in an utterly constrained space, that of the "I think, I am," as the place of the hierarchy of ideas, Descartes had no alternative but his proof. Let me read you this proof again.

PROPOSITION II

The existence of God can be demonstrated a posteriori merely from the fact that we have an idea of God within us.

DEMONSTRATION

The objective reality of any of our ideas requires a cause which contains the very same reality not merely objectively but formally or eminently (Axiom V). But we have an idea of God (Def. II and VIII), and the objective reality of this idea is not contained in us either formally or eminently (Axiom VI); moreover it cannot be contained in any other being except God himself (Def. VIII). Therefore this idea of God, which is in us, must have God as its cause; and hence God exists (Axiom III). (2:113–117)

The purely formal unfolding of the proof is merely an ordered reading of the axioms, an implementation, in a certain order, of the materials available. The point of suture is the exclusion of the possibility that the objective reality of an idea can be caused by the objective reality of another idea. What would now be the supporting points for the proof, not contained in the axioms? The most important point, which is not strictly speaking in the axioms, is that the "I am" is finite. Clearly, if the "I am" were not finite but infinite, it could be the eminent cause of the idea of the infinite. But Descartes refers to Axiom VI here.

So let's begin with this omission and ask what the foundation of the finiteness of the "I am" is. It can't be empirical reality: the finite duration of my existence has nothing to do with the "I am." It's an empirical given of the self, of the body. Remember that the "I am" only exists to the extent that I think it, and at the moment that I think it. It is without duration, a category that could therefore not be an attribute of the "I am," let alone be the basis of its finiteness. The "I am," which is a point of enunciation, is unrelated to the duration of human existence. What matters is not that the "I am" lasts but rather that it is a point. The "I am" is finite in that it is in eclipse, in that it is empty. Its finiteness is based on its emptiness, not on its fullness.

The underlying axiom is therefore that the empty punctuality of the "I am" is finite. That's what guarantees the proof: the idea of God as such is finite, as is the "I am," but its differential marking, its weight of being, is infinite. We certainly don't have in our heads, in the punctual cogito, an infinite idea of the infinite God. But *what differentiates this idea from the others is infinite.* And what differentiates it from the others? Its hierarchical place in the multiplicity of ideas. It's this place that differentially "infinitizes" the finite idea of the infinite God. The hierarchical system of ideas, which is mediated by their "objective reality," their differentiated weight of being, is brought fully into play here.

Our idea of the infinite, attested as existing in the finite space of the "I think, I am," is immediately two-sided: as an idea it is finite, but as an idea placed in the hierarchy of ideas it is infinite. There is a being of the idea that is not its immediacy as an idea but is related to its objective reality and thus to its place in the hierarchy of ideas. Therefore, the infinite exists.

Let's accept that and focus on lack. We should note, first of all, that the "I am" is finite, that the essence of this statement is that the pure empty point of the enunciation is finite. But what is excluded by this assertion? Well, it's the infinite as infinitely small, as an infra-finite differential. The thesis that the disappearance contained in the "I think, I am" is finite is self-evident only if we exclude the possibility that there can be an *infra*-finite infinite and if we see the *supra*-finite as the sole infinite. The infinity of the disappearance itself, which is inaccessible to the finite, is thereby excluded in an excessive but also differential way. The vanishing differential term, "I think, I am," can be said to be nonfinite, or falling short of the infinite.

At this point, you can see how a detailed comparison—which we won't have time to make—would be necessary, a comparison with Pascal's famous text on the two infinites. Pascal says that the being of the "I am" is suspended between two types of infinites, the large and the small. So, for him, there's a double abyss rather than a sole hierarchical superiority of the infinite. As you can see, we once again find here the point-by-point opposition between Pascal and Descartes. For Pascal, the concept of the infinite is twofold, and Pascal's thesis deals a major blow to Descartes's proof of God's existence, which, as I've shown, assumes that the infinite is completely bound up with largeness. This is because, for Descartes, it is impossible for the infinite to be a sign of surplus, that is to say, that there could be anything in the idea of the infinite other than the restriction of our ideas, to such an extent that it is ultimately the (empty) concept of the Whole. Descartes rejects the idea that the void of the enunciation should be counted as one. He leaves it outside the multiple. Neither the One of the void nor the Whole of the multiple can therefore give rise to the idea of the infinite. Thus, there's a leap from the Subject, as the only existent, to the big Other, hypostasized as the sole real referent of the (finite) idea of the infinite.

With these remarks we'll take leave of the great and prudent Descartes, who holds that the One unfolds only at the point of the subject, in the confrontation with the Other, that Other that is nevertheless related to the subject, because from the latter's mere existence it can be inferred that its Other will offer it, with nothing tangible in return, the guarantee of Truth.

Session 5

January 10, 1984

After drawing attention, with Descartes, to what I called an inaugural text concerning the category of subject as such, I am now going to turn, retrospectively, as it were, to a text from an earlier era, the Greek era. One of my intentions is to show that, while the question of the subject is missing from the title, it nevertheless appears punctually in the text. The text we'll be dealing with, Plato's *Sophist*, retrospectively validates the thesis I'm putting forward, which is that, broadly speaking, philosophy's object, even in the absence of its signifier, is the subject.

This dialogue is not some marginal text. Indeed, it's an extremely famous text, famous for the simple reason that it is the first to bring to light a theory of nonbeing that remains ontological and is not, like the theory in the *Gorgias*, purely sophistic. It is the first text in which nonbeing becomes an explicit category of being and in which the aim is to establish the thesis that nonbeing is. Naturally, it is through this being of nonbeing that, as I see it, Plato will implicitly propose his doctrine of the subject.

The *Sophist* is a dialogue that follows a rather complex strategy, whose apparent objective is not exactly the question of nonbeing. It's not an abstractly dialectical dialogue as is, to a certain extent, the *Parmenides*, the dialogue we'll focus on next. Its aim, its ambition, is to define the character of the sophist. Empirically, a sophist was a professional, a professional teacher of the art of giving effective speeches. He was someone who, for a fee, taught well-bred young men how to handle themselves in political debates. So he was a character connected in an important way with the democratic space, a space in which deliberative, public politics happened, such that political decisions were discussed therein and what was at stake in them wasn't monopolized by a small group, at least not apparently. The sophist would teach the tricks of the trade to well-to-do young men intent on pursuing a career in politics: how to defend a position, then its opposite, how to deal with any circumstances, how to switch sides elegantly, and so on. So this is what the dialogue seeks to grasp, in its proper being, particularly as regards the question of language, since that's what the sophist was primarily a professional of.

The *Sophist* was originally part of a trilogy in which three characters were introduced: the sophist, the statesman, and the philosopher, each of whom gives its title to a dialogue. We don't have the last one, the *Philosopher*, which is a real shame. It is not certain, moreover, that it was ever written.

Be that as it may, all throughout Plato's career the sophists were his key interlocutors and adversaries. They're involved throughout his work, in a kind of very complex interlocution. The sophist is essentially a negative figure, with whom Plato has a very unusual relationship of critical fascination, which is the guiding thread of an important part of his thought. We know, moreover, that Plato wasn't a democrat, and the two things go hand in hand. He wasn't a democrat since he thought, for one thing, that politics had to be based on truth and, for another, that truth was one and couldn't be subjected to the arbitrariness of contrasting arguments. It was as though something about sophistic nihilism was a sort of perpetual reminder for Plato of the improbable vitality of the question of truth, especially in the political field.

In *Theory of the Subject*, I point out that the militant nihilist, whom we encountered in the 1960s and 1970s in the guise of the anarchistic radical leftist, the one I called "anarcho-desiring," is an essential character, an indispensable interlocutor, in the search for a true politics. There is a similar affinity in Plato's relationship with the sophist. Criticizing the sophist is an endless task that is never settled once and for all, as though it were necessary to sharpen the thought of true politics, of just politics, through a critical intimacy with those who embody the skeptical version of it in the broad sense, or more precisely, the democratic-skeptical version.

In Plato's view, the sophist is fundamentally characterized by his ability to present the false as true and the true as false. In modern terms we could say that the sophist is the master of semblance, the one who introduces semblance into mastery. Plato's question is the same as the one that gave its title to one of Lacan's seminars: What is "a discourse that would not be pure semblance?"[1] This is the same as asking "What is a discourse that would not be the sophist's?" since the sophist is the master of semblance, the one who masterfully deploys this ability to present the false as true.

This will immediately lead to two groups of questions on Plato's part.

First, what is the essence of this presentation? How can the false be presented as true? Since it is indeed possible to present the false in the form of an imitation of the true, to formulate a theory of sophistic presentation you necessarily have to begin by formulating a theory of semblance, i.e., of imitation, mimesis, simulacrum, and this is what Plato will do.

But this problem leads to another one. If the false can be presented in this way, even as an imitation, it's because it has a being, since nothing that has no being is presentable. The master of semblance shows that semblance is presentable as the mimesis of truth, and if it's presentable, it's because it *is*. On the other hand, the false *is not*; indeed, it is in exemplary fashion that which has no being. For Plato, the true statement is a statement about being, and the false statement a statement about nonbeing. Therefore, if the false is presentable, it's because, in a way, it *is*, which leads to the need to establish that there is a being of nonbeing. So it's not possible to complete the description of the sophist unless you have an ontology of nonbeing, unless it's made possible, thinkable, that, in one way or another, nonbeing is.

The stakes are very high. They are political because, for Plato, the doctrinaire theorists of pure being, those like Parmenides and the Eleatics who refuse to accept that nonbeing is, force the philosopher into a hopelessly defensive position vis-à-vis the sophist. Indeed, they lack the tools of sophistry, which, in reality, operates in nonbeing, in the false presented as true. Thus, far from being pure negative philosophical speculation, establishing something that makes it possible to overcome sophistry is a crucial challenge for Plato. This is why the main thrust of the *Sophist* will be, on the one hand, to establish that there is a being of nonbeing, and, on the other hand, to criticize as antipolitical the philosophical heritage of the theorists of pure being. This battle on two fronts is reminiscent, for me, of the way Kant sets out his thought—which he calls "critical"—between dogmatism, which runs from Plato to Leibniz, and skepticism, which runs from Carneades to Hume.

⸺⸘⸺

The *Sophist* features four characters: Theodorus, Socrates, the Eleatic Stranger [or, as he is called in some translations, the Visitor from Elea], and Theaetetus.

Plato begins with a vast panorama of all the philosophies of his time. He will identify four broad tendencies, which the dialogue presents before arguing against each, one after the other.

1. The proponents of the original multiple, who think there is an original, irreducible plurality in being. The concept of being is not a simple one; it has to be divided. These are the pluralists.
2. The proponents of the One, namely, Parmenides and his school. For them, being is absolutely one.
3. The materialists. Being is inherently corporeal.
4. The "Friends of the Forms," that is, the dogmatic Platonists— Plato's own right wing. They accept an original multiple system of intelligible ideas, but this system is immutable.

1. The proponents of this first tendency don't posit *the* multiple as such; rather, for them, there is *multiplicity* in being. They can be compared to those who think that being is two, such as, for example, certain Ionian physicists, who believe there's a duality of hot and cold, etc. They are immediately criticized on the grounds that they're unable to think what being is, once being is the Two that they introduce. Actually, they count being as three: being and its two components. If you conceive of being as Two, then being appears as a third thing hidden behind the two constitutive terms. There always remains a vanishing "extra something," which precludes saying that it's the two that's originary. In the passage I'm going to read you, the criticism is put in the mouth of the Visitor from Elea, whose present interlocutor is Theaetetus but who claims to be directly addressing the proponents of the tendency he's attacking.

> VISITOR: We should ask of them, as if they were here with us, "So come on, you people who claim that all things are hot and cold or some other such pair of things: what exactly are you saying about them both, that is, when you say both and each of them are? What are we to take this 'being' of yours to be? Is it a third thing

alongside the two you started with, so that we're to count you as
saying that everything comprises not just two things but three?
After all, I don't suppose you're calling one of them being, if you
say both equally are; whichever of them it was, that would pretty
much make them one, not two."

THEAETETUS: True.

VISITOR: "So," we'll ask them, "is it both of them together you
want to label as being?"

THEAETETUS: Perhaps.

VISITOR: "But, friends," we'll say to them, "in that case too you'd
very clearly be saying that the two are one."

THEAETETUS: Quite correct. (243d–244a)[2]

You can see how interesting this passage is in terms of the logic of
lack. The predicament that Plato forces the representatives of this
first tendency into is that they have to either count two as three or
count two as one, but they're unable to count the two as two. For
them, being is a term either in excess or in default.

⸺

2. This thesis was dealt with throughout the *Parmenides*, where there
are two arguments concerning the problem of the One, the multiple,
and being, one of which has to do with language and the other with
the relationship between the One and the Whole.

(a) As regards language, we find the old argument. If being is one,
the One cannot be said since to do so would be to introduce the
Two. Either the name "one" is, and therefore there is the Two, or
being is merely its name, and to say that being is one is to make a
name into one. To put it another way, if being is one, naming being
immediately introduces a vacillation, because if the name *is*, then
being must be only the name since it is one, but in that case the
name no longer is, since it is what it names, i.e., being, and if the

name is not, then it couldn't be said as one. Hence being drops out of the discourse if the name is not. To say that being is one is to make being vacillate in its name, by making it either unsayable or evanescent.

Here's what Plato tells us, still speaking through the Visitor, who continues to address Theaetetus:

> VISITOR: If he posits the name as something different from the thing it belongs to, he is presumably talking about two things.
> THEAETETUS: Yes.
> VISITOR: And yet if he posits the name as being the same as the thing, either he'll be forced to say it is the name of nothing, or, if he's going to claim it as the name of something, the name will turn out to be merely a name of a name, not of anything else.
> THEAETETUS: Just so.
> VISITOR: So the one, being just one, will turn out equally the name of the one and the one of the name. (244d)

In this (rather . . . sophistic!) discussion we catch a shadowy glimpse of Plato's thesis that in order for language to be possible there must be an articulated place of being, not being as such. Otherwise, it would be impossible to say anything at all and, in particular, to say that being is one. The thesis that being is one is self-destructive: it's tantamount to blocking language. It's a paradoxical thesis in the logical sense because it cancels itself out. Consequently, there must always be a preexisting articulated place—a *topos*, for Plato—a place of ideas, a place of an intelligible multiplicity. Thus, you'll see that, with Plato, too, we find, in the absence of any reference to the subject, the thesis that there is always a primacy of the place. The concept of the One necessarily implies the concept of the place for which there is One. As a result, the Parmenidean thesis is untenable because it purports to be exclusively punctual, to give the point without the place of the point, to think an outside-place without a place, a radical outside-place. That's why it's a radical-leftist thesis.

(b) The One and the Whole. Here, Plato will attempt to show that if you think that being is one, then you won't be able to produce the concept of the Whole. Either being is Whole or it's not Whole. If it's Whole, that's because it's multiple—it has parts—and therefore exceeds the One, and so being is in excess over itself: being is lacking itself while the Whole exceeds the One and therefore being.

Here's how the Visitor continues his demonstration:

> VISITOR: And yet if what is is not a whole through having acquired the attribute of oneness like that, and at the same time the whole is, by itself, then what is turns out to be lacking itself.
> THEAETETUS: It certainly does.
> VISITOR: And by this argument, what is will turn out not to be, if it is deprived of itself.
> THEAETETUS: Just so.
> VISITOR: Moreover, all things once again become more than one, what is and the whole having each acquired its own separate nature. (245c)

In short, there is therefore an excess of being over itself in relation to the Whole, and a lack in relation to the One. In what follows, the Visitor will continue to put forward the paradoxes that support his thesis. But what should we make of this dialectic? The paradoxes used here in my opinion don't mean exactly what Plato has them say but rather that the One and the Whole are not concepts that "work" on the same plane. The One-Whole relationship is a relationship of torsion rather than correlation.

What I myself think is that if we want to think the One and the Whole in a relationship of correlation, we come to a dead end. That relationship needs to be thought in torsion, in the form of an internal exclusion. In the *Sophist*, the discussion swirls around a bit because it reflects the lack of an explicit concept of the subject. This concept is traced here only through its absence: only its presence as a nexus would make the articulation thinkable. The nexus between the One and the Whole is precisely the subject: that's what my own thesis is. In the dialogue, without torsion and without the subject, Plato is perfectly right: all we have is a dialectic devoid of any stability.

⸺⸺

3. So far we've dealt with the critiques of dualism and monism. Now we're going to turn to the critique of materialism.

The "Friends of the Earth" is how Plato refers to the materialists. He will paint a literary portrait of them, a portrait that is the source of the portrayal of materialists in general throughout the whole academic history of materialism. He imagines that he's got an affable materialist before him, and he simply offers a weak, strictly literary refutation, which amounts to forcing him to admit the idea that there are incorporeal things. The materialist will agree, for example, that justice is incorporeal. As the Visitor says, "if they are willing to admit that among the things that are there is even a little bit of a thing that is without body, that will suffice" (247c8–d1).

It's interesting to see how, as soon as the materialist appears, the scene become literary. It's no longer dialectical or refutational. Less than a philosophical position, the materialist represents a character, and he is treated, with his supposed friendliness, as a dramatic or novelistic invention. Plato doesn't hide the fact that a real-life materialist wouldn't let himself be refuted, that he wouldn't be open to Plato's arguments. So what we'll witness is not a real discussion but rather a scene, in all the senses of the word. Here, the "scene" is about justice.

⸺⸺

4. The "Friends of the Forms." Historians have wondered who they might be. My thesis is that they're the Platonists, in a figure that—ironically, and since it's an Eleatic who's supposed to be speaking—Plato identifies as the rigid aspect of his own thought. Remember that the *Sophist* is a dialogue of Plato's maturity and that he therefore already had ossified disciples. They are people who admit that there is an intelligible topos, a primordial place of the thinkable, and who oppose that to the world of becoming, to what is changeable, alive. They conceive of the place of the thinkable as separate, eternal, unchanging. Plato will say that that opposition is antidialectical, too extreme, and that becoming should be conceived of as a category of the intelligible place itself. The place should be thought of as a living place. Plato shows how knowledge itself is a process, governed by a certain type of becoming: the intellect, the knowing soul, is a living principle that cannot be separated from the categories of change. So there is a dialectization, an implementation of the intelligible place itself. In Plato's view, the place of the intelligible mustn't just "sit there." It is not opposed to becoming the way death is opposed to life.

Here's a brief summary of Plato's argument, presented, as ever, by the Visitor to Theaetetus.

> VISITOR: But—Zeus!—what is this? Are we in any case going to be
> so easily persuaded that change and life and soul and wisdom are
> truly absent from what completely is, and that it does not live,
> or think, but sits there in august holiness, devoid of intelligence,
> fixed and unchanging? (249a)

You can see that, at this stage, we have an ontological horizon, which consists of three principles that, in Plato's eyes, can be taken for granted:

1. We must reject strict dualism, that is, the idea that being is intrinsically double or multiple. There is indeed a single

category of being. Being is a simple idea. In short, there is a count-as-one of being.

2. We must accept that there is an articulated, intelligible place, on the basis of which something can be said about being. And we must therefore posit that there is a dialectic of being, but that it is sayable only in a field of thought having a complex articulation, or system of relations.

3. Change—that is, life, thought—is one of the fundamental categories of being. It's not related solely to the degeneration that occurs in the sensible world.

So it will be necessary to posit an intelligible multiple, which I call the "articulated place of the thinkable" and which is not the sensible world or the whole of the sensible or the one of the sensible but is instead the horizon of thought as dialectical thought. And being will have to be placed in this horizon. Let me mention in passing that the complete process of placement of being in accordance with this place will require nonbeing to be.

——— ⬥ ———

The question Plato will begin with is as follows. Assuming that the condition of thought is that there is an intelligible multiplicity, an articulated place, what is the order structure of such a multiple?

Is the multiple thinkable otherwise than through the thinking of order, hierarchical thinking? That's an important philosophical question. It is at any rate certain that, for Plato, the answer to this question must be yes. The crux of our dialogue is to achieve the placement of being by proposing a figure of order, a foundation matrix. The demonstration is complicated, and the development in the dialogue is hard to follow. Even if I don't always agree with him, let me refer you on this subject to Jean-Claude Milner's definitive article "Le point du signifiant," which appeared in *Cahiers pour l'analyse* (no. 3, May 1966).[3]

Let me summarize Plato's argument. It is assumed that there is a multiplicity of ideas, forms, kinds. Every time you think that something is, you're thinking of the idea of being, and whenever you think that something is moving, you're thinking of the idea of motion. If this multiplicity is articulated (the ideas have a structure of relationship/nonrelationship with each other, otherwise nothing is sayable), then operators of connection, principles of composition, an internal composition law are needed. Plato calls this "mixing." Some ideas can mix, and others are unable to combine with each other.

I'm now going to reconstruct in a somewhat formal way what happens in the dialogue. We will denote as $m(x, y)$ the existence of a possible mixture of idea x and idea y. Plato distinguishes two classes of ideas: there are those that mix with all the others and those that are such that there exists at least one with which they can't combine. The first class could be called the "universal expansion class" and the second "the limit point class."

In logic, the first class corresponds to the universal quantifier class. Let a be a particular idea. It has the property of universal expansion if we have:

$$(\forall y)\ m(a, y)$$

The second class corresponds to the existential quantifier class, connected to negation. Let b be a particular idea. It has the property of the limit point if, with $\neg$ being the sign of negation, we have:

$$(\exists y)\ \neg\, m(b, y)$$

The problem will be to find the representatives of these classes. So Plato will look for a core set of fundamental ideas.

Being is the typical representative of the first class: every idea is characterized by being, and being thus mixes with all the other ideas. But being is not the only representative of the universal expansion class: the idea of the same—self-identity—also belongs to it, since every idea is identical to itself. Motion is the representative of the second class because there is at least one idea with which motion cannot combine: the idea of rest. I should mention in passing that this is something that will be disproved later on by differential calculus, thanks to which rest can be thought of as a limit of motion and motion as a differential of rest. In Plato's view, there is a negative relationship between the two constituent relationships of their idea, since it confirms their membership in the limit point class and their exteriority to the universal expansion class. Indeed, to know what motion is, a second idea needs to be thought, its limit point, i.e., rest. The second class is completely determined by the example of these two ideas. Being, however, insofar as it is the paradigm of the first class, is mixed with both rest and motion.

For the time being we have three fundamental ideas: being, motion, and rest. But things are not so simple. We've made sense of the two broad classes, *provided that being, motion, and rest are in fact distinct*. To think distinction as such, we obviously need to be able to think the same and the other. Which means that, to understand the overall structure, we'll have not three ideas but five.

I'll explain all this in detail next time.

Session 6

January 17, 1984

The chief aim of the *Sophist* dialogue is to establish the being of nonbeing. But this has to be done in an intelligible place, whose proper essence is to be multiple. After criticizing the opposing theses, Plato begins by asking the question of how this place is organized, of what might be called the syntax of the Ideas.

We know from many of the Master's other dialogues that real things "participate" in the ideas, and that it's this participation that identifies them. This thesis, however, is not syntactic but semantic: a good deed is, through participation in the Idea of the Good, a local model of that idea. It's an interpretation.

The *Sophist* is not concerned with that semantic doctrine of participation. What its structure is concerned with are the intrinsic articulations of the intelligible place and therefore its syntax. The theory of participation is vertical; it has to do with participation in transcendence, whereas the combinatory theory of the *Sophist* is a horizontal theory concerning the relationships of ideas with one another, a theory of the connection of ideas with one another.

It can be said (I refer you to Milner's article) that this syntax is generative: the aim is to determine the small number of greatest ideas that will provide the matrix of this syntax from a few Ideas, in order to obtain the general law, which is generated by this core syntactic set.

As I mentioned earlier, Plato, in the disguise of a Visitor from Elea, ultimately retains five ideas: being, motion, rest, the same, and the other. We note that the Good does not figure in the list, and this sheds light on the astonishing statement in the *Republic* to the effect that the Idea of the Good is not an idea.

The combination of these five ideas, or "greatest kinds," provides a scale model of the whole syntax of the Ideas. In this respect, in isolating a small core combinatorial set to elucidate a huge question, the *Sophist* is very much a structuralist dialogue.

The problem that arises is why there are five greatest kinds. Indeed, five is an interesting figure, a figure that's much less common than Parmenides's one, Aristotle's two (matter and form), Kant's three (pure reason, practical reason, and judgment), or the four with which Hegel, at the end of his *Logic*, quantifies the true dialectic. Following Milner, we end up with a reconstruction of the Platonic thinking as to this question.

The starting point is as follows: to think combination, an operator of combination (of ideas) is necessary. As we have seen, Plato calls it mixing or communion, or combination. In any case, what's behind it is the possibility of combining. We will write $m(a, x)$ to say that idea *a* mixes with idea *x*. We've seen that, as a result, the "greatest kinds" can be classified, and so ultimately can all the ideas, into two classes: class C_1, shall we say, the class of universal expansion (the ideas that mix with all the others) and class C_2, the class of the limit point (the ideas for which there's another idea with which they can't mix).

Class C_1 is therefore represented by an idea that can combine with all the others. This will be the idea of being, since every idea is characterized by being. The formula of this class is:

$$(a \in C_1) \leftrightarrow \forall x\, [m(a, x)].$$

Class C_2 is the class in which is found an idea that does not combine with another. It is represented chiefly by motion, which can't combine with rest. The formula of this class is (¬, again, is the sign of negation):

$$(a \in C_2) \leftrightarrow \exists x \, [\neg \, m \, (a, \, x)].$$

This requires the Three. Indeed, what doesn't motion mix with? So far we have the two representatives of the two classes, C_1 and C_2, being and motion, but that's not enough to base C_2 on. The third term will be that with which motion doesn't mix, and the kind that doesn't mix with the idea of motion is *rest*. Motion and rest are both in C_2 because they are mutually limiting.

We had one kind, being. To have two, we needed the Three. So these three greatest kinds are being, motion, and rest. They are identical and more or less differentiable, i.e., identical to themselves, which gives them their consistency. What's more, there's no confusion possible between the one and the other two: these three kinds are unequivocally differentiable.

The fact of having three kinds and thinking them as both identical and differentiable in turn requires two ideas, identity and difference: the *same* and the *other*. To be assured of the three, the five will be necessary. So the list of ideas, of greatest kinds, had to be supplemented.

The question that immediately arises is then: are the same and the other in class C_1 or in class C_2? The same should seemingly belong to C_1 since every idea is the same as itself, and the other should belong to C_2 since it is other than everything, except that it is not other than itself, or else it would be nothing. The other is therefore its own limit point.

But things are more complicated than that!

Let's first make a detour through the operator of mixing. Is mixing an idea? If so, what class is it in? Is it one of the greatest kinds? Now, Plato uses mixing to define the dialectic. Let me read you the passage:

VISITOR: So then given that we've agreed that kinds too mix in such ways as these, must a person not have some sort of expertise to progress in his arguments if he is going to show correctly which sorts of kinds are in harmony with which and which are not receptive to each other, and further, whether there are some that hold them together, running through them in such a way as to make them capable of mixing; and again, in cases where they divide off, whether there are others similarly running through them all that cause the division?

THEAETETUS: Yes! He certainly will need expertise—pretty much the most important one of all, probably.

VISITOR: So what are we going to call this expertise, Theaetetus? Or—Zeus!—have we stumbled, without noticing, on the very expertise that makes a person free? Can we possibly, in searching for the sophist, actually have found the philosopher first?

THEAETETUS: What makes you say that?

VISITOR: Are we not going to claim that dividing according to kinds, and not thinking either that the same form is different or, when it is different, that it is the same, belongs to expertise in dialectic?

THEAETETUS: Yes, we will claim that. (253b–254a)

The mastery of the category of mixing and difference is the dialectic; consequently, the mastery of mixing implies the mastery of the dialectic. And yet Plato never presents mixing as an idea. This is an apparent riddle, which has only one solution: mixing is a *meta-idea*, an operational type of existence, so to speak, which is different from the ideas and can't be aligned with the ideas themselves. Thus, mixing belongs to a superior category.

Being, motion, and rest are ideas, that is to say, what makes it possible to say about things that move or that are at rest that they *are*. So an idea is something whose semantics is real. But mixing is a thinking of syntactic relation, and therefore it's a concept of the dialectic, which implies the place of ideas without being itself an idea, since it's the meta-idea of the relationships among ideas. Mixing—like the Good—doesn't belong to the same series as being, motion, and rest, i.e., the first series, the basic series, of the intelligible universe.

Plato's intelligible place is therefore a stratified place, and our question can be formulated as follows: are the other and the same ideas or meta-ideas? This is a question of the utmost importance for the Platonic theory of the subject—a theory that, as I said, is present in absentia. For if the same and the other are ideas, they are consequently operators of participation (or a category of what gives itself to be thought) for Plato, but not dialectical concepts. As a result, they can be aligned, for example, with being, or motion, depending on whether you put them in C1 or C2. But can the other be aligned with being? If so, there is no theory of the subject; there is only, Althusser would say, a process without a subject. If, however, the other is the outside-place [horlieu] of being, we have a completely different philosophical system.

Plato treads a fine line with respect to this issue. It would seem that the five greatest kinds form a list, divided into C1 and C2. But can the other, the very concept of difference, be included in the list of terms that it differentiates between? So? Stratification or alignment, or something else? Plato will deal with this issue because the Visitor from Elea, his Eleatic marionette, is suddenly very interested in the question of the other. Let me read you the passage:

> VISITOR: Greatest, certainly, of the kinds we have just been talking about are this very one, namely being itself, and rest and change.
> THEAETETUS: Yes, much the greatest.
> VISITOR: And now two of the three we say are, themselves, unmixed with each other.

THEAETETUS: We do, emphatically.

VISITOR: Whereas being is mixed with both of them, since both of them presumably are.

THEAETETUS: Obviously so.

VISITOR: So they make three.

THEAETETUS: Of course.

VISITOR: So each of them is different from the other two, but itself the same as itself.

THEAETETUS: Just so.

VISITOR: What then about the things we're speaking of now, when we talk like this—the same and the different? Are these two more kinds, other than the three we already have, yet always necessarily mixing with them; and should we inquire into them on the assumption that there are five kinds, not three? Or are we referring to one of the three with this talk of "the same" and "the different," and just not noticing? (254d–e)

Plato's first demonstration will consist in saying that the same cannot be being. The second is that the other cannot be being either. Next time, we'll examine the difference between these two demonstrations: the same is different from being, and the other is also different from being. We'll see that they are essentially asymmetrical, an asymmetry from which nonbeing will emerge.

Session 7

January 31, 1984

As I mentioned at our last session, in addition to the three fundamental kinds—being, motion, and rest—two others appear: the same and the other. The basis for this emergence is that each of the first three kinds must be able to be identified and differentiated or else it would be impossible to count them as three. Identification will be based on the same while differentiation will be based on the other.

The main problem will be the status of these two new terms compared to the other three. Are they of the same or of a superior type, and should they be aligned with level 1 [ideas] or with mixing, which is a metalogical term, a meta-idea? At first glance, they seem to be instances of mixing since they're apparently relations. Being, motion, and rest are intrinsic attributes, whereas the same and the other are relations. Actually, the problem is a lot trickier, not just in Plato's work but in and of itself.

Indeed, there is a fundamental asymmetry between the same and the other. It makes its appearance in Plato's text as soon as he attempts to distinguish between the same and the other, on the one hand, and the being/motion/rest group, on the other. He introduces the same and the other in order to *distinguish the first three from one other.* Yet no sooner has he done that than he attempts to *distinguish the same and the other from those first three*, which is not the same operation. He begins by ascertaining that the same and the other are really necessary and not already present in the other three. So he tries to differentiate difference, that is, to show that there is not already a concept of difference, that difference is really a different concept.

The crucial point, then, is that the same is not being, and neither is the other. There are philosophers who argue the contrary. For Parmenides, for instance, being and the same are the same thing. Being is the same as itself, incapable of being anything other than the same as itself. Sartre's thesis will be that identity is an essential property of the in-itself, and this excludes any alterity. Being is the same. Conversely, in the Hegelian dialectic, since being is negativity, being is the other. It can therefore be understood as the ability to distinguish itself from itself. For Heraclitus, being is constant self-transformation. Heraclitus and Parmenides differ in that for the former, being is other and for the latter, being is the same.

Plato launches into a long polemical demonstration on this subject aimed at ruling out the opposing theses of Parmenides and Heraclitus.

> VISITOR: But again, if "is" and "same" don't indicate anything distinct, when we come to say that change and rest both are, we'll be talking about them both as if they were the same thing.
> THEAETETUS: And that is certainly impossible.
> VISITOR: In which case it's impossible for sameness and being to be one. (255c)

What is the crux of this demonstration? It has already been established that motion and rest can both be combined with being, since being is in the position of universal expansion. Furthermore, "the same" means "identical." But if being is said to be identical, then motion and rest must share in the identical since they both mix, in the same way, with being. Yet this is impossible since they're different, both of them belonging in this regard to class C2.

Next:

> VISITOR: But should we be thinking of being and sameness as one thing?
>
> THEAETETUS: Possibly.
>
> VISITOR: But again, if "is" and "same" don't indicate anything distinct, when we come to say that change and rest both are, we'll be talking about them both as if they were the same thing.
>
> THEAETETUS: And that is certainly impossible.
>
> VISITOR: In which case it's impossible for sameness and being to be one.
>
> THEAETETUS: Pretty much.
>
> VISITOR: Are we then to posit sameness as a fourth form, over and above the three we already had?
>
> THEAETETUS: Yes, absolutely. (255 b–c)

The real crux of the demonstration is that it is impossible for there to be the identical in itself, endowed, like being, with universal expansion. That would mean that all things are identical and that there is therefore nothing but the One. So the crux of the demonstration is the retention of the prior distinction.

In conclusion, the identical must be considered as simple self-identity, and there is no principle of universal expansion beyond the relationship to self. In other words, to think the same, an idea must be related to itself. The universality of the position of the same comes down to this ability to relate an idea to itself, to identify it twice. The same is therefore always the Two of the same in its conceptual operation. Therefore, it is essentially the relational operator of repetition. Since the essence of the same is repetition, we need to be able to think the same term twice, that is, to repeat it. But the fact that the same is not being can be inferred from the fact that there is the unrepeatable. If the same is able to be the concept of repetition, it is because there is the unrepeatable. Paradoxically, the essence of the same is that there is the unrepeatable. If everything were repeatable, we'd be in the general sphere of identification. For example, motion doesn't repeat rest. Why? Because it disrupts it, because it ends it. The fundamental underlying dialectic of the same is the dialectic of repetition and disruption. The same is the concept of repetition. If the concept of repetition is needed, it's because there is nonrepetition; otherwise, being would be sufficient. But being is not sufficient because what disrupts *is*, in the same way as what is repeated, but, on the contrary, is not the same as what is repeated. Repetition is not coextensive with being. There is disruption—which *is*—and this requires that there be the same, as a concept distinct from being.

Note that "same" is purely symbolic here. So we'll have to distinguish, as Plato does, between the same and the similar: what falls into the imaginary is the similar. The same—strict repetition—is ended only by disruption. It is, as we'd put it with Freud and Lacan, the "automatism of repetition," which is a category of being. It follows that the same can be posited as a repetitive relation, which is to say that it serves to think what has the capacity to be reinscribed, repeated. This is very profound because the same is not caught up in ontological closure. It does not simply signify pure self-identity.

Does this mean that the same is an idea like the others, located on level 1? It has been disrelationed, as it were. Its intrinsic capacity to be repeated has been identified. The problem now is to determine which class it belongs to. Is there a typical representative of this capacity to be repeated? I'd be tempted to say no. This capacity for repetition is the essential functioning of the symbolic in general. Nor is it the real, since what is at issue is the reinscription of the mark. It is different from being, motion, and rest. The same is the ability to write something twice and be sure that it itself *is*, since it's been written twice. The same can be replaced by any term as long as it's a term. The same is thus in the position of an ideational variable, x, and is never specified in any term already given. The same is the indeterminate of ideas as ideas, as repeatable, the x, y, z of the domain of ideas, replaceable by any one of them. So level 1 can be supplemented by adding to it this indeterminate variable: the same.

—⊶⊷—

What can be said about the other now? The other is clearly different from being. It is the other, this time, that will truly differentiate difference. The other is involved in its differentiation. The demonstration is very complicated. Its underlying axiom is an axiom prohibiting repetition: the other is in the fundamental register of the Two, meaning that it forbids repetition. If A is the operation of the other, it's clear that we can't have $A(x, x)$ but only $A(x, y)$. The other imposes the other; it requires a different term. The essence of the demonstration of the fact that the other is not being is therefore another way of saying that nothing is other than itself, that nothing is self-differentiation, that nothing is pure difference, that nothing is non-self-identity.

This is very strongly emphasized by Plato:

> VISITOR: What about difference?[1] Should we say it's a fifth form? Or should we think of this and being simply as two names for one kind?
> THEAETETUS: Perhaps we should.
> VISITOR. But I think you agree that of the things that are, some are spoken of in and by themselves, while others are always spoken of in relation to others.
> THEAETETUS: Why would I not?
> VISITOR: And that difference is one of the latter—right?
> THEAETETUS: Just so.

VISITOR: It would not be, if being and difference were not very much distinct. If difference shared in both forms in the way that being does, then among the differents, too, there would be a different that was not in relation to something else, whereas as things are we find that whatever is different simply cannot fail to be what it is, namely different, in relation to something else.

THEAETETUS: Yes, as you say.

VISITOR: The nature of the different, then, we're to treat as being fifth among the forms we're singling out.

THEAETETUS: Yes.

VISITOR: And moreover, we're going to say that it is a nature that pervades them all; for each one of them is different from the rest not through its own nature, but rather through its sharing in this other form, difference. (255c–e)

Plato's demonstration consists in foreclosing what is non-self-identical, and, as a result, the other emerges as distinct from being. As for me, I will say that the non-self-identical is the real of the other, because it is its own particular impossibility. The fact that the other is distinct from being has as its impossibility, and hence as its real term, the non-self-identical.

What Plato does here is to align the other with being, in the C_1 universal expansion class. The other is distinct from being but combines with all the ideas since they're all different from the others, so they all share in the other. If we follow Plato, there would be three terms in the C_1 universal expansion class (being, the same, and the other) and two in the C_2 limit point class (motion and rest).

But this comes at the cost of foreclosing the non-self-identical, which Plato passes off as self-evident. It's up to us to reopen this foreclosure. We've got to analyze Plato and bring to light what has been repressed in the symptom.

There is indeed a being underlying the other, namely, the non-self-identical, which to my mind is the real principle of the other. The non-self-identical is obviously not representable, since to represent it would be to identify it. But it's nonidentifiable since it is not self-identical. *The ontological class of the other is therefore the empty class, the one from which no representative can be selected.* In Plato's view, as long as it's the empty class, it doesn't have to be taken into account: since it is nonrepresented, it is foreclosed. But we assume that something can be, without being represented or representable. It's true, the non-self-identical will never be represented by a term. The other cannot represent its class. An empty class must be added, the true place of nonbeing, under which the other, which is radically unrepresentable in the universe of level 1 terms, is subsumed.

Plato thus aligns the other with the other four "greatest kinds" and makes it the placeholder for the foreclosed empty class, which, as a result, it represents. But he will say that this representation is immediately dispersed, and this amounts to instituting the other as an unstable term. No term can properly represent it since it has no principle of alterity within it. Thus, on the one hand, it is aligned but, on the other, no sooner is it aligned than it disperses.

The ontology behind this operation is the foreclosure of the empty class. In the article by Jean-Claude Milner that I mentioned to you, he divides this foreclosure, this function of the unalignable, into two. For Milner, the other has two functions: a function of *delimitation* [cerne] and a function of *abyss* [gouffre]. According to Plato, around each term there is an infinite presence of the other. The function of delimitation means that, since each term is different from all the others, the others delimit it. That's the other of level 1, that is, as pure differentiation of the multiple. As for the underlying function of abyss, foreclosed by Plato, it is the other as empty class, the other from the standpoint of its real, i.e., pure difference, nonbeing. For

Plato, delimitation is the placeholder of the abyss. But the abyss is unnamed, unclassified. I, on the other hand, will say: for difference to prevail, there must be the void. Naturally we'll find the trace of this in Plato, which is that difference disperses into the infinite. The infinity of difference testifies to the unnamed abyss. This latent unlimited quantity of nonbeing is related to the fact that, for it to prevail, the abyss, which Plato tries to do without, is necessary. He only identifies its symptom, i.e., the infinity of difference.

Of course, what we see here is the point of the subject, which is both named and revoked, the point of the subject inasmuch as the other, which is not presentable as such, only appears in the gap between the other terms, the general gap between all the terms, hence what Milner calls the function of delimitation. We can discern the subject by its being in the gap, by its being in eclipse, between these terms. But there's an ontology of this point that, in Plato, or even in Milner, is incomplete. Indeed, to exist as a gap there has to be the point of the empty set. It's not enough to say that there's a gap; you have to be bold enough to say that there's a being of the gap. This ontology of the eclipse that can be punctuated in the empty class is neither named nor recognized by Plato. We will see how this empty class will be classified in relation to our two levels (ideas and meta-ideas). But first we need to establish a basic ontological point: there is a being underlying the other. Actually, the empty class is *the* term of level 2. Mixing, another level 2 term, is in actual fact not a term but a relation. In addition to mixing, there is, on this level 2, a term, which really *is* a term, but is so qua empty.

We cannot do as Plato does and pretend to believe that only level 1 terms exist. For there are the relations among ideas. Nonetheless, it is true that even on level 2, the level of relations, or meta-ideas, there must be a term designating the gap function as such and not just relations. The empty class, which ultimately means the being of the other, is the empty term proper to level 2.

We'll continue to make our way bravely through this labyrinth next time.

---oxxo---

Someone in the audience: *Isn't restoring a being of the other in the guise of the non-self-identical conceding something to Parmenides, namely that the other is not nonbeing? Isn't there still a sort of ontology of presence?*

---oxxo---

I'd be quite willing to say that Plato's position is an ultimately moderate critique of Parmenides. Plato still maintains his theory of difference (of the other) within the theme of presence. He can't bring himself to ontologize difference: he registers its inevitable presence but not its being. The other is everywhere present; it is endlessly dispersed. The impetus for the dispersion is to preserve the other as the representative of nonbeing. But what returns is the latent contradiction between wanting to articulate a principle of differentiation and retaining the presuppositions of presence. The upshot of this contradiction is a strange dialectic, in which the non-self-identical is evoked (it would otherwise be impossible to distinguish between other and being, and we'd remain in Parmenides's sphere) but only to be immediately revoked.

---oxxo---

Someone in the audience: *But isn't there nonetheless a logic of absence?*

---oxxo---

Regarding absence as Plato attempts to theorize it, all his efforts are aimed at identifying it as presence. The glorious Parmenidean plenitude will be lost. An articulation will be gained, a dubious and uncertain gain. The other is precisely the structuring of this loss and gain, an articulation that refuses to be based on the absolute subtractive point, the non-self-identical, or empty class. So Plato will lose more and more being, without, however, gaining enough nonbeing.

———— ✧ ————

Someone in the audience: *What idea of politics is involved here?*

———— ✧ ————

The question comes down to how the notion of other, the gap, the non-self-identical, works in political thought practice. What's important to see, to speak in more empirical terms, is that, for example, the gap between politics and economics is not a gap between instances, a systemic difference, in Althusser's sense. Indeed, the operations of politics are so intricately linked with the economic structuring that they can't be disentangled from it, since they are bound up with it as with a system of conditions of possibility. Nor is it representable in different instances: it cannot be said that organized labor is the instance of the economy and the party that of politics. The gap is greater, but it's also more unified. You can't think any of this without an ontology of the non-self-identical. The terms of politics can't be aligned with those of the economy, but this doesn't mean either metalanguage or a higher instance or "determination in the last instance." It means that there is an *internal differentiation* that produces a constitutive gap, a gap of being in which the political subject resides: the proletariat, for example, whose whole being, Marx claims, is to be nothing.

Session 8

February 7, 1984

What the *Sophist* shows in exemplary fashion is that there is necessarily a stratification of the operators in the conditions of possibility for thought. Unity of plane is impossible. In the *Timaeus*, one of Plato's last dialogues, there is one below type 0, which does not itself constitute a type and could be called the "pure relationship" or "the undifferentiated." Plato calls it "the errant cause." No reference is made to a minimum degree in the *Sophist*, which is concerned with types 1 and 2, ideas and meta-ideas, or ideas and relations among ideas.

In the *Timaeus* we've got a global cosmological structure, hence the need for a totally undifferentiated general material, for raw existentiality, for a difference in which nothing is specified, a purely passive difference, the passive receptacle of determination in general. Here we might think of Merleau-Ponty, who, echoing Husserl, speaks of the "flesh of the world," which is both involved in all experience and indeterminate with respect to that experience.

The *Sophist*, by contrast, deals with the type 1 structure, which is that of "ideal logic." It is only dialecticized, set in motion, by the so-called mixing operator, which sets the conditions for two type 1 terms to combine. Hence the latent existence of a type 2, the type of relations, or meta-ideas.

Where, in this context, do we find the Platonic idea of the other, on which the thesis of a certain existence of nonbeing is based? A distinction will need to be made between what is explicit in Plato and my own explicitation. For Plato, the other and the same are aligned with the first three: being, motion, and rest. So it's as if there were five type 1 terms, the type merely being divided into two classes, the universal expansion class and the limit point class. This is the absolute matrix of the thinkable, of ideal logic.

For me, by contrast, there are, strictly speaking, three terms: B (being), M (motion), and R (rest). Each term represents a class, that is, things that can be selected or chosen. There's a fourth term, the same, that is not a representative but a variable for the representatives. It denotes the representable, everything that can be in a position of representation. The same is the x that can be replaced by one of the other three.

The other has a double status. If, like Plato, we attempt to consider it a term, it refers, as a term, to the empty class, but since the empty class is not representable, insofar as nothing can be chosen from it, the other is not a term in the same sense as the other three. Actually, it's a pure name, the name of the nothing. Being the name of the nothing and being the representative of a class are not the same thing. The other is a nonrepresentative name. It is consequently a proper name, the others being common nouns. The name of nothing can only be a proper name. As a proper name, it cannot be aligned with the terms, not even, as is the case with the same, as a variable.

This is the issue that Plato dodges but at the same time makes use of in his demonstration, i.e., that the whole (the variable, the same) and the nothing (the other, the non-self-identical) limit classification, prohibit the aligning of the five terms, and require that there be at least two stratified levels in the ideal world. The whole disperses in the variable, and the nothing becomes a proper name.

So the general law of stratification can be formulated as follows: *every stratum generates a proper name whose referent is a void located in the stratum above.* Thus, we can say that this proper name is the name of the stratification itself. Rather than say that it denotes a term of the stratum, we'll say that it denotes the empty term of the stratum above. Where terms are concerned, the relationship between one stratum and another is always that between the void and a name.

Plato isn't interested in the ontology of the gap, in a statement such as "For difference to prevail, there must be the void." So he'll attempt to posit the other as an always determinate difference, as the difference between one term and another. Actually, this attempt fails, since, for Plato himself, the real of the gap—the point of impossibility—is necessarily the non-self-identical. The other is unable to establish itself as a pure relation between terms because its axiom is nonexistential. So that brings us back to the fact that the other is necessarily the name of the gap, not only between the terms but also between levels 1 and 2.

The other is indeed what creates a gap, but to do so it must name the gap between the strata—in order to be the concept of the gap, of difference. Difference can only be structured if you can name its stratification.

The other is what supports the intelligibility of the stratification, the stratification between logic (terms, ideas) and dialectic (relations, meta-ideas). This is a very general statement. Every logic implies a dialectic, and there is always a name for the gap between them. This name—which is here "the other"—is neither a term in the logic nor a relation in the dialectic. It's not like mixing, identity, rest, motion, being. It's an operator of local nihilation [*néantisation*] used to name the gaps, especially the irreducibility of the dialectic to logic.

This statement is quite far-reaching because the fields can be specified. Take political logic. To be structured, it requires a dialectic, namely, class struggle, which occupies the position that Plato assigns to mixing. Furthermore, there is necessarily something in the position of other. Marx called it the proletariat, which is neither a term nor a relation. If you try to specify it as a term, you run into the void of the stratum above, because it's impossible to "fill" the proletariat. That said, it is in a linking position between logic and political dialectic. It is always declared, in a sense, that the proletariat doesn't exist, only that it *should* exist: "We are nothing, let us be all!" says the political Other.

Plato's genius was to have discovered this point and to have concealed it by declaring that the other was a term (aligned with the other four) or a relation (the nonexistent gap between the terms). He wavers between the two.

———

Someone in the audience: *But is it really concealed? You're not talking about the* Theaetatus. *Why are you, who wrote* Theory of the Subject, *returning to the tradition of not talking about the* Theaetatus? *You don't budge, you're Alain Badiou, but you can't be the person who wrote* Theory of the Subject. *You're presenting Plato to us in his logic, in the Platonic, Kantian framework. One thing is blatantly obvious: Plato knew very well what was what. In the* Phaedrus *he says that the link between intellect and soul is love.*

———

I'd be delighted to talk about the *Theaetetus* with you, and about Theaetetus himself, as he is, the Visitor's main interlocutor in the *Sophist.* We need to be good spectators of Plato's texts, not just good readers. I'm convinced that Plato wanted us to laugh at Theaetetus in the *Sophist.* We know that Plato is quite capable of depicting strong interlocutors, tough opponents. But Theaetetus isn't Callicles; he is, on the contrary, a caricature of the disciple, explicitly so. Why is there this caricature, neither disciple nor opponent? Well, because the *Sophist's* argument is not certain of its own mastery. To have a true disciple, there has to be a true master. Is the Visitor a true master? His argument is unsure because the need for Plato to deduce the other, i.e., the intricacies of the negative, is not something he's happy about. He would doubtless have preferred to avoid it. Because once nonbeing is unleashed, the whole system is endangered. The *Sophist* is a precarious dialogue, which explains why, for its staging, a weak interlocutor is needed: your beloved Theaetetus.

Now let's return to the text:

> VISITOR: What is not, then, must necessarily be, both in the case of change and with all the kinds, because with all of them, the nature of the different, by rendering each a different thing from being, makes it something that is not; and in fact in accordance with this same reasoning we'll be correct in talking of all of them too as things that are not—and then again, since they share in being, in saying that they are, and talking of them as things that are.
> THEAETETUS: Probably.
> VISITOR: In relation to each of the forms, then, there is a lot of what is, and an unlimited quantity of what is not.
> THEAETETUS: It seems so.
> VISITOR: And even what is, itself, has to be said to be different from the others.
> THEAETETUS: Necessarily.
> VISITOR: So even what is is not, as many times over as there are other forms; not being them, it is the one thing it is, itself, but conversely it is not all the unlimited number of others. (256d–257a)

All this takes place after the other is deduced. So we've got to assume as established fact what we've seen. Why "both in the case of change and with all the kinds"? This is a dig against mobilistic ontologies (such as that of Heraclitus): the foundation of nonbeing is not change. This is not just an idle remark, because the "mobilists" admit the non-self-identical. A thing is at the same time itself and something else. It changes; it is capable of being different from itself, quite apart from the relationship to change. In this polemic against the mobilists, there's a trace of the rejection of the non-self-identical as a means for introducing the other.

What Plato says is that every thing, every idea, is and is not. It is, because it shares in being, and it is not, because it shares in the other. This is a destratifying statement. If the other were only difference, only the gap, then the conjunction "and" would be true. Given two ideas, each is *and* it is not. Not being is the edge of the gap that makes one differ from the other. What's glossed over, however, is the impossibility of the non-self-identical, which must found difference. There must be the void, but it is foreclosed here by "and." There is something that Plato doesn't take into account: the elements of the void *are not*. The class of nonbeing is not an element of the gap but of position. The empty class is required in the construction of the other. The absolute dispersion of nonbeing is the main issue. If it isn't attached to the empty class, which is its One, it falls into absolute, infinite multiplicity, the infinite multiplicity of differences from all the others. If nonbeing is not anchored in the One of the empty class, it disperses.

As we can see, Plato doesn't establish a being of nonbeing. He doesn't count it as one since he's forced to count it to infinity. There is a Platonic avoidance of the One of nonbeing, the attribute of the One remaining reserved for being (and for the other ideas). We're dealing here with a pretheological figure that's at the root of the tradition of Platonic theology, which is indeed a theology inasmuch as the predicate One is reserved for being. Atheism begins when nonbeing is counted as One. The only thing that's appropriate to the void is a proper name. There is no concept, but there is a name. Plato, however, doesn't want one, even though he invents one: the other. But contrary to what he says, the other is the name of the void, not of difference. To found difference, the void is necessary and so is its name, but a proper name, not a concept of the same type as motion or being.

———— ✦ ————

I'd now like to return to the excerpt I already referred to, to help you appreciate the importance of the challenge to Parmenides and of Plato's awareness of it.

> VISITOR: So do you realize that our disbelief of Parmenides has taken us beyond his prohibition?
> THEAETETUS: How so?
> VISITOR: We have shown him more than he forbade us to look into, pushing still further on with our investigation.
> THEAETETUS: How?
> VISITOR: Because he says, I think, "For never shall this prevail, that things that are not are; I tell you, keep back your thought from this path of inquiry."
> THEAETETUS: Yes, he does say that.
> VISITOR: Whereas we have not only shown that what is not is, but have declared what the form of what is not actually is; for having shown up the nature of difference as something that is, cut up into pieces over all the things that are in their relationships with each other, we took our courage in our hands and said of the part of it that is contraposed to the what is of each thing that it was the very thing that what is not really is. . . . Someone needs to challenge us and . . . say both that the kinds mix with one another,

and that since what is and difference pervade them all and one another, difference, with its share in what is, *is*, because of that sharing, while at the same time it is certainly not what it has that share in, but rather something different from it; and since it is different from what is, he'll have to say that it is in the clearest conceivable way necessary for it to be possible for it to be what is not. What is, for its part, because of the share it has in difference, will be different from the other kinds, and in being different from all of them it is not each of them, nor all the rest together, only itself, so that what is, in its turn, indisputably is not myriads upon myriads of things. Similarly the other kinds, whether taken one by one or all together, in many respects are and in many respects are not. (258c–259b)

The importance of the challenge has two correlatives in the text:

1. First of all, its solemn, intimidated and intimidating prose. The protagonist is the Visitor as a character. He is introduced as Parmenides's disciple, and we might wonder why he has no name of his own but is simply the Visitor from Elea. What bars the proper name from Plato's fiction? I would say that this visitor/stranger is a sort of theatrical emblem of the non-self-identical inasmuch as he is a stranger to himself, to his own being. It's Parmenides himself, as is clear, yet other than himself since he supports the theory of nonbeing, thereby becoming a stranger to himself. He is an Eleatic tasked with splitting the Eleatic doctrine whose proper name is Parmenides.

The character is introduced at the very beginning of the dialogue. Indeed, at the end of the *Theaetetus* they had arranged to meet up with Theodorus the following day. And this is mentioned right away at the beginning of the *Sophist* by Theodorus himself, who makes the introductions as follows: ". . . also bringing with us this person here. He's a visitor from his native Elea, where he's a friend of the followers of Parmenides and Zeno; the man is very much a philosopher." In what follows, Socrates will disappear completely, and Theodorus, who had arrived with the Visitor, won't take any further part in the dialogue, so it takes place between two interlocutors, Theaetetus and the Visitor. Right from the beginning, then, the latter character is steeped in a semisacred atmosphere. He represents a sort of fictionalization of strangeness to self, originary strangeness, pure strangeness.

2. The second textual correlative of the challenge to Parmenides is the famous passage on parricide, which is indeed a remarkable text:

VISITOR: And there's this other thing I'd ask of you even more.

THEAETETUS: What's that?

VISITOR: That you don't take me to be turning into some sort of parricide, as it were.

THEAETETUS: How so?

VISITOR: In order to defend ourselves we're going to need to cross-examine what our father Parmenides says and force the claim through both that what is not in a certain way is, and conversely that what is also in a way is not.

THEAETETUS: We must obviously fight hard for that sort of conclusion in the coming discussion.

VISITOR: Obviously! Apparent even to a blind person, as they say. So long as these things are neither stated nor agreed, we will hardly be able ever to talk about things said or believed and say that they are false, whether we call them images, or likenesses, or imitations, or just apparitions, nor will we be able to talk about any expertises relating to these, either, without being forced to contradict ourselves and make ourselves the object of ridicule.

THEAETETUS: Very true.

VISITOR: For that reason we must take our courage in our hands and go for a frontal assault on the paternal claim. It's either that

or leave it totally alone, should we hesitate for some reason to do
the deed.

THEAETETUS: I can tell you, there's nothing whatever that is
going to stop us from doing it!

VISITOR: Well, there's a third small thing I have still to ask of you.

THEAETETUS: You have only to ask.

VISITOR: When I was talking a few moments ago I think I said
that I've always found mounting a challenge on these matters too
much for me, and never more than now.

THEAETETUS: You did say that.

VISITOR: Well, that makes me afraid I'll seem mad to you for doing
an immediate about-turn. In fact it's for your sake that we'll be
setting about challenging Parmenides' claim, if we actually manage it.

THEAETETUS: Well, I certainly won't think you are acting in any
way inappropriately if you proceed straight to this challenge of
yours, and your proof, so carry on, with confidence on this score
at least. (241e–242b)

Plato chooses the paternal metaphor to set out the debate. He uses
the murder of the father as a metaphor for the assumption of the
son into the realm of the symbolic. It is telling that this stage of the
conflict deals with being and nonbeing. It is all overdetermined by
the need to have to "force the claim through." So this is a space of
violence. What is shown here is that there is no assured mastery in
the field thus opened. They may be confronted with a rationality
without any guarantee, maybe even with madness. The murder of
the father is always a space of hesitation and potential madness.

It should be noted that this is the only passage in which Theaetetus will play a key role. The Visitor wants to assure himself of the
obliviousness of youth, which is supposed to assure it of the courage
required for the action. Theaetetus has no fear because he doesn't

realize what's at stake. He is the blind emblem of speculative courage. The Visitor will say that this refutation is beyond him. Parricide
is too much for him. If it's Parmenides as a stranger to himself, then
it's beyond his identity. So a mediator, preferably an oblivious one, is
needed. Hence the resort to the obliviousness of youth. The Visitor
will move forward, supporting himself on the young man's shoulder,
and afterwards the young man will be able to say "Yes, yes, yes . . ."
We might think of Mao and the Red Guards here. What is happening is so serious that the blindness of youth is required.

But let's be clear: the Visitor will fail in his challenge. The paternal law is more or less preserved, inasmuch as the One will remain
reserved for being. What Plato shows is that being is not what is
other, but he doesn't exactly show that nonbeing is. Syntactically,
the question of being is not the question of the other: the statement
about the other is not exactly identical to the statement "Nonbeing is." He has actually remained in the element of multiplicity and
linked being with the One.

So it's a compromise that leaves the monopoly on being to
the father, Parmenides, and gives nonbeing to the son, like some
chump change. That's the hidden point—the essence of compromise
is always to hide something—which naturally and very precisely
concerns the subject. It's true that the subject is only visible in the
eclipse between two terms, but it must be based on a stratifiable
excess. The subject is not only structured like a language; it is stratified like a dialectic. Something is in excess over the logic in which
it has its place. The endpoint of this excess, its limit point, is something other than the gap.

In the *Sophist*, the subject is the other. But that's not enough.
There is something other than the other, which is unrepresentable
and therefore unrepresented, even by a signifier for another signifier, which returns only as to a higher level, by exceeding the signifying law of representation, that is, in one way or another, by making

a scission emerge with regard to the law of representation. This is why, as there are two statuses of the other, the subject, too, comes about with a dual status, which Plato doesn't manage to distinguish between.

We'll try to identify this double subject in Kant by examining the Kantian category of the transcendental subject and then that of the subject of the moral action.

But before attempting to identify the subject in Kant by examining the Kantian category of "transcendental subject," we'll devote two more seminar sessions to Plato, using the *Parmenides* dialogue as a basis.

Session 9

February 28, 1984

As I mentioned previously, the excerpt I'll offer you is from the *Parmenides*. It will allow us to go further in connection with a different dialectic from that of the same and the other, by dealing with the dialectic of the One and the Whole. Today the session will be devoted to presenting, to contextualizing, the dialogue, and next time we'll get into the heart of the matter.

The *Parmenides* is very unusual in that it's the only one of the dialogues in which Plato puts someone he considers a great philosopher on stage. He will therefore let him speak, but with all sorts of precautions. This is unique in Plato's dialogues, because even when there are real people in them, they are either supporters or opponents (Sophists in particular). Here, we have the figure of someone who is in the position of master for Plato. The *Parmenides* is a dialogue of the master, the father. Yet this master is a figure that must be overcome, as we saw with the *Sophist*. A number of Platonic dialogues revolve around Parmenides and the Eleatic doctrine and thus around the affirmation of the fundamental unity of being. These dialogues represent a truly ontological moment since they are concerned with neither the theory of knowledge, nor politics, nor morality or ethics: they are devoted to a great exploration of the question of being. And the figure of Parmenides is emblematic of this question, while it is at the same time what must be overcome.

Roughly speaking, the *Parmenides* deals with the question of the One. It is a completely aporetic dialogue, which means that its conclusion is negative through and through. It's a dialogue that, on the surface, creates nothing but an impasse. It doesn't even indicate the real of the impasse; it remains within the structure of the impasse, as evidenced by its very conclusion, which I'll read to you:

> Then let this be said, and also that, as it seems, whether unity is or is not, both it and the others are and are not, and appear and do not appear to be all things in all ways, relative both to themselves and to each other.
>   Most true. (166c)[1]

Parmenides is present in this dialogue, directing the aporetic process from start to finish. What's unusual, though, is that we're dealing with a very peculiar implementation of his thought: the Parmenides of the *Parmenides* dialogue doesn't really speak on behalf of his own doctrine. When Parmenides comes in, it is actually to propose a dialectical "exercise," which is precisely what a master does. This exercise will lead to the complete unfolding of an impasse, the impasse of his own thesis on the absolute unity of being: Being is One. But this thesis isn't stated as such; it's merely the pretext for an exercise.

Parmenides, in short, comes in not as the master of truth but as the master of the conceptual debate. So he's present in the dialogue as the master of knowledge, not of truth. He's in a way the Academy of himself, the virtuoso of dialectical knowledge, but he doesn't claim to have insight into truth. The dialogue deals with the possible and therefore not with the question of truth but with that of knowledge.

In the *Parmenides*, Plato imagines a very old Parmenides, who has become for a little while the master of a very young Socrates. Let me read you the passage in which Parmenides introduces his thesis and explains how he's going to proceed. He addresses Socrates and speaks to him about Zeno, who is present:

You undertake to mark off something beautiful and just and good and each one of the characters too soon, before being properly trained. I realized that yesterday, when I heard you discussing here with Aristoteles. Believe me, your impulse toward argument is noble and indeed divine. But train yourself more thoroughly while you are still young; drag yourself through what is generally regarded as useless, and condemned by the multitude as idle talk. Otherwise, the truth will escape you.

What is the manner of training, Parmenides? he asked.

The one you heard Zeno use, he replied. Except for this: I admired it when you said, and said to him, that you would not allow inquiry to wander among the things we see nor concern them, but rather concern those things which one would most especially grasp by rational account and believe to be characters.

Yes, he said, for it seems to me easy enough, the other way, to show that things which are are both like and unlike, and affected in any other way whatever.

And you're right, Parmenides replied. But it is also necessary to do this still in addition: to examine the consequences that follow from the hypothesis, not only if each thing is hypothesized to be, but also if that same thing is hypothesized not to be, if you wish to be better trained.

How do you mean? he said.

Take, if you like, Zeno's hypothesis, if many is. What must follow for the many themselves relative to themselves and relative to the one, and for the one relative to itself and relative to the many? If, on the other hand, many is not, consider again what will follow both for the one and for the many, relative to themselves and relative to each other. Still again, should you hypothesize if likeness is, or if it is not, what will follow on each hypothesis both for the very things hypothesized and for the others, relative to themselves and relative to each other. The same account holds concerning unlikeness, and about motion, and about rest, and about coming to be and ceasing to be, and about being itself and not being. In short, concerning whatever may be hypothesized as being and as not being and as undergoing any other affection whatever, it is necessary to examine the consequences relative to itself and relative to each one of the others, whichever you may choose, and relative to more than one and relative to all in like manner. And the others, again, must be examined both relative to themselves and relative to any other you may choose, whether you hypothesize what you hypothesize as being or as not being, if you are to be finally trained accurately to discern the truth.

An extraordinary procedure, Parmenides! I don't at all understand. Why not explain it to me by hypothesizing something yourself, in order that I may better understand?

You impose a difficult task, Socrates, he said, for a man of my age. (135c–136d)

As you can see, the exercise proposed is hypothetical. Its structure consists in hypothesizing an existence and drawing the consequences from it, then hypothesizing a nonexistence and drawing the consequences from it as well. All this is strangely similar to sophistry. The dialectical training in question takes no position on the validity of the hypothesis. This is not unlike Plato's criticism of the Sophists for defending two different things one after the other. Parmenides hardly differs from them. So it's an exercise that's not in the regime of truth.

On this basis, the *Parmenides* takes the next step, the moment when Parmenides's thesis will be criticized, although Parmenides himself remains uninvolved. He is caught up in strangeness to himself and appears in the guise of an imperious master of knowledge who has come to train right before our eyes. Hence the need for the dialogue not to be conclusive: it's simply a matter of having done all the exercises. The aim is not to conclude but to be complete. To put it another way, it's all about completeness, not about discovery. I'd be tempted to say that we've got a sort of *Art of the Fugue* of the dialectic here. The result is an absolutely extraordinary, unbelievably complicated mise-en-scène. Actually, this mise-en-scène aims to veil rather than to unveil, in keeping with the taboo surrounding the character of the master. This is accomplished via a system of screens and indirect removes.

1. *Temporal remove.* What Parmenides says had been said fifty years before. So it exists at a great temporal remove. Consequently, there is a precariousness and remoteness to its transmission. A number of screen characters will be introduced. The narrator, who comes in right at the beginning of the dialogue, is Cephalus. He arrives in Athens along with some philosopher friends and there meets Adeimantus, a friend of his. Adeimantus's brother, a man by the name of Antiphon, used to know a certain Pythodorus. *He* had been a student of Zeno, Parmenides's first disciple. So he's a third-generation Eleatic. Antiphon belongs to the fourth generation and is only interested in horses. As for Pythodorus, he had been present at a discussion in his home among four people: Parmenides (already very old); Zeno; Socrates (very young, which was historically impossible, so this is clearly fictional); and Aristoteles, a reactionary politician who was a tyrant and had taken part in the Conspiracy of the Thirty. Pythodorus had learned by heart everything that was said and had made Antiphon do the same. The result was this dialogue: it took place at Pythodorus's home, was memorized by him and was

transmitted to Antiphon, who will relate it to Cephalus and his friends from Clazomenae.

The dialogue will thus begin in the indirect style, a style that becomes increasingly direct as it goes on. Antiphon is a lousy narrator because he's no longer interested in any of this. He's only doing it to please his brother. Pythodorus is an equally lousy intermediary since he plays no role. He doesn't say a word. He represents late Eleaticism, the Eleaticism in which transmission has degenerated to some extent. So the dialogue is related at a great temporal remove, but it should be noted that, as a result, there's no risk of interference in the transmission, of an altered transmission, since these disciples have no agenda.

2. *Structural remove.* The dialogue unfolds in three parts.

In the first part, Socrates has arrived at Pythodorus's house, where Zeno is reading from his works on the paradoxes of the One and the Many. In them, he refutes the many. Quite remarkably, Parmenides has gone out. Why does Plato feel the need to tell us this? Well, because he absolutely does not want Parmenides to approve of what Zeno is saying. You'll notice that there is this constant effort not to involve the master of truth in the disciple's loquacity. Zeno is in his forties and quite smug. Plato really dislikes him. He likes the master but not his disciples. So he implies that Zeno already represents a serious decline. Parmenides comes back in just as the reading concludes.

Then begins the second part. A young and hot-headed Socrates attacks Zeno's arguments quite vehemently, saying they aren't worth much since Zeno has shown these paradoxes of the One and the Many from the standpoint of the things themselves. What would be meaningful would be to show that the One in itself is many, that the essence of the One contains the many. This is when Parmenides intervenes, and the third part begins.

In this third part, Parmenides begins by admiring Socrates's impulse toward argument, but, immediately thereafter, he tells him that his theory of forms is not as simple as all that. He launches into a series of serious objections to the Platonic theory itself, the theory of Ideas, of Forms, which was put in Socrates's mouth as a refutation of Zeno's arguments. Socrates is quite distraught. Parmenides then suggests that Socrates lacks training in the dialectic. So everyone present implores Parmenides to give an example. He eventually gives in. The exercise he'll present will take up two-thirds of the whole and deals with his doctrine, that is, with the One. Incidentally, he chooses as his interlocutor the youngest of the attendees, Aristoteles, who will be an utterly weak interlocutor.

The *Parmenides* will thus examine the question of the One, and it is the nine hypotheses about the question of the One that make up its central structure. The fact that there are nine hypotheses has given rise to countless interpretations. You'll find a very interesting text concerning the classification of these hypotheses in *Cahiers pour l'analyse* no. 9. It's an article by François Regnault entitled "Dialectique d'épistémologies," which I'm drawing on.[2] The hypotheses are classified according to three criteria:

1. Existence: either the One exists or it does not exist.
2. Relation: either one examines things from the standpoint of the One as regards the others or from the standpoint of the consequences as regards the others in relation to the One.
3. Absoluteness or nonabsoluteness of the presumed existence: either one thinks that the One is absolutely, which means that it does not share in any other idea, or else it is "shareable," that is, it shares in other ideas.

By combining the three criteria, we obtain eight hypotheses (I'll say a word later about the third hypothesis, which does not figure in the table below):

EXISTENCE	ONE/OTHERS RELATION	OTHERS/ONE RELATION	ABSOLUTENESS	HYPOTHESIS
1	1	0	1	1101 (I)
1	1	0	0	1100 (II)
1	0	1	1	1011 (V)
1	0	1	0	1010 (IV)
0	1	0	1	0101 (VII)
0	1	0	0	0100 (VI)
0	0	1	1	0011 (IX)
0	0	1	0	0010 (VIII)

Hypothesis I is the most fully developed. The One, which exists, is examined in relation to the others under the condition of absoluteness. This examination will serve as a model for the briefer examination of the other hypotheses. Then the order becomes blurred, zigzagging through the underlying structure that orders them, for reasons that have to do with the liveliness of the dialogue. This type of approach is found very often in Plato, who in this way achieves displacement effects, which impart philosophical and literary expressiveness at one and the same time. This voyage through the structure is quite different from what we'll find in Aristotle.

In the structure, as I mentioned, there are eight hypotheses, whereas in Plato's text there are nine. Indeed, in hypothesis III, the One is posited as being *and* as not being. So the hypothesis is not subject to the original dichotomy. The One is actually posited as becoming, as change. The third hypothesis is therefore the analysis of change, of instantaneousness, of the One of change as instantaneousness.

Something very strange results from this: a passage that's completely heterogenous with the rest. In it, Plato presents the instant as a possible figure of the One, as a differential in time, time as pure change. It's a diagonal hypothesis relative to the others. It is remarkable, we should note, that what is in excess is time.

The passage we'll examine is from hypothesis IV. In it, the One, which exists, is seen from the standpoint of the others, and it is relative, "shareable." This hypothesis is conclusive as regards the One as being [*étant*]. It thus occupies a pivotal position, just after the aberrant hypothesis about change.

I'll begin with two comments. The first has to do with a comparison between the *Parmenides* and the *Sophist*. The second situates things in terms of the aim of all this for Plato as well as our own aim, the aim for us "moderns."

1. In the *Sophist*, the later work, Plato, as we have seen, focuses on five basic ideas: being, motion, rest, the same, and the other. The question that arises is whether this can be compared with the *Parmenides*. It's quite a complicated question since the principles of connection between the dialogues are often tricky; the principle of transition, of circulation, has to be identified based on the reader him- or herself.

Take the Plato (alias Parmenides) who considers that the One is. The consequences of this hypothesis will determine a position of the One in relation to a number of concepts, such as identity, difference, motion, and rest. We should be able to find the basic ideas in these concepts, in what will structure the consequences. But we find many more than five. Thus, in order:

--Questions having to do with spatial position: figure and location
   (an essentially geometrical issue)
--Questions having to do with temporal position: before/after; the
   problem of eternity

--Motion and immobility

--Identity and difference

--Similarity and dissimilarity: the problem of the same and the other

--Equality and inequality

--For self and for others

--Limitation and limitlessness

--Being and nonbeing

This is the concept list in which the whole dialogue operates. It's the complete contents of the exercise in the *Parmenides*: structure; journey through the structure; concept list.

Now what's the connection with the list in the *Sophist*?

We find:

--Being, motion, and rest, the same and the other, but divided into many types.

To which are added:

--Time and space, which will lead to the examination of the missing third hypothesis.

--For self and for others. Actually, this is the same and the other, in an interesting variation.

--Limitation and limitlessness. This is significant since it's a major point of difference between the *Parmenides* and the *Sophist*. Indeed, the structure of this pair is the One/Whole relationship. The most important thing about the *Parmenides* is this dialectic.

2. Taking all this into account, what can Plato's aim be, and what will my own aim be?

Plato's aim isn't easy to grasp because the dialogue ends in an impasse. Clearly, it's not just an exercise. Scholarly commentators have seen it as a sort of scholastic exercise, but we should be wary of such a conclusion, given the complicated theatricality set in motion by the presentation. I, for one, think that for Plato the aim of the *Parmenides* is to show that there is no conceptual access to the question of the One and the Many, no access through a philosophically thematizable question. My thesis is that in the *Parmenides*, precisely because of its complete exercise aspect, it is not possible truly to present a living, real dialectic of the One and the Many. To be sure, this dialectic structures all the thought, but it cannot be thematized in a formalized exercise. The question of the One is, as a result, the dialogue's impasse. The dialectic of the One and the Many takes place in the real movements of thought, but it's not something that can be turned into a conclusive academic exercise. For philosophy, this question is in a transcendent position: it constitutes the field of philosophical investigation, but it's not a theme that can be isolated or specified. There is no philosophy unless this question is addressed, and yet it cannot be isolated conceptually without going outside of philosophy and thereby entering into a sophistical framework. This explains why Plato comes so close to sophistry in this dialogue and blames this proximity not on his spokesman, Socrates, but on old Parmenides, who can't do anything about it.

The counterproof is given us by the *Timaeus*, in which the thesis defended will be that, when it comes to connecting the One and Many, only a God (a "demiurge") is in a position to do so. This completely confirms my hypothesis, i.e., that this question, if you want to examine it on its own, is either infra- or supra-philosophical.

As for what my own aim is, I'd be in agreement with the Plato of the *Timaeus* in maintaining that the fulfilment of this question is mathematical, and also in saying that it is always partly a fulfillment rather than a thematization. Mathematics does not theorize the One and the Many even though it constantly operates within that conceptual pair. I also think that the question of the One and the

Whole is a different question, which is constituted as a philosophical question in the shadow of the previous one. It will be necessary to establish the difference between them. The problem of the One and the Whole actually pertains to the question of the subject, hence to a philosophy whose object is the subject. Traces of this can be found in the *Parmenides* in connection with what is said in it about the One and the Whole and is not at an impasse. That's a way out of the dialogue's impasse.

I said that the dialogue was globally aporetic, but it isn't always so locally. It offers solutions, though not concerning the One and the Many. Clearly, the One is the connecting concept between philosophy and mathematics because the One/Many pair is mathematical whereas the One/Whole pair is philosophical. This is an extremely important point. But the problem in Plato is that this is not resolved. The One is treated as though it were in a single dialectical space. But it can't be treated as a unity of plane; its inscription in heterogenous spaces must be accepted. The One must be grasped in its division, in the heterogeneity of its functioning with regard to separate conceptual fields. If that isn't done, we get the *Parmenides*, a magnificent dialogue but one that comes to a complete standstill.

Session 10

March 13, 1984

The supporting text that's been handed out to you is an excerpt from what Plato presents as an example of dialectics performed by a then very old Parmenides before an audience that included a very young Socrates. I'll read it to you. Parmenides is the one who puts forward theses, and Aristoteles—not to be confused with Aristotle—is the one who responds to him.

But clearly, it would have a share of unity, because it is other than unity; otherwise, it would not have a share, but be unity itself. But as it is, it is impossible, I take it, for anything except unity itself to be unity.

Yes, it is.

But both whole and part necessarily have a share of unity: for it will be one whole of which the parts are parts; and again, what is part of a whole is one given part of that whole.

True.

Now, things that have a share of unity will have a share of difference from it?

Of course.

But things different from unity are, I take it, many; for if the others than unity were neither one nor more than one, they would be nothing.

Agreed.

And since things that have a share of the unity of a part and things that have a share of the unity of a whole are more than one, is it not forthwith necessary that those things that get a share of unity are, just in themselves, unlimited in multitude?

How so?

We may observe that when things are getting a share of unity, they neither are nor have a share of unity.

Clearly.

Then they are multitudes, and unity is not in them?

Yes.

Well then, if we in our mind should subtract from such things the fewest we possibly can, must not what is subtracted be a multitude and not one, since it would not have a share of unity?

Necessarily.

Now, whenever we examine alone by itself the nature of difference from the characteristic, as much of it as we ever see will be unlimited in multitude?

It will indeed.

Moreover, when each part becomes one part, they forthwith have a limit relative to each other and to the whole, and the whole a limit relative to its parts.

Exactly so.

Then it follows for the others than unity that from the communion of unity and themselves, something different, as it seems, comes to be in them, which provides a limit relative to each other. Their own nature provides, in themselves, unlimitedness.

It appears so.

Thus, things other than unity, both as wholes and part by part, are unlimited and have a share of limit.

Of course. (158a–d)

As the theme of his dialectical exercise Parmenides chose the idea
of the One, an idea crucial to his own philosophy. His thesis is that
the One is an intrinsic attribute of being, which is essentially averse
to differentiation. This thesis is deduced from the absolutely primary ontological statement "Being is." The prologue to Parmenides's
poem instructs us to stay away from any road where a being of nonbeing might be found. We must posit that nonbeing is not and take
the only path left: being is. The inferences that follow are that all
the attributes of the multiple and of transformation (destruction,
change, multiplicity, etc.) are unassignable: they are matters of opinion. The dialectic of the whole and the parts is not applicable to
being. To say that being is One is, explicitly, not to say that it is
Whole. The gap between One and Whole is a Parmenidean gap:

Nor is it [What Is] divided, since it is all alike;
and it is not any more there, which would keep it from holding
together,
nor any worse, but it is all replete with What Is.
Therefore it is all continuous: for What Is draws to What Is.[1]

It is clear that for Parmenides "all alike" means "self-identical,"
which is one of the central theses of the One. Nothing of the non-
identical, understood in Platonic terms, can be found in being: there
is no other. The One is foreign to all operations; it has a strictly
ontological dimension, and so the One is ultimately synonymous
with being. They are interchangeable. It is the One that is being, not
in the sense that being would have to be counted as one but because
of an originary consubstantiality.

My own thesis, as you know, is that it's not the One that is being
but the void. Parmenides's metaphor is one of plenitude. Sartre uses
it again at the beginning of *Being and Nothingness* when he speaks of

the "solidity" of being-in-itself.[2] It's a metaphor for the compactness of being, which has no fissures, cracks, or gaps. I, for my part, think it's the void that is being, i.e., the unpresentable, what cannot be subsumed under any plenitude.

The One is what counts the void as existent, which is to say as the nominal event of the unpresentable, because counting the void as one—which is the ontological gesture—is an event, not a being. For me, the One is fundamentally an operator. The structure of the event always means that an unpresentable is counted as one in a place of count, that is, in a regulated place. The structure of the event is always of this sort: there is an unpresentable that's the index of being, and there is the count-as-one that's in a place. That's what an event is, and, of course, there is, strictly speaking, only the event. There's no point in saying that there is being. There is never anything but the Two, a Two constituted by the event (1) counted as one (2).

Retroactively, since there is only the Two, what was counted as one is the Two, naturally: it's the unpresentable that is never presented, it's the "there is." Since it's the "there is" that's the structure of the unpresentable, it's the Two that is counted as one. A structure is always the count-as-one of a Two. The structure's appearance, its structural effect, is not the event. The nexus between the structure and the event is the fact that the event is the count-as-one of the unpresentable, therefore the Two, but that this Two is always counted as one. The structure is what counts the event as one. The formula of any structure is: *two combine into one*. One, on the other hand, divides into two, and this irreducible Two is always the count-as-one of the unpresentable.

The fact that the Two was counted as one returns as a symptom in the structure. That's what the subject is. The subject is the symptom of the Two of the event, inside its count-as-one, and thus, necessarily, in the form of a breakdown of the count-as-one.

Let me give you two examples.

1. To begin with, a mathematical paradigm. Take the statement "The empty set exists." The void connotes the unpresentable since nothing can be shown that represents it. The impasse of presentation touches being, and "exists" is what registers this point. What exists is radically unassignable. "Exists" connotes that we have touched "set" being: it is the count-as-one, in a regulated place, which is set theory. The void exists as one qua set. The event means counting the void as one, which is to say, calling it a "set." As a result, in fact, we'll act as though we had counted "there is this set" as one, and we'll forget being, since it's an unpresentable that we have counted as one.

What we have here is a structural operation, by which I mean that it is the "there is" that is counted as one. The structure is: there is the unpresentable that is nothing, there is the count under the name of "set," and the event. The empty set is the Two of these two things, of the zero and the one, the unpresentable and its count. Subsequently, this Two will always be counted as one as the empty set.

The event of being is that the nothing emerges as a name with an index of existence: the empty set exists. This event causes being to be Two as to its occurring: the void and the name, the unpresentable and the One. Then this Two is repressed by the pure and simple count-as-one in the place, which is set theory. The symptom of this repression is later found as the marker of the subject operation. The main symptom is that the empty set is part of any set, as is shown by set theory. This radically singularizes the empty set. The void, which is the point of being, fits every set: it's included in every set, which is true of no other set. This is what confirms it as originarily unpresentable. (I prefer to say "unpresentable" because it's more radical than "unrepresentable.")

The subject process is the operation of the Two, or the gap that the designation as one seemed to eliminate, presented in an indelible symptom: inclusion in anything at all, omni-inclusion. This shows that in set theory, being has been touched: it is present everywhere as the indicator of inclusion.

───◦◦◦───

2. This time, the paradigm is political. When the laid-off Talbot workers exclaim, "We want our rights!," that's a statement that I say has an event structure, which is not true of every statement.[3] What is unpresentable? What is the point of the void here? It is worker-being as such. In the capitalist structure, it is not presentable. What is presented is labor power as a commodity. Moreover, worker-being is essentially without rights, devoid of rights, since it's simply a commodity in the capitalist sphere. It has no rights, but it does have a price. There is no worker-being as such: it is a void in the regime of exchange-value law. So when the Talbot workers say "We want our rights!," they are counting themselves as one, they are counting the unpresentable as one. They are saying nothing about what they are, except through empirical evidence such as: "We've been working here for twenty years." In this way, an event occurs, since there's the structure I mentioned before: worker-being is counted as "rights," even though everyone objects that what the workers are declaring is only a name. Besides, they themselves wouldn't be able to say what their rights are. The gist of the matter is that an unpresentable being has been counted as one: worker-being has been counted as one as "rights."

This is really an eventful split. Everyone sees this situation as a Two, the Two of the workers' resistance, which is unpresentable, and of the statement about rights. It's the unpresentable and the One. But this will be repressed. It will be reabsorbed into the social sphere. If there had been no event, the "there are laid-off workers" would not be counted as one. Only the "there are" is counted as one, not the foreclosed workers. Yet in the event, what was counted was precisely that: that "worker" was foreclosed. But this will gain ground. The Two will gain ground as a symptom, as a subject operation.

What is the symptom that insists after the complete empirical forgetting of the episode? Well, that symptom is a periodization. After this event, the question of workers' rights will become an essential subjective component of every workers' situation, even if *they* are unaware of it. In the period of general workers' struggle that is beginning, the Talbot workers, too, like the empty set, are in a position of general inclusion: they're a part—a subjective part—of every situation. Every future situation will try to be commensurate with the Talbot situation. This is an insistence that reflects the political sequence, in the form of the subjectivity of the situation.

Here is the general thesis now, as a theorem:

When there has been an event, that is, the count-as-one of an unpresentable, two things necessarily happen:

1. There is repression of the Two of the event by the count-as-one of the "there is" and not of the unpresentable, not of the event. This is the effect of structure.

2. There is an indelible symptom: a general inclusion, an omni-inclusion, of the unpresentable under its name in every situation that is homogeneous, in the place, with the evental situation.

The event is included in and insists as a subjective part of every situation of the same structural type, a situation that is not necessarily an evental one.

I'll conclude this digression of sorts now.

———— ⚭ ————

I said that the Plato passage was part of the fourth hypothesis. That hypothesis is defined by three axioms:

1. The One is. This is opposed to the other possible axiom: the One is not.

2. The One is examined from the standpoint of the others than the One. This differs from examining the others from the standpoint of the One.

3. The One is shareable. This means that it has a relationship with the others, that it's not absolutely separate from them. The idea of the One can combine with the other ideas. This differs from the transcendent absoluteness of the One, which interacts with nothing and is a mystical thesis.

More specifically, the chosen passage examines the problematic in relation to the One, the whole, and the parts. This is of particular interest to us because the fact of counting the unpresentable as one has specific implications for the whole and the parts. Whenever there is an event, a part that is universal, a part that's a part of everything in the whole, emerges in the structure.

Parmenides aims to establish, via Plato, that, in the context of the fourth hypothesis, the intrinsic determination of the proper essence of everything that is not the One but the unlimited is the infinite, ἄπειρον (apeiron). Clearly, the unlimited, for Plato, for a Greek, is strictly the unpresentable, almost in the moral sense of the term. For the infinite is what cannot be thought, let alone be presented or represented. As a result, Plato's demonstration will be as follows. I'll summarize it in terms of its objective. If something given in whole/parts form is counted as one, we notice, in the context of this fourth hypothesis, that what is, by itself, hence the being of what is given in whole/parts form, is given in limitlessness, in a principle of absolute indeterminacy. This is a backwards step, the reverse of the one I was talking about a moment ago.

The Greek word for the unlimited is a privative term referring to πεῖρας (peiras), which is usually translated as "the limit." But it is the limit in the sense of finitude, of the closure of what presents itself as determinate, as a possible object of thought. Everything that is presented is presented insofar as there is *peiras*, closure, and therefore characterized by the essential finitude of Greek ontology. The *apeiron* is the unpresentable, hence the unthinkable, since nothing is thinkable except in terms of its limit, its finitude.

For Plato, this is obviously a paradox, which will reveal the impasse aspect of the fourth hypothesis, and of the eight others as well. Plato absolutely rejects the idea that being is the void. Nor does he think being is the One, but in any case it is certainly not the unlimited. This difference in emphasis is important, and, insofar as we're dealing with a refutation *ad absurdum*, I think it's an excellent demonstration. Here it is:

The original relation is participation. To participate in the One means to be counted as one. Here, the One functions as an operator: if something participates in the One, it can be counted as one. The demonstration is in several steps, which I'm summarizing since the text is quite convoluted.

The first step. What participates in the One, considered in itself, is not one in itself, since it is one only insofar as it participates in the One. Only the One is one in itself. The others can only be one if they participate.

This could be glossed by saying: *a* participates in the One; *a* is considered among the others than the One; ergo *a* is not the One; *a* participates in the One but is not the One.

Participation will allow the unit *a* to be counted as one, but naturally, considered in itself, extricated from the retroaction of the count-as-one afforded it by its participation, *a* is not one. This means that *a* will be considered either in its being, εἶναι (*einai*), or in terms of its participation in the One, μετέχειν (*metechein*). This gap between the two will be where the whole dialectic is grounded: it is the Two from which to set the dialectic in motion.

The second step. It's demonstrative. Plato takes as an example of *a* the whole and the parts and examines the implications of counting

either a part or a whole as one. For him, whole and parts participate in the One. When the whole participates in the One, we have
a whole. The same is true for a part that can be identified as a single
part of a whole.

The third step. We apply to this example the general statement
from a moment ago, that is, the whole and the part are not one
in themselves but only as a result of their participation. In other
words, what should be counted as one is not, for this very reason,
one. There is the one and the count, and only the fact of counting as one results in the thing being one. So they are not one but
many.

There's a sleight of hand here. Plato explains it as follows: if they
are neither one nor more than one, they are not at all. Now, they are
not one, so it could be said that they are not. What's missing here is
an intermediate dialectic dealing with the question of whether they
participate in being. Plato sticks to the line that lets him avoid the
zero, the empty set. He disposes of the case in which the Whole is
empty. The empty set is precisely what is neither one nor many. This
is the evasion of the void.

The fourth step. This step consists in establishing that this multiplicity is unlimited, which means that it is not a number. This "many"
swells infinitely. The demonstrative method is "infinite descent."

Let me read you the last phase of the argument again:

> Well then, if we in our mind should subtract from such things the
> fewest we possibly can, must not what is subtracted be a multitude
> and not one, since it would not have a share of unity?
>
> Necessarily.
>
> Now, whenever we examine alone by itself the nature of differ-
> ence from the characteristic, as much of it as we ever see will be
> unlimited in multitude?
>
> It will indeed.

Moreover, when each part becomes one part, they forthwith have a limit relative to each other and to the whole, and the whole a limit relative to its parts.

Exactly so.

Then it follows for the others than unity that from the communion of unity and themselves, something different, as it seems, comes to be in them, which provides a limit relative to each other. Their own nature provides, in themselves, unlimitedness.

It appears so.

Thus, things other than unity, both as wholes and part by part, are unlimited and have a share of limit.

Of course. (158c–d)

What is the crux of the argument? The whole and the part, grasped intrinsically, are multiples. If now, in my mind, I divide up the part, if I de-totalize the Whole, if I try to grasp the constitutive atom, then my argument can begin again: since nothing participates in the One, everything is still multiple. Infinite descent. This multiplicity is limitless since it's never bounded by the One. This is why it's an unlimited multiplicity. Stopping would mean counting as one. The infinite descent no longer allows us to present anything (cf. "the nature of difference from the characteristic"). We end up beyond the thinkable: "their own nature" is unlimitedness. We no longer have "any idea" about it, we're beyond the thinkable; being is different from the idea. But for Plato being *is* the idea. We end up in being beyond being, the unlimited, that is, the unpresentable.

So Plato concludes that we're at an impasse. The figure of being, if the count-as-one is subtracted, is the unpresentable: if we undo the relationship, we end up with the unpresentable. Here Plato's dialectic, by its own strength alone, reveals that if you assume that the One is, you realize that being is not one but unlimited. The means for this demonstration are the whole and the parts, and we touch on a fundamental structure, the One, the Whole, the unpresentable (for the unlimited One). What Plato should conclude from this is that the true hypothesis is the third one, the outlier. It's the only hypothesis to say that the One is *and* is not, whereas all the rest say that the One is *or* is not. Because the One functions as an operator insofar as there is the count-as-one, but since what is counted as one and is being is not one, the One is not, because, by its own nature, it is unpresentable, unlimited, not-one—which does not, however, mean multiple.

So the third hypothesis is the only valid one, the only one that says that the One is an operator. The unlimited is the unpresentable that comes into being as the One through the event of its count-as-one, and this event is not an operation of being but actually the original marking of the subject.

Someone in the audience: *How does this differ from the Lacanian S1/S2 matrix of the subject?*

Lacan doesn't completely unpack the evental implication of that figure. In a certain way, in the early Lacan at any rate, there's an element of structural conflation of it; the S1 and S2 are considered as the signifying difference, as the place of the Other. I myself think there's complete heterogeneity between the unpresentable and the count-as-one rather than a difference in the domain of the signifier. I'd say: there is the place, there is the signifier, and there is the figure of the event. The figure of the event means that, at some point, something unpresentable is counted as one. The concept of primary repression isn't what I mean by "figure of the event." Lacan won't say that it touches being. To fully develop this, the relationship between the category of being and that of the real would have to be examined. There is a relative isomorphism, closeness. But clearly, for Lacan, something drops off the chain into primary repression. That's not what I say.

—⊷⊷⊷—

Someone in the audience: *But with regard to the subject, where are the structure and the event positioned respectively?*

—⊷⊷⊷—

The first count-as-one is the structure of the event. When I say that it must be counted a second time as one, that's the law of the structure. But there's more to it than that, because the symptomal figure of the event is indelible. Lacan doesn't say as much since he would then be saying that it's being that's involved. But he doesn't say that. The essential figure for him remains the figure of the signifying difference. The subject is what is represented by a signifier for another signifier: this, for him, is a major structural point. But it's not what I say.

What I say, on the contrary, is that what is subject is assignable only in terms of failure of presentation. Speech errors, slips of the tongue, and so on are simply malfunctions in the chain. With Lacan, nothing malfunctions. He has no theory of dysfunction. The symptom is what exposes the functioning. For there to be a theory of dysfunction, a theory of choice is not enough; a theory of excess is necessary. There is no schize of the place in Lacan's work. Perhaps there was one at the very end of his life, when he circled around the idea of the real, but that was the erratic part . . .

The symptom (sinthome) is the skewing of truth. It is telling that when Lacan refers to the sinthome, it is by way of the metaphor of lack: it is actually a hole and is assignable as a border effect. When *I* call something that testifies to a subject a "symptom," I mean a principle of division in the operation of the chain itself, a fissure in the symbolic itself. I say that there is no complete conflation possible between articulation and division. For Lacan, there is a primacy of the causality of lack. Dysfunctionality denotes a periodization of the historicity of the place, a schize within the place itself. If you say, "Where it was, there something shall happen," it's still "where it was." It can't be said that, for Lacan, something happens. Something always happens where it was. You can of course twist it and still find everything in it. But there is no theory of the event in Lacan, no theory of the double count-as-one, no theory of periodization. The instance of interpretation does not periodize. Between repetition, truth, and event, there is something, in the Lacanian framework, that leaves no place for the inception of the subject as such, except as primary repression. To see this in its ontological dimension, we'd have to approach it in terms of the question "What does the Two identify as the real?" What it identifies I think of as atomistic. I think the real is pure, undifferentiated multiplicity, which is to say the possible repetition of the count-as-one in the realm of chance, or, to put it another way, that in connection with which there is some One.

Session 11

March 20, 1984

Where Descartes is concerned, the subject, even in the absence of the term itself, is a philosophical concept. By contrast, even if from our own perspective we can detect a kind of trace of the subject operation in Greek philosophy, that function is not isolated as such. The subject remains a hidden operational concept. So when it comes to the question of the subject, it is Descartes who inaugurates modernity. Lacan in fact says that the subject of the unconscious is nothing other than the Cartesian subject. If Descartes is the inaugural figure, if he represents the first period of the modern concept of the subject, this first period is only substantiated through the retroaction of the second period. It is undeniable that Kant represents that second period, which leads to a very interesting question as to what occupied the time between Descartes and Kant and was both eclipsed and represented in this period of a century and a half.

I'd like to examine this principle of retroaction in its own right. Broadly speaking, the following can be said. What is presented in the first stage—here, the concept of subject—does not present its presentation. The presentation of what is presented is not itself presented. In Descartes the subject is presented as a concept, but something about the gesture of presentation is concealed. We had noted this Cartesian concealment at work between the moment of the "I am" and the moment of the "what I am." God is the operator of this concealment. Now, what is presented is presented in its presentation only when it is represented. What happens must be represented in order for us to have access to its presentation. So the second stage is that of representation, the purpose of which is to present the first presentation through the mediation of what has been presented.

The most important aim of Kant's work is therefore not the rehabilitation of the Cartesian framework or the attempt to draw the consequences from it. It is, rather, with regard to the question of the subject, to deal not just with the presentation of a concept, with its inception, but with what is at stake in the presentation itself of the subject. Here, I'd agree with Heidegger when he says that Kant's fundamental question is the ontological question, in the form of the question of the subject. Whereas, in a way, Descartes's question is that of certainty, of the subject's involvement in the problem of truth, not that of the subject's involvement in the question of being. In Descartes, the question of being is hypostatized as God. Descartes in this sense represents the modern form of the system, created by Aristotle, that Heidegger calls "onto-theological."

Kant's question is entirely different. It is: What is the status of being, from the now inescapable standpoint of the subject? This is indeed why he can be said to re-present the Cartesian subject, but with a view to the radical question of its being. We will see that what necessarily happens, and is the most radical and trickiest point, is that, when the representation of a concept is involved, what was presented has to be desubstantialized, disenclosed from its seeming closure, because this closure actually stems from the fact that the concept was originally only presented. There is always a second stage, a desubstantialization, a dis-closure of what has already been presented. Hence Kant's explicit polemic against the idea that the subject can be apprehended as an object, that is, as a closed figure. He criticizes Descartes for this.

This could be formulated as a general theorem. A novelty—here, a conceptual one—is only confirmed by its second stage: what is involved is first of all the *act* of presentation. The obligatory next step is a critique of the closure of what was first presented. Throughout history, there have been very many pairs of two-stage presentation. These include, among others, Christ and Saint Paul in connection with the foundation of Christianity; Marx and Lenin, with communism; Freud and Lacan, with psychoanalysis. In each case, that specific operation of dis-closure representative of the initial presentation comes into play. For example, it could be said that in the shift from Christ to St. Paul, the person of Christ is thematized according to its operation and no longer according to its being, which is why it is reduced to the resurrection. Where Marx and Lenin are concerned, the question is what becomes of the concept of class in its properly political dimension, which implies that, to a certain extent, it is detached from economics. Finally, from Freud to Lacan, the concept of the unconscious undergoes a radical desubstantialization: it becomes analogous to a language effect; it is "structured like a language."

Kant's aim is to dismantle—to "deconstruct"?—the Cartesian subject by treading a fine line, that of the extremely difficult distinction between the empirical and the transcendental subjects. He will dismantle the Cartesian subject and transfer the One to presentation, to sensory phenomena, which will revolve around the transcendental subject. Or, to follow up directly on what I said earlier about Descartes, Kant will eliminate the "what." He criticizes and does away with the step represented by the move from the "I am" to the "what I am." As a result, the subject will fall into the pure void of its logical function, but this will at the same time be its assumption into ontology. It will become a category of being and of the count-as-one of being. This takes the form of an explicit critique of Descartes, on the specific grounds that, in Kant's opinion, Descartes's first stage is still a matter of rational psychology. The Cartesian "I" is still a psychological "I."

This issue of the critique of psychology (or of what Husserl calls psychologism) is a crucial gesture, which is endlessly repeated throughout the history of philosophy. The accusation of psychologism is repeatedly leveled against the predecessor. There is something like an endless purging of the psychological empiricity of the subject. For example, however respectful Lacan may be toward Freud, it could be said that one of the features of Lacan's task, too, is to eliminate the traces of psychologism in Freud. Husserl's entire oeuvre is driven by this critique, by the attempt to extract a pure theory of the subject, of consciousness, from psychologism. Psychologism: that's the enemy where the theory of the subject is concerned. It is as though psychologism were its flip side, its permanent threat, the purging of which is never complete. Let's look at this passage, where the notion that we can move, as Descartes does, from the manifold of ideas to a unified "I am" is directly challenged, where the operation of the cogito is therefore defined as a pure paralogism:

> In the *first class* of syllogisms, from the transcendental concept of a
> subject that contains nothing manifold I infer the absolute unity of
> this subject itself, even though in this way I have no concept at all of
> it. This dialectical inference I will call a transcendental *paralogism*.[1]

Kant's language, even through his translators, is far from being always crystal clear. You have to make a real effort. It's a language whose technical sophistication makes it the first technical language of philosophy, the founding language of a substantial portion of modern philosophy's lexicon, which actually comes from German romanticism.

Here, though, is a passage explicitly directed against Descartes:

The "I think" is, as has already been said, an empirical proposition, and contains within itself the proposition "I exist." But I cannot say "Everything that thinks, exists"; for then the property of thinking would make all beings possessing it into necessary beings. Hence my existence also cannot be regarded as inferred from the proposition "I think," as Descartes held (for otherwise the major premise, "Everything that thinks, exists" would have to precede it), but rather it is identical with it. It expresses an indeterminate empirical intuition, i.e., a perception (hence it proves that sensation, which consequently belongs to sensibility, grounds this existential proposition). (B 422 n., p. 453)

What can be said about this passage? A spearhead is immediately aimed at a weak point in Descartes's argument, namely, the move first from the "I think" to the "I exist, I am," and then from the "I am" to the "what I am." Kant sees clearly that, in terms of "rational psychology" (this, as I said, is how he characterizes Descartes's and his successors' project), there is nothing here but a "constant circle," given that "we must always already avail ourselves of the representation of it [the subject, the "I" of the "I think"] at all times in order to judge anything about it" (A 346). In other words, I cannot go outside the subject to describe the subject (to say that it exists or that it is substance), since the subject is already involved in any representation or any description.

In this way, for Kant, the so-called originary point on which Descartes bases his demonstration is an empty point, *and remains so.* There is no extension of knowledge in it. I can expect nothing new from the "I think," which is nothing but the subject of the enunciation, implied in any statement, since there is nothing in it that I can count as one and thus distinguish from the subject.

To count something as one, I must in fact have *the experience of something else.*

Kant's formal summary of Descartes's project is interesting in this respect, especially if it's compared to Descartes's presentation of his "proof" of God's existence. I'll read you this summary and Kant's commentary:

> The procedure of rational psychology is governed by a paralogism, which is exhibited through the following syllogism:
> **What cannot be thought otherwise than as subject does not exist otherwise than as subject and is therefore substance.**
> **Now a thinking being, considered merely as such, cannot be thought otherwise than as subject.**
> **Therefore it also exists only as such a thing, i.e., as substance.**
> [. . .]
> In the first premise, things are talked about that cannot be thought of other than as subjects; the second premise, however, talks not about **things**, but about **thinking** (in that one abstracts from every object) in which the I always serves as subject of consciousness; hence in the conclusion it cannot follow that I cannot exist otherwise than as subject, but rather only that in thinking my existence I can use myself only as the subject of judgment, which is an identical proposition, that discloses absolutely nothing about the manner of my existence. (B 410–412n, pp. 447–448)

To use the vocabulary of *Theory of the Subject*, I would say that mere subjectivation does not itself give the subject any consistency. There is no principle of consistency in subjectivation that would allow for the count-as-one of what would deserve to be considered, in Kant's terminology, a "thing."

The problem already existed for Descartes, and consistency was only saved by God. Kant says: of course, the "I think" is involved in the totality of experience, but it is impossible to count it as one as if it were a consistent entity. This identification "reifying" thought, substantializing the subject, is a paralogism: something not possible. So subjectivation is not equivalent to count-as-one.

In sum, Kant posits an obligatory desubstantialization of the subject. This is why he distinguishes between what is a "subjective condition" and what would be a "concept" of the thinking being. The subjective condition is the "I think" as the pure condition of all possible experience, which is not the same thing as the "I think" as realizing the concept of the subject, as giving something to be thought. That said, what will be counted as one? The condition. And that's where the problems begin for Kant, because the count-as-one of the condition is not the count-as-one of the concept.

To say "I think" is to indicate a virtual condition but to define it as empty. Thus, the idea that the "I think" produces a concept of the subject will be eliminated. Dis-closure is effected, in opposition to the substantialization that had allowed Descartes to present the subject as a thinking thing.

It remains to be seen what a condition is. How can it be counted as one, even if just the one of a condition? And yet it must be, if the subject is to be salvaged. This is a tricky problem for Kant. In the condition we already find the prefiguration of the modern idea of the "eclipse" of the subject, which is neither being (in the sense of a thing) nor nonbeing (in the sense of nothingness, of effectlessness).

Now what is a condition? Two of its attributes can be singled out. First, a condition always concerns a possible experience, and, second, it is what, with respect to this possible experience, of whatever kind, is in a position of necessity. So it will appear as purely logical. The condition is not given in any experience. Therefore, the condition of an experience is necessary for that experience but is not given in any experience. This is what Kant generally calls the *transcendental*, which is a key concept of Kantianism. For me, as we will see, it's *structure*. It is what, with respect to experience, is in a position of conditional necessity but is never presentable as an object of experience.

Recourse to the transcendental appears whenever there is necessity. It appears in particular when a count-as-one is necessary, when, with respect to the possible experience, this experience's principle of unity is necessary. For only the transcendental principle makes it possible to guarantee both unity and necessity. Pure experience is nonunity—diverse, multiple, changing—and nonnecessity. The attributes unity and necessity cannot be ascribed to experience. The same goes for the subject of the enunciation. It is multiple (there is nothing to guarantee it as one), and it is not necessary (for the cogito to take place). It is consequently impossible to ground certainty in the "I think," which has neither unity nor necessity, and therefore impossible to find presentation in it. Descartes presented the subject empirically, in the framework of rational psychology, and thus got caught in the sterile circle of the paralogism. Breaking out of it requires dividing the subject into an empirical (structured) consciousness and a transcendental (structuring) consciousness. Here is Kant's move:

All representations have a necessary relation to a **possible** empirical consciousness: for if they did not have this, and if it were entirely impossible to become conscious of them, that would be as much as to say that they did not exist at all. All empirical consciousness, however, has a necessary relation to a transcendental consciousness (preceding all particular experience), namely the consciousness of myself, as original apperception. It is therefore absolutely necessary that in my cognition all consciousness belong to one consciousness (of myself). Now here is a synthetic unity of the manifold (of consciousness) that is cognized a priori; and that yields the ground for synthetic a priori propositions concerning pure thinking in exactly the same way that space and time yield such propositions concerning the form of mere intuition. The synthetic proposition that every different **empirical consciousness** must be combined into a single self-consciousness is the absolutely first and synthetic principle of our thinking in general. But it should not go unnoticed that the mere representation I in relation to all others (the collective unity of which it makes possible) is the transcendental consciousness. Now it does not matter here whether this representation be clear (empirical consciousness) or obscure, even whether it be actual; but the possibility of the logical form of all cognition necessarily rests on the relationship to this apperception **as a faculty**. (A117, p. 237)

The subject itself cannot be counted on to count itself as one; the principle of the empirical consciousness cannot be found in that consciousness itself. This is why I, for my part, introduce the thesis that Kant's transcendental is quite simply the possibility of the count-as-one operation applied to the subject. A transcendental principle must be found for the unity of consciousness, and this principle is the point from which the subject is counted as one, where it is guaranteed in its consistency.

Let's agree, as I already suggested, to call *structure* the field of operations of the count-as-one. The first aspect of the Kantian revolution is this: if you want to count the subject as one, so that it makes sense to speak of subjective unity, so that the subject is not dissolved in the multiplicity of its successive experiences, then that has to be an effect of structure. It is given neither in an experience nor in the form of presentation in which the One would emerge in its form of being.

You have the empirical consciousness, which is the place Descartes starts from. Now, there needs to be a structural support for the count-as-one of this consciousness so that it's an effect of structure. It is only on this condition that the diversity of the empirical consciousness can be grasped as unity. That's why a place of the condition is necessary, a transcendental, structural place.

What is remarkable is that Kant also calls this structural place a subject, indeed a consciousness. In other words, there is a distinction between transcendental subject and empirical subject, with the transcendental subject being the structure whereby the empirical subject can count itself as one. But we might then ask: what counts the transcendental subject itself as one?

Actually, the real definition of structure is counting the two as one. This will be expressed in the following way: from the place (from the point) of the structure (of the transcendental) the two of the transcendental subject and the empirical subject is counted as one (there is no count-as-one of the empirical subject alone). The transcendental subject, counted in this way, will be empty. What will be counted as one is the correlation between the empty being of the subject (as "transcendental subject") and the evental nature of the empirical subject.

This, it must be said, is partly concealed by Kant. The truth of Kant's subterfuge is that the dismantling of the Cartesian subject, of the "I think" as pure enunciation, gives rise to the schize between the transcendental and the empirical subjects, and the real problem for Kant is how this schize is counted as one in its turn.

So we've got three things:

1. The transcendental place = the structure.
2. The transcendental subject. As the empty point of unity in the structure, it occupies the place of lack.
3. The empirical subject = a multiplicity that, from the standpoint of the transcendental subject, can be counted as one.

To recap: the transcendental subject, as the empty point of the transcendental place; the empirical subject, as a multiplicity counted as one; and the transcendental place, as what counts the empty and the empirical simultaneously as one.

All of the foregoing represents a considerable revolution, because, for the first time in history, the category of subject emerges through its correlation with the function of the void. At the same time, this shows retroactively that, as I mentioned, this was already the case with Descartes. But Kant represents the actual foundation, because it is the first time that the operation of structure will be involved, an operation that had been replaced, in Descartes, by the divine machinery. Kant is simultaneously the founder (including retroactively) of the subject as empty point and as count-as-one. As far as the void is concerned, he is the founder of structuralism. It is a fact that there's an important link between the theory of the subject and the effect of structure. The extreme modernity of this revolution must be appreciated. Kant dominates our modernity just as much as Hegel, whose structural correlative he is. Hegel founds historical dialecticity and Kant, structural dialecticity. The Kant/Hegel pair is in equal measure the inaugural pair of philosophical modernity.

―――⊷∞⊷―――

Now what about the question of being? As usual, the question of being is the question of the void, in a specification that explicitly links it to the question of the subject. What is called transcendental subject is really the point of the real for the subject: it's something that is not in empirical diversity, nor is it assimilable to the transcendental as structure. It is neither the empirical nor the place, neither the imaginary nor the symbolic (thus, it is the real). We could say that, with the set of transcendental place/transcendental subject/empirical subject, we have the three instances that identify the question of the transcendental subject as the point of impasse of the real.

When we appreciate the extreme sophistication of all this in Kant's work, the question of its origin inevitably arises. Where could this have come from? It's unclear. The same is incidentally true of Descartes. In Descartes we find the heroic dimension of the founder, of the one who takes the first step, taken with an instantly recognizable fearlessness. Heidegger sees in Descartes the figure of the hero, of the person who makes a clean sweep of everything. Kant is a different figure. He represents the painstaking work of the second founders, those who always have to deal with complex issues of the system. In addition, this occurs for the first time in history as the ascension of the academic scholar. There was nothing like this with Kant's predecessors. With the Greeks, philosophical mastery had nothing to do with such a figure, even if there may have been a difference between Parmenides's poem and Aristotle's work. We saw how things were with Descartes. As for Spinoza, he represents the aberrant figure of the expelled Jew, and Malebranche, the reverend father, while Leibniz remains a man of the court, a philosopher influenced by diplomacy. With Kant we witness the emergence of the dull figure of philosophy, the educational technique with a narrow focus, and this will continue with Hegel.

Kant was an extraordinary character. His life was regulated like clockwork. There was probably no woman in his life. He was a man whose breadth of knowledge and intellectual rigor were truly astonishing. He created his technical apparatus from scratch, and his works are veritable construction sites. I recommend reading Thomas de Quincey's book *The Last Days of Immanuel Kant*. It's of course a fictional account, but it's fascinating, and I refer you to his writings not only on Kant but also on the Sphinx, or on Macbeth, for example.

With Kant we witness—and this is what fascinated de Quincey—the advent of the prosaic figure of the philosopher, the bourgeois character, the academic philosopher. He is in this respect the figure of the second stage, which is a stage associated with institutional questions. And that makes the extraordinary speculative fearlessness, so little apparent in the man, even stranger. In this respect, he resembles Haydn, a modest figure by comparison with the extraordinary musical revolutions he instigated.

Before dealing with Kant in detail, we should also bear in mind what transpired in the interim with regard to the question of the subject. What were the mediations that make it possible to contextualize the Kantian revolution? Actually, there's a double line of descent from Descartes, which corresponds to the divided interpretation, typical of all great founders. This line of descent is split between the Continental and the English currents.

The Continental current attempted to reconstruct complete metaphysical systems on the Cartesian foundations. This was as true of Malebranche as it was of Spinoza or Leibniz. Kant labeled them dogmatists, a dogmatism that can be seen in their effort to reconstruct, in the element of the Cartesian revolution, philosophical systems comparable to those that came before Descartes. These efforts were split between their effective contemporaneity and a profound nostalgia for restoration. The aim was to restore a conceptual order so as to bring the Cartesian revolution to a close and to draw the conclusions from it, sometimes even against Descartes himself. What at any rate is striking for us is that we see that the category of the subject was abolished. The conclusions were thus drawn from the Cartesian revolution through the eradication of the category of the subject. Indeed, that category was absent in the work of Spinoza, who was nevertheless the most forward looking of them all. As for Malebranche, he abolished it through divine intervention. In the case of Leibniz, a multifaceted and complicated philosopher, the category of expression and form completely supersedes the void of the cogito. His is a philosophy of full multiplicity. In dynamic terms, or in terms of ontological dynamism, it might be said that all these post-Cartesians refounded philosophical systematicity at the expense of the original void on which Descartes had based it.

The English current was represented by Locke and Hume, who were quite different from each other. This line of descent completely preserved the problematic of the subject but in the element of the empirical subject. If there is subjectivity, then there is nothing but that, i.e., experience, and they would try to reconstruct everything on that basis. It was an absolutely post-Cartesian current, which retained from Descartes the empirical character of experience rather than the void of the cogito. It was also a corrosive, critical, skeptical current in its deepest tendencies, because the validation of truth is always precarious. Its final incarnation was Hume, who directly attacked the concepts of unity and necessity.

A significant segment of this current, which was fundamental for Kant, was interested in the relation of causality. There was still the problem of the count-as-one of the Two, since it was a matter of counting as one the Two of the multiplicity of experience. One thing is the cause of another: that was the matrix. Hume rejected any structural framework and asserted that there is actually only the Two. It is counted as one only out of habitual association. It's only out of purely subjective habit that the Two of cause and effect becomes the One of necessity. There's no guarantee of being in this. The operation (causality) is as empirical as sensory things are. Which, by the way, comes back to the fundamental idea of every empiricism, namely that there is no One, that there is only the multiple. It might be said that empiricism is a philosophy that establishes that there is no One.

Before addressing the question of Kant's position with respect to these two currents, let me give you a few bibliographical references.

--*Critique of Pure Reason* (1781), followed by its "summary," the *Prolegomena to Any Future Metaphysics* (1783). We're reminded of Marx, who wrote *Wages, Price and Profit* as a synopsis of *Capital*. The idea is that people will understand the short treatise better than the long one.

--*Critique of Practical Reason* (1785). Deals with morality, along with its summary, the *Groundwork of the Metaphysics of Morals* (1797).

--*Critique of the Power of Judgment* (1790). Deals with aesthetics. It is an augmentation of *Observations on the Feeling of the Beautiful and the Sublime* (1764).

Kant was a disciple of Wolff, who was himself a disciple of Leibniz, whose thought he rigidified. In his precritical period, Kant was therefore in the Continental tradition. However, reading Hume had a devastating effect on him. We know that Kant said that Hume awoke him from his dogmatic slumber. What guarantees the necessity of the count-as-one (cognition) of the Two (the thinking subject and the thought world)? Basically, Kant intended to restore the One, but to found it with the acute awareness that he had to respond to Hume. His approach was to found the necessity of the count-as-one of the Two while avoiding a twofold danger: that of doing so only through experience (like Hume) and that of trying to found the count-as-one of the Two on a dogmatic demonstration, which would mean that the count-as-one of the Two could be inferred from the principles of being. According to Kant, the position that comes from experience is skeptical, and the one that comes from being is dogmatic. Both were to be avoided. Kant adopted a synthetic position, which he called, oddly enough, "critique." In Kant's work there is an operating system of the count-as-one that is neither the being itself of things, which would be equivalent to a reduction to the real, nor the semblance of experience. This third term is the action of the structure, which has autonomy and which he called the transcendental system. This system reinstated what the other two foreclosed, that is, the original void of the subject, of the cogito. It was likewise opposed to the subject's dissemination in multiplicity.

———— ⦿ ————

In all of this there is one key word for Kant: mathematics. Kant's relationship with mathematics is a fascinating, essential question. What is this function of mathematics, and how can it be explained?

Kant says that Hume, in attacking the cause-effect relationship, concluded that its mainspring was habit, but he failed to see that the same was also true of mathematics: mathematical judgments also effect a count-as-one of the Two of relationship. We can refer to his comment on 7 + 5 = 12. Something in the concept of 12 combines 7 and 5 without my being able to say that what is stated is already contained in 7 and 5. I thus go beyond the strict analytic content of my initial givens. There is a synthetic operator that ensures that in mathematics itself there is a count-as-one of the Two. Now, says Kant, if Hume had seen this, i.e., that it extended to mathematics, he would have recoiled at the extent of his skepticism. Mathematical judgments are indeed indisputable, and Hume himself would have understood that his psychologico-skeptical account was no good. Before the majesty and absoluteness of mathematical science he wouldn't have been able to say that it all dissolved in pure empiricism or the psychology of habit.

So we're dealing with an unusual operation, which consists first in radicalizing Hume's critique and then in saying that this empirical critique actually goes farther than Hume himself imagined.

We're touching here on the problem, so important in philosophy, of the peculiar status of the mathematical referent: this referent is a mediation of the radicality of thought. When a philosophical operation must be turned against itself, mathematics is often the mediation of the radicality of this turn.

Kant will therefore address the question: How is pure mathematics possible? And he does so with the profound conviction that when it comes to mathematical necessity, no one doubts. We've already seen this conviction in Descartes, who needs the evil genius, actually a deceiving God, in order to suspend mathematical truths. Kant will trace back the chain from the point of radicality. And he will formulate the question in this way: "How are a priori synthetic judgments possible?" Using my terminology, I'll replace "judgment" with "statement," "synthetic" with "count-as-one of the Two," and I'll understand *a priori* to mean "not able to be inferred from experience." Thus: How is the count-as-one of a Two possible, insofar as it is necessary and so does not derive from experience?

A priori synthetic judgments are necessarily possible, since mathematics proves that they exist. Hume would have denied that there are any, Kant says, but we don't have to ask ourselves the question since mathematics has settled it for us, and Hume himself would have had to agree. So the question of how, rather than what, arises. That's what the position of critique is. The question of what (the existence of a priori synthetic judgments) is settled by the very fact of mathematics. What should be retained from Hume's critique is the question of how. To answer it, the transcendental system, that is, the constitutive character of structure, will have to be introduced.

This is the perspective from which we'll approach the texts next time, with a very important question: If the transcendental system, hence a structure, allows us to tackle the question "How are a priori synthetic judgments possible?," what becomes of the real in this cognitive process? For the dogmatists and the empiricists alike, this question has already been settled. For the empiricists—i.e., Hume— the real is what is given in the diversity of experience, while the dogmatists—i.e., Descartes and Leibniz—claim they have a direct argument for being and immediately infer the question of being from the philosophical system.

Kant doesn't decide on this immediately. He treads a fine line, precisely because his is a critical philosophy. We will call "critical" any philosophy that begins with the question of how and deals with the question of being on the basis of the system of how. Often, the critique lags behind and is constantly threatened by weak relapses, most often into empirical figures, but sometimes into revivals of dogmatism. Kant's genius was to hold to the fine line and propose a true doctrine of the real.

It's this Kantian real that we'll be dealing with next time.

Session 12

March 27, 1984

K ant, as we have seen, boils down the questions from the confrontation between dogmatism (Descartes, Leibniz) and skepticism (Locke and Hume) to one big question, "How are a priori synthetic judgments possible?" *Synthetic* meaning, may I remind you, what adds something to experience, and *a priori* denoting an intrinsic necessity.

A priori synthetic judgments are possible—in fact, they have to be, since they exist, as mathematics shows—so long as experience is not a passive operation but a structured one. Indeed, experience is structured, organized, by the transcendental subject (the structure), and as a result, experience is possible under universal subjective conditions, which apply to all possible experience.

This means that what is universal about judgment does not concern the object but the subject. The guarantee of this universality must be sought in the structure, that is, in the subjective conditions. This is what Kant called a "Copernican Revolution." It is in fact a fundamental operation of decentering: whereas the necessary guarantee of cognition was once sought in being, it is now sought in the objective structure itself. This places the concept of subject, as far as cognition is concerned, on the side of its ultimate guarantee, its universality and its necessity, all things that, for Kant, do not come from experience but from the structure (the transcendental).

A comparison with Descartes should be made here. For Descartes, the subject is not first in terms of the universality of cognition. It is first in the order of certainty: it is the first certainty. The subject is simply an indisputable point of being. For Descartes, the subject's emergence on the scene is ontological because the subject is the first absolutely undeniable existent. But this subject guarantees nothing as to judgment. To guarantee the universality of judgment, Descartes needed the second existent, the one called "God," namely, the Other, in the strict sense. The subject is merely a transitory, existential necessity, a point of being needed in order to gain access to the real, which only the proof of God's existence can provide. I will infer from my existence as subject-that-thinks the existence of the big Other, which in its turn will guarantee judgments, specifically mathematical judgments. So the Cartesian subject is in no way a structure conferring its validity on all possible experience.

The Cartesian system consists of I/God/the world, that is, three terms and two schizes, two fissures. I/God: the fissure of the Other's incommensurability, since the I is finite while God is infinite. This fissure is filled by the proof of the existence of the I, from which the existence of the Other is inferred. God/world: the fissure opened up by the Christian dogma of the Creation. The world comes from God. For Descartes, it even comes from him all the time: that's his dogma of "continuous creation." This set of five concepts—I, God, world, proof, creation—constitutes the space of truth. These five operators are needed.

The Kantian system is completely different. The subject is structure. It is a system of conditions for possible experience. Experience is the mediator; it is what is structured. As for being as such, we know nothing about it, at least in terms of cognition.

So we are dealing with two systems with schizes, but the latter are entirely different from each other.

Descartes:

--The I is the original existent point.

--God, the existent as Other than I, will represent the possible guarantee of judgment.

--The world, the supposedly external real correlative of my judgments, is the third term.

--The covering-over of the first schize is the ontological argument: it's a movement from existent to existent.

--The covering-over of the second schize, God/world, is a relationship of creation, and the correlation is therefore theological.

---∞---

Kant:

--The transcendental is the place of structure. So, from the outset, it is the point of guarantee of the universality of judgment.

--Experience: there is no schize between the transcendental and experience. Experience is where the operation of the transcendental takes place.

--Being is the thing in itself, the objectivity of the object. It is what lies behind representation and experience. Here there is a true schize.

--The object of the operation = X, which is a variable.

---∞---

In Kant the universality of judgment is guaranteed by the intricate relationship between the transcendental that structures it and experience. The transcendental is universal, but it's a subjective universality, the structure of the subject of all possible experience.

In Descartes there's a guarantee of being, but it is transcendent, in the position of Other in relation to the I. So there is a theological punctuation. In Kant there is a guarantee of universality but no guarantee of being. We are in the space of representations.

At this point, then, we could say that the category of subject remains ontological in Descartes and is subordinated to a guarantee of being, while the concept of subject in Kant is epistemological or critical but not ontological, since the ontological is the X, the indeterminate correlate of a possible experience. So between Descartes and Kant a "shift" occurred in the category of the subject, a change in philosophical register: the switch was from the point of being, from the existent, to the structure, that is, to a system of conditions—hence a subject that is not only desubstantialized but also deexistentialized. Its whole being is in its operation, in the structured character of experience.

The traditional view holds that the category of subject remains marked by dogmatism in Descartes, whereas with Kant the subject emerges as a critical figure. Kant really signals the end of ontology as a relevant question. Indeed, since being qua being is outside the scope of experience, nothing universal can be said about it. The category of subject is the critical operator of the end of ontology.

I think it is one of the great merits of Heidegger to have been the first to assert that, despite appearances, Kant's big question is actually the ontological question, that his fundamental question is the question of being, and that the movement of critique is itself a movement toward this question, a clearing-out of the question, since there is a critique of its pretense and a description, at best obscure, of the point where this question can actually be formulated as a question.

I'd like to explain how it can be claimed that Kant's question, initially epistemological, maintains and raises afresh the ontological question, i.e., what can be said about being itself. There are two approaches to this very important problematic because, paradox-ically, what is involved is the materialist nature of the category of subject itself. If, in a way, the category of subject is fundamentally linked to its critical destiny, if it is not intertwined with the onto-logical question, well, then, its destiny remains idealist. Indeed, the category of subject operates only in order to found universality in the subjective, to detach universality from any principle of being. To hold a purely critical view of Kant, as Lenin, with some justification, does in *Materialism and Empiriocriticism*, is to see in Kant a hybrid figure of idealism, because it amounts to separating cognition from being and to compromising the category of subject with idealism.

For anyone who, like me, wants to confer a materialist status on the category of subject, it is interesting to see how it can be shown, with regard to Kant, that ultimately, and through complications that are all his own, it is being itself that is at stake in his work.

In this respect, Heidegger's take on Kant is of interest to me. He extricates Kant from the traditional critical epistemological prob-lematic by taking two steep, twisting paths. The first concerns the Kantian category of the object, the concept of object, while the sec-ond concerns the question of the being of the subject. The difficulty lies in the link between the two.

Concerning the first point, Kant holds absolutely that experience is correlated with being, and that there is a schize in the order of cognition: experience does not give us cognition of being, only of phenomena. That said, since being is a condition of experience, we will retain our three terms in any actual experience. How do things present themselves? Our representations, that is, experience, require objects. Experience is correlated with the notion of object, because it is objects that are represented. This representation does not pro-vide access to being in itself because representation is subjectively structured and I cannot go beyond this structuring. There is one thing that subjective conditions do not structure: the existential index of representation, i.e., not the object itself but the objectivity of the object. The fact that the objects of experience are in a position of objectivity does not depend on the subjective conditions. Objectivity is not a subjective category, even though it is a category of representation. The position of objectivity in experience is not inherent in the structure.

In this way, being is presented but not cognized—I can only cognize objects—in the figure of the objectivity of the object, in the fact that the object presents itself to experience. Here in Kant there is a doctrine not of the cognition of being but of its presentation, which is naturally immanent to experience. Thus, we won't say, either, that there is an experience of being, because being would then have to be an object, since being is the objectivity of all possible objects. But there is no experience of objectivity, only of the object; it's a pure presentation to cognition of what is cognized.

So it can be argued that, for Kant, thought is ultimately subordinated to being, not as an object but as presence. Significantly, he uses the word *thought* at this juncture, to be distinguished from the word *cognition*. Cognition is subordinated to objects. Thought, for its part, is faced with what presents itself to cognition and pertains to being. What Kant introduces is the distinction between thought and cognition, which will resonate strongly throughout Heidegger's work. The thinking of being underpins cognition, in the form of a presentation of objectivity.

Let me read you a passage from the very beginning of the "Preface to the 1st Edition of the *Critique of Pure Reason*":

> It is entirely contradictory and impossible that a concept should be generated completely *a priori* and be related to an object although it neither belongs itself within the concept of possible experience nor consists of elements of a possible experience. For it would then have no content, since no intuition would correspond to it though

intuitions in general, through which objects can be given to us, constitute the field or the entire object of possible experience. An *a priori* concept that was not related to the latter would be only the logical form for a concept, but not the concept itself through which something would be thought.

If there are pure *a priori* concepts, therefore, they can certainly contain nothing empirical; they must nevertheless be strictly *a priori* conditions for a possible experience, as that alone on which its objective reality can rest. (A95–96, p. 227)

This text tells us the transcendental, that is, *a priori* concepts, is necessarily related to a field of objectivity. There has to be an objective field of all possible experience. If there were not, we would be dealing not with concepts but with the purely logical form of concepts. This is a key point: in order for a concept of the transcendental domain to be the basis for a thought, before this thought is specifiable as cognition, there has to be a field of objectivity. Otherwise, we're dealing with pure logic. And this means that structure, in Kant's sense of the term, is not a pure logic *since it requires a givenness of objectivity, a "there is" of being*. The pure "there is" of being alone ensures that the structure is not a pure logic—hence the anticipation of the Lacanian idea that the real is the impasse of formalization. Kant formulates it in the following way: the concepts that structure experience are only thoughts in relation to a "there is." Thought is in this sense onto-logical, if we admit that "onto"— the principle of the "there is"—is, here, the point of excess over "logic." The operation of thought is the logical at the impasse of the "there is."

However, we can go much deeper still regarding the scope of being of thought. The ontological question will turn back on the subject itself, present here in the figure of the objectivity of the object. If the word *subject* simply means the conditions of experience, their

structured system, the transcendental, the transcendental relationship, the organizing category of judgment—if, therefore, the subject
is the subjective conditions—how can I count this subject as one?
I can of course take *subject* as an adjective and speak of the subjective conditions. But in what sense can I count it as one and speak
of *the* subject? This question has no answer in terms of experience
since experience is in the figure of the object, under the sway of its
structuring by the subjective conditions. Yet it emerges as a necessary question because experience, for its part, is counted as one.
Experience presents a unified world to me; there is an obvious stability to experience. So I need to find the principle whereby I can
count the subject as one. I don't have the means for this within the
framework of strict Kantianism, as presented thus far, because it is
instead entirely subordinated to multiplicity, that is, to the subjective conditions of experience: time, space, causality, etc.

Kant addresses the question in the following way:

> No cognitions can occur in us, no connection and unity among them,
> without that unity of consciousness that precedes all data of the
> intuitions, and in relation to which all representation of objects is
> alone possible. This pure, original, unchanging consciousness I will
> now name transcendental apperception. . . . The numerical unity of
> this apperception therefore grounds all concepts *a priori*. (A107)

I have to count the subject as one (note the term "numerical unity")
because there is cognition. Without this count-as-one, there would
be no cognition, only a juxtaposition of noncomparable and uncon-
nected spheres of representation. Once Kant gives up counting
being itself as one (given the schize between "object" and "being"),
Kant, unlike Descartes, has no guarantee of unity where the world,
being, God is concerned (and where he nonetheless wants to found
the unity of cognition—our representations do not present chaos

to me, and I am not the subject of such chaos, even if it were structured), and the One must reemerge in relation to the subject; the subjective conditions must be counted as one. So there is necessarily the One of the subject because of the structured character of cognition. However, the fact that this is necessary doesn't tell me where this unity comes from, and calling it "transcendental apperception" doesn't solve the problem.

Yet this problem of the count-as-one of the subject is, as Kant very clearly recognizes, a crucial question for any theory of the subject. Indeed, it is the most complex question, given that it is one thing to make the subjective operation emerge and quite another to guarantee its count-as-one. Just because there must be subjectivity doesn't mean there is *a* subject. We can see Kant grappling with this question at the very end of the *Critique of Pure Reason*. It's a sort of extra question. In the book itself, Kant deduces, classifies, and organizes the transcendental place. The body of the work is structural. Then comes the moment when the necessity of the subject is deduced: Kant describes a multiplicity of conditions, but as an extra question, the count-as-one is necessary. This follows immediately after and will gradually become his main question.

As far as I'm concerned, the question of the One of the subject is precisely what dictates the question of subjectivation and the subjective process. The hypothesis of a unity of lack is introduced in connection with subjectivation. The question of the One as concerns subjectivation is related to lack as an algebraic correlation. As regards the subjective process, it is concepts of consistency, therefore of a topological nature, that guarantee the One. In a way, algebra and topology, lack and consistency, structural and historical causality, are concepts organized around the question of the count-as-one. Much more difficult than the need to identify the specificity of the subject process is the question of being able to say that it is indeed *one* process.

In politics, for instance, the question of the count-as-one of sub-jective processes quite simply concentrates all the difficulties of the question of organization. And we know that the question of orga-nization is key, since organization, philosophically considered, is the only known measure of unity of a political subject. It's not the question of the subject in general but that of its One. This is why it's a very complicated question. If there is an ontological question regarding the subject, it is always from that angle. What procedures make it possible to count the subject as one? From the standpoint of the question of the subject, ontology is immediately in the space of the One and the multiple because it's not a technical but a mathe-matical question in a broad sense.

In Kant the problem is the following: it is a matter of examining not the conditions of an experience but those of the empirical con-sciousness, the conditions of an experience that can nonetheless be counted as one. It's not the same problem. You can know why there's an object in the experience without having solved the problem of how your experiences are consistent with one another under the law of the One of the subject. As Kant says, "The synthetic proposi-tion that every different empirical consciousness must be combined into a single self-consciousness is the absolutely first and synthetic principle of our thinking in general" (A117n). So for Kant, the first principle of our thinking in general is that the various empirical experiences must be combined into a single experience of myself.

It is absolutely clear, however, that the unity of the subject cannot come to it from outside since that would mean it could be thought as the unity of an object. But the unity of an object is a unity internal to experience; it is in representation and does not bridge the schize between objectivity and its structuring. The unity of an object can-not guarantee the unity of the subject since it presupposes that unity.

This is the moment when the ontological question will enter into torsion. The unity of the object itself is bound up with the unity of consciousness, which alone can guarantee the One of the object. There's no hope of finding in the object the guarantee of the count-as-one of the subject. On the contrary, I must presuppose it in order to think the One of the object, because, as far as experiencing it is concerned, I always experience it immediately, which is to say, always *already* structured. Furthermore, the One of the object has no guarantee of being since "object" is a category of representation. For example, there is no One of the being-chair since the chair is an object of experience and that's all. So the count-as-one of the subject must come not from representations but from the relationship between the different representations, hence from the subject. When I say that the count-as-one of the object is linked to the count-as-one of the subject, it's not at the level of experience or at the level of cognition. It's when I want to *think* that there is the count-as-one. The "formal unity of consciousness"—the Kantian term—is the point where the fact that there is a unity of the object is grounded. And it's in the realm of necessity. Therefore, this count-as-one of consciousness is itself transcendental, necessarily, since it cannot be empirical, given that there is no empirical experience of the unity of the subject as such.

Consequently, the count-as-one of the subject is transcendental (there are only two alternatives: either empirical or transcendental), which means that it, too, is a subjective condition of experience. It follows that the count-as-one of the subjective conditions is an extra subjective condition.

So, I say that this extra something is a condition of being, not a condition of structure, and I will show this. The condition that the I be One, which is supernumerary with respect to the subjective conditions that organize experience, is what allows these conditions to be counted as one, and therefore to close them off, to totalize them, by using an existential boundary that is necessarily a point of being (the subject *is* One) and not a point of structure.

We now know, negatively, that the count-as-one of the subject is not an experience, not a self-consciousness in the sense of an experience, not a reflection. We know that it is not something self-evident guaranteed by the Other. By the way, let me remind you that in Descartes the fact that the subject is One was also contingent on God. So it is a subjective condition, or even a faculty of the subject, a *sui generis* faculty that ensures that the various actual (empirical) consciousnesses are in the position of the One and can be counted as one. When Kant uses the term *faculty*, it's because he wants to underscore the fact that, of course, it's a subjective condition, but that there's a big difference, a gulf, compared to the other subjective conditions. There's a situation of excluded inclusion. The count-as-one is a subjective condition, but it is a faculty because it is supernumerary inasmuch as it totalizes the other transcendental determinations. This is the totalization about which Kant, in the passage quoted above, says: "This pure, original, unchanging consciousness I will now name transcendental apperception."

Where will this condition, this "transcendental apperception," be located? It's connected with the transcendental, which is to say, with the nonempirical. It is not exactly the structure, since it doesn't operate on objectivity; it only operates on what is presented. It is necessarily connected with the subject as being since it's not connected with the subject as a structured operation of experience. This is why Kant calls it "pure, original, and unchanging." He thus indexes it to being. Finally, if there is some One in objectivity, it is really because of a guarantee that comes from being—except what indexes being is the transcendental, not as structure, not as operation, but grasped at its point of existential limitation, which is the subject as being.

Finally, the faculty of transcendental apperception is how the One of being presents itself, from the standpoint of the subject—how Kant returns to the Parmenidean reciprocity between being and the One.

Finally: the pure identity of the subject, its count-as-one as such, is how being's power as One presents itself in the form of the One of the object. It is here that the two paths indicated—that of the objectivity of the object and that of the count-as-one of the subject as regards its being—intersect. It is here that there is some One in objectivity and that the objectivity of the object is thus capable of the One. The original apperception is in every sense the very presentation of being, the point of being in Kantianism—a presentation that is neither an experience nor a concept nor an irrational presupposition.

Since the unity of the object is only guaranteed by the count-as-one of the subject, and since this count-as-one is a faculty, i.e., transcendental apperception, which is necessarily assignable to being rather than to structure, it follows that the unity of the object does indeed have its guarantee in being. However, this being can legitimately be named the being of the transcendental by virtue of the correlation that ensures that it is the point of being of the structure; the object in general, capable of the One, can therefore legitimately be called a transcendental object and the transcendental object is ultimately what underpins the objectivity of any object, the other ontological correlate. Let me read:

> The pure concept of this transcendental object (which in all of our cognitions is really always one and the same = X) is that which in all of our empirical concepts in general can provide relation to an object, i.e., objective reality. Now this concept cannot contain any determinate intuition at all, and therefore concerns nothing but that unity which must be encountered in a manifold of cognition insofar as it stands in relation to an object. This relation, however, is nothing other than the necessary unity of consciousness. . . . (A109)

Thus, we twist and complete our chain. The count-as-one of the subject is of the same order of being as the transcendental object X.

It, too, is an X. Therefore, it is one and the same thing as the original apperception and the objectivity of the object. The conditions of experience are subjective, but the condition of the One of experience, that is, the original apperception, pertains to being—not that being is known, but it is presented and effectuated here in a unity of givenness that ensures a sort of correlation between the One of the subject and the One of the object. So Kant's materialism can be said to consist in making the subject and the object communicate in the sphere of being, through the mediation of the One. Between the two there is the structure, i.e., the transcendental as place.

So we've got the transcendental as place/the transcendental subject/the empirical consciousness/the object/being (in itself).

Thus, the Kantian ontological network is created by these five categories (transcendental, subject, empiricity, object, being). The complete Kant, as Heidegger saw, is the intersection of two questions. The question "How are a priori synthetic judgments possible?" can only be truly answered by a further question: "Where is the unity of judgment grounded?" This intertwining of the ontological and the epistemological questions is at the heart of the Kantian question. It remains to be seen what is presented of being in original apperception.

Kant undertakes a critical sorting out. Since the Kantian approach to the question of being is original apperception, the question of what is presented will first require ruling out certain hypotheses. This will be the "critique of the paralogisms of rational psychology."

Kant's solution consists in saying that everything presented under the sign of the One is purely empty. The apparent simplicity of what Kant calls the I lies in the fact that this entity is empty. It doesn't represent anything but functions as the One referent of all givenness of things. I, for one, would see here the idea of the name of the void as the subject's suture to being. In any case, transcendental apperception is neither intention nor concept, which are the two major categories of what presents itself to cognition. The I is a pure empty form that "accompanies" every representation. I think there is tremendous depth to this metaphor: the subject is neither an object of intuition nor a conceptual synthesis, yet it accompanies the totality of experience as its empty part, its indeterminate element.

Thus, Kant strategically paves the way for psychoanalysis, because the central thesis of psychoanalysis, known as the unconscious, is to understand this function the subject has of accompanying being. For psychoanalysis, in its Lacanian development, the subject is in fact neither the object of an intuition nor the correlate of a concept. Psychoanalysis developed in opposition to the pretensions of rational and introspective psychology. Now, to this negative task, which clears up the question of the subject, Kant gave the name, through the critique of paralogisms, "the destruction of rational psychology." Kant is in this sense one of the great modern thinkers. The purely empty function of accompaniment that he identifies, which is grounded in being itself, is what has the ability to anticipate what, in a contemporary way, can be called a subject. In this sense, as far as the question of the subject is concerned, I would say that we're still in the age of Kant, as reconfigured by psychoanalysis with a Lacanian emphasis.

Session 13

April 17, 1984

Today, we're going to see how Kant returns to the question of the subject after having dealt with it successfully, or so it seemed, in the *Critique of Pure Reason*.

It is characteristic of Kant's work that, given a problem, each of the conceptual solutions he proposes generates a problem more radical than the one dealt with before. The solution at the same time opens up a chasm, a new fissure, a new schize, hence the need for a new bridge. This shows how crucial an ontological question the One and the multiple is for Kant, a question that he never manages to treat to his complete satisfaction and that he deals with through a network of subsidiary questions: How is mathematics possible? What is a moral action? How can aesthetic judgments be understood? Underlying the system of the three *Critiques* is that of a recovery of the One where the immediate solution of the problem had resulted in a split, a manifold of faculties. This movement of recovery is characteristic of the Kantian trajectory and of this thinking that divides, splits apart, discriminates, and immediately wonders how the One can be recovered in the element of this scission.

The *Critique of Practical Reason* deals with the question of moral action introduced with regard to the subject, a question that remained unaddressed in the doctrine of the transcendental subject.

We will see later on, in connection with the question of art, how the question of the subject should be re-counted for a beyond of its theoretical and practical treatments.

The movement of the *Critique of Pure Reason* is, as we have seen, as follows: being—Kant calls it the thing-in-itself, the noumenon, the supersensible—is subtracted from representation, or, in other words, our experience gives us no access to being qua being. Representation, that is, the totality of my experience and cognition, including both sensibility (space and time) and concepts (the categories), is an order governed by the structure of the transcendental. However, there remains a trace of the ontological subtraction, which constitutes the border of representation: there is only one idea of representation, or, in other words, there is a *single* disposition as to the objectivity of the object. The subjective foundation of this unity, that is, the name as subject of this trace (nothing can be said about it from the standpoint of being, only from the standpoint of the subject) is original apperception. That is the name as subject of the trace, in representation, of the fact that being-in-itself is subtracted from representation.

It is a fundamental philosophical thesis: the One is always the name of being-as-subtracted. If, ever since Parmenides, there has been a linkage between the One and being, it is because the One denotes the subtraction of being. As empirical consciousness, original apperception is nothing. It is neither representable nor represented. But it can be deduced from the fact that there is unity of representation, a trace to be interpreted as resulting from the subtraction of being.

Incidentally, this really shows that Kant, in line with what I think, is convinced that the transcendental subject, insofar as it is opposed to multiple empirical consciousnesses, insofar as it can be counted as one, must be found, or deduced. The subject, in Kant, is indeed a product of thought. It is not the original given, which is experience as organized by structure.

To sum up: being subtracted from representation returns in connection with the One and as the name of the void, from the standpoint of the subject. In this sense, as Heidegger maintains, there is an originary linkage between the subject and being. So the Kantian doctrine of the transcendental subject is indeed an ontology.

If we try to express this from the standpoint of being, we will say that being is a traced subtraction, since it is named in its void under the sign of the One. But there's something unsatisfactory about this, a failure to hold together, an unnoticed torsion. Being, which was subtracted, underpinned, *as subtracted*, the objectivity of the object. It was what ensured that representation, as the field of experience in general, was that from which being is subtracted. The sign of this subtracted presence is that the objectivity of the object is guaranteed for us. But we find this being in connection with the One of the subject under the name of original apperception. How can this double occurrence of subtracted being—objectivity in connection with the object, the One in connection with the subject—in its turn be counted as one? We don't know what guarantees, here, that we can count as one the being that underpins the objectivity of the object and the being that is the name-as-One of the subject. Are they the same, and in what sense? There is, to be sure, a linkage between subject and being, since the subject is at the edge of being, but what is the One of this edge effect?

The ontological trajectory distributes being between what is subtracted (the thing in itself, the noumenon, the supersensible, the unrepresentable) and what we find in this count-as-one that's like the invariant transcendental of the empirical consciousnesses. There are at least two names for being here. Clearly, a dialectic of this duality is needed. A relationship must be established between the One of the subject and the supersensible as such. Otherwise, being remains Two, even if in all cases it is being that's involved. To use Kant's language: is there a subjectivation of the supersensible?

If not, a chasm will have been opened up within being itself—a chasm between being under the sign of the One, the naming of the void, on the one hand, and the thing-in-itself, the supersensible, the noumenon, on the other. Kant demands of himself that the whole problem be reexamined in order to try to bridge the chasm opened up by the *Critique of Pure Reason* between the initial subtractive occurrence and the final occurrence of the count-as-one of the subtractive void.

For Kant, the One of the subject, which is the edge of being, is considered as existence in the strict sense, as what ek-sists to experience, as what is a necessary assertion that is not contained in (that ek-sists to) experience, since it is, qua transcendental apperception, the first condition of experience itself. But does *being* exist? The question is not self-evident, and it is central for Kant, as Heidegger showed. For in order to ek-sist in this sense, the "sistence" with respect to which there is ek-sistence must be defined. "Sistence" is the transcendental field, experience, from which being is subtracted. The fact that it is subtracted and that it ek-sists are not equivalent operations. The subject ek-sists to experience since it counts it as one, but being does not count experience as one. It is supersensible and is therefore not a given of sensory experience. To be and to exist are not the same thing.

Being is described as subtracted from representation, the transcendental subject as an empty point counted as one. Are subtraction and the void the same thing? This is a fair question to ask. Does being exist? Because to say that being is is not necessarily to say that it exists. Can the subtractive and the void really be counted as one? Are we able to count as one the count-as-one and subtraction, existence and being?

It is an absolutely general characteristic of modern (by which I mean post-Cartesian) philosophical discourse that anyone who counts being and existence as one necessarily does so under the name of "freedom." Freedom is the philosophical name of the count-as-one of being and existence. Kant was the first to clear up this question, but it can already be found in Descartes, for whom the starting point, the "I am, I think," results from anything that precludes the absoluteness of my negative freedom.

"Freedom," in Kantian terms, is the name of the subject's relationship to the supersensible; more generally, it is a definition of the philosophical concept of freedom to say that "the name of the void is also a name of being." This is why Kant's problematic necessarily becomes a problematic of freedom and why the second stage of the Kantian investigation will be to seek its inner dynamic not in cognition but in action, in practical reason.

Let me just say a word about method. When Kant creates a category field, he always does so based on what he considers to be facts. In the *Critique of Pure Reason*, for instance, the fact is the existence of mathematics. Thus, he feels a deep humility toward facts: he always begins with historical, practical, proven facts, and it's on the basis of the possibility of one such fact that the structural system that will account for the conditions of possibility of the fact in question is implemented. The existence of mathematics is proof of our capacity for making a priori synthetic judgments. Then the conditions of possibility of such judgments are developed.

In his new structural setup, Kant will begin with the fact that "there is duty." This means that a binding law with regard to action is everywhere evident. He posits—in the sense that he notes its existence—that every reasonable being is called upon to obey a strict imperative, a "you must." Kant starts from the assumption that everyone is well aware that there are good actions and bad actions and that, with respect to a decision to be made, there's a generic "you must" that lets you know if you've acted well or badly. To deny as much would be the act of a scoundrel as well as a liar.

In what sense is duty a fact? It is not an empirical fact, or, to put it another way, it is not what manifests itself as an object of experience. Kant shows this clearly in the *Groundwork of the Metaphysics of Morals*. The use of duty can be inferred from ordinary consciousness, whereas the *Critique of Pure Reason* makes reference to the knowing consciousness. Duty is a fact, but there's not a single piece of evidence that can be cited in its favor, nor can it be said that any action was done out of duty. Dutiful action cannot be experienced. It is not an empirical fact in the sense of ordinary action, nor is it a paradigmatic fact that could be derived from a certain number of examples. Let me read you a very clear passage:

> If we add further that, unless we want to deny to the concept of morality any truth and any relation to some possible object, we cannot dispute that its law is so extensive in its import that it must hold not only for human beings but for all *rational beings as such*, not merely under contingent conditions and with exceptions but with *absolute necessity*, then it is clear that no experience could give occasion to infer even the possibility of such apodictic laws. . . . Nor could one give worse advice to morality than by wanting to derive it from examples. For, every example of it represented to me must itself first be appraised in accordance with principles of morality, as to whether it is also worthy to serve as an original example, that is, as a model; it can by no means authoritatively provide the concept of morality.[1]

Consequently, duty can only be a fact of pure reason. The factuality of duty resides entirely in the subject. It has no objective index; it is a nonempirical factuality. But what is a nonempirical factuality if not a structural factuality? In the case of mathematics, we had the established fact of mathematics. But in the case of duty, we're dealing with a fact that is already structural, and no object can be considered as constructing the structure. The fact of morality cannot be presented in the form of the object of the morality of the action, so its presentation is itself subjective. The structure is originary.

The relationship between the moral question and the question of science could be thematized in the following way. In the case of science, there is fact and there is structure, of which the fact is an effect. In the case of morality, there is structure and there are facts, actions, but it cannot be known to what extent the latter are effects of the structure. Action, and this is a very important point, will always be morally undecidable. As far as science is concerned, the Kantian doctrine is a doctrine of decidability, whereas in the case of morality, since the structure is originary, there is, generically, undecidability. We who have been trained in modern logic know—this is a very profound idea—that it's when we begin with the formal that we find the undecidable. When the original fact is structural, there is a trace of undecidability as to the facts. Conversely, when the fact is empirical, the structure is there to produce decidability as to the fact.

It remains to construct the structure from the purely subjective fact of duty.

Kant begins by working backward from duty to the concept of will. For there to be duty, there must be will. In other words, the capacity whereby duty exists is called will. Here's what Kant says in the *Groundwork of the Metaphysics of Morals*:

> Everything in nature works in accordance with laws. Only a rational being has the capacity to act *in accordance with the representation of laws*, that is, in accordance with principles, or has a *will*. Since *reason* is required for the derivation of actions from laws, the will is nothing other than practical reason. (4:412, p. 24)

Another consequence of this shift is that the position of representation will also change. In cognition, the *representation* of the object is based on laws. In the field of morality, law is *what is represented*. The representation/law/object system is thus completely upended.

In the cognitive sequence, there is the object and the representation, a representation that is always an object representation and only occurs in a system of law, since there is the transcendental structure of representation. In the moral sequence, representation concerns the law, and action, i.e., the object, results from the representation of the laws. The structural schemas are completely transformed. The will is the capacity to act in accordance with the representation of the laws, not of objects. But as a law is a structural fact, *the will is a structure upon a structure: it is a metastructure*. It is, structurally, a representation of structure. That's why it will be in a position of formalization, because it is the structural operating on the structural, not the structural that operates on an object.

I think this is a very profound idea. To understand what the will is, what decision is, we need to look not to some internal force but to the formal. The will is not an impulsion, an affirmative force, a gushing spring, but rather an instance of formalization. This is why, in politics, the party is the will (if one is Kantian, at any rate), that is, not the representation of a class but its revolutionary political formalization. It is Kant who thought most forcefully that the will is always a formalization.

A second concept, coming after the concept of will, will be the concept of imperative. It's the name of the subjective representation of the law. It's the will in its metastructural position, the way in which the metastructure operates. Let me read:

> The representation of an objective principle, insofar as it is necessitating for a will, is called a command (of reason), and the formula of the command is called an **imperative**.
>
> . . . Therefore imperatives are only formulae expressing the relation of objective laws of volition in general to the subjective imperfection of the will of this or that rational being, for example, of the human will.

Now, all imperatives command either *hypothetically* or *categorically*. The former represent the practical necessity of a possible action as a means to something else that is willed (or that it is at least possible for one to will). The categorical imperative would be that which represented an action as objectively necessary of itself, without reference to another end. (4:413–414, pp. 24–25)

An imperative can be defined as the minimum unit of representation of a law that is presented as binding on the will. This doesn't mean that the imperative binds us: we are dealing with the will as formalization, so we don't have the constraint but the *form* of the constraint. This means that the will can only conceive of the categorical imperative as binding; it can only conceive of the law as law.

As regards the hypothetical imperative, there is a conditional constraint. If this is how it is, then.... In logic, this is an implication. This concerns the question of the logical form of the constraint, too. The categorical imperative represents an action as intrinsically necessary, that is, as independent of its outcome. It is a pure, unconditional form. Kant also says that the hypothetical imperative is heteronomous. Heteronomy describes a law that includes the other, since the legislation is subordinated to an outcome, to a principle of alterity. The categorical imperative, on the other hand, is autonomous, which means that it is self-binding, that it isn't bound up with an alterity, isn't internally split by this alterity.

Finally, in this structure that combines will and imperative, the structural fact, which used to be called duty, has been renamed *the categorical imperative*. In other words, the fact one begins with—that everyone knows that there is a moral duty—can now be stated this way: there is a categorical imperative. As it is a fact, we will say "There is," but the content is: There is an unconditional imperative, an autonomous command.

Now we know why it's not empirical: it's because it's formal. In contrast to the hypothetical imperative, which is heteronomous, that is, dependent on the outcome, and in which there consequently remains a primacy of experience on which the formal is dependent (for example, if I want to quench my thirst, I must drink), in the case of the categorical imperative, the formal is not dependent on any experience, hence its total autonomy.

The fact of duty is an autonomous formalization, the form of nothing, except of every possible act. So the question is what an autonomous formalization is and how it operates. Kant's question won't be, as before, the question of possibility. To be sure, the categorical imperative plays in the *Critique of Practical Reason* the role played by a priori synthetic judgments in the *Critique of Pure Reason*. But the symmetry stops there. In the case of a priori synthetic judgments, the question was whether they were possible. In the case of the categorical imperative, everything has been said once it's been said that it is a pure form.

This time, Kant will work downstream from the original fact. In the case of cognition, there was the fact (mathematics and, more generally, science), and he went upstream toward its possibilities. In the case of the categorical imperative, there is also the fact (duty), but, downstream, he'll have to ask what the operation of a pure form can possibly be. How can a law be enacted concerning an action if that law is indifferent to the outcome? So Kant will put forward a very complex theory of the power of form in action. The tension he introduces stems from his claim that there is a universality of the moral principle of action but that the assured, objective character of this universality remains undecidable. On the one hand, the power of form in action will be supreme inasmuch as it is universal and opens for us what cognition alone is incapable of: access to the supersensible. But at the same time this power can never be validated in experience, by its real effects. It remains, in its very power, undecidable as to its particular existence in a concrete action.

Session 14

May 15, 1984

L et me repeat, in shorthand fashion, what I proposed as the Kantian conception of being: Being is subtraction (because subtracted from representation), traced (because representation is not the representation of nothing), then named in its void (what emerges from it is the count-as-one) under the rule of the One. Ultimately, between the subtractive and what is referred to as the One (original apperception), what is the dialectic? What type of unity do they have? This is the question of the count-as-one of the count-as-one. And if we use the term *supersensible* for being, we can say that the new question becomes: Is there an existential dialectic of the supersensible? Or, in simpler terms: Does being exist? Or again: Is there a link between the transcendental subject and the supersensible as such, i.e., as subtracted from any rational cognition produced, precisely, by the transcendental?

You then have two symmetrical, fundamental questions:

1. Can we say that the subject, which exists (it is the name of a void), *is*? What can the meaning be of this designation-as-being of the subject?
2. Concerning the being that is subtracted, can we say that it exists?

The first is a very important and difficult question regarding the theory of the subject. The predication of being with respect to the subject is the focus of a major revolving-door philosophical debate, which is fully developed in Sartre, for example, who considers existence the nihilation of being. In a way, this question, first introduced by Kant, is more fundamental than Descartes's question about the "what I am" of the subject. The being of the enunciation "I think, I am" is not examined as such in Descartes. The "is" of the "I am," the "I is" [*j'est*] of the subject, the gesture [*geste*] of the subject, the "is" [*l'est*] of the subject that am [*qui suis*], is not interrogated as such. We are reminded here of the famous Latin translation of the divine utterance *Ego sum qui sum*, "I am who am," which glosses over being, the "is," with its grammatical first person.

Kant's more demanding approach is driven by the idea that the answer to this question cannot be found in cognition. As regards the subject, exploring the sphere of cognition reveals nothing to us beyond its existence, that is, beyond the description of its emptiness and its function as One. Therefore, the question of the subject's being is an essentially practical question.

This is a very remarkable approach. To a certain extent, an ontological question can only be assigned to the realm of practice, and what will determine the point of being of the subject belongs to the sphere of action. But be careful: this doesn't mean that the subject is action!

Kant will begin by constructing a structure other than the cognitive one, which is essentially a transcendental structure of the object, of object representation. Let me remind you of the steps of his approach. He begins, as usual, with a fact. The first fact, this time, is duty, the pure imperative, the "voice of conscience," a term borrowed from Rousseau. As a pure subjective fact, duty is not an empirical given. The factuality of this fact is its pure existence, its undeniable presence at the very point of the existence of any consciousness, of any subject counted as One.

Just as an aside, this conception is inherent in the Kantian vision of man, in Kantian anthropology. What is man for Kant? Pure mathematics and the pure imperative. Without the former there would never have been any enlightened understanding; without the latter, never any moral action. More fundamentally, these are the only paths to ontology itself, and this allows the ontological question to be formulated.

In a scientistic anthropology, what distinguishes humans from animals is language and tools, with a possible dialectic between them: language as an instrument, as the capacity for communication; tools as the capacity to invent the means to an end, which allows us not to be bound, in terms of the ends, to bodily immediacy. We thus have a communication/transmission, means/ends complex.

It can't be said that things are entirely different for Kant. On the one hand, mathematics for him is very much a matter of language: judgments, assertions, statements. But in no way is communication involved. What's involved is language, but language embedded in mathematicity, so that we're no longer in the realm of communication but in that of inscription. This is why mathematical judgments are synthetic and a priori. As for the moral question, it is indeed a matter of means and ends: we're in the practical, instrumental realm. But duty is both the means and the end, or, if you like, it's an end without means. So we could say that in Kantian anthropology we're dealing with language in itself (without communication) and with the end in itself (without regard to the means). There is something like a hyper-anthropologism in Kant's philosophy.

This is what he summarizes in the extremely famous passage from the conclusion to the *Critique of Practical Reason*, which I'll read to you:

Two things fill the mind with ever new and increasing admiration and reverence, the more often and more steadily one reflects on them: *the starry heavens above me and the moral law within me.* . . .

The fall of a stone, the motion of a sling, resolved into their elements and the forces manifested in them and treated mathematically, produced at last that clear and henceforward unchangeable insight into the structure of the world which, with continued observation, one can hope will always be extended while one need never fear having to retreat.

This example can recommend that we take the same path in treating the moral predispositions of our nature and can give us hope of a similarly good outcome. We have at hand examples of reason judging morally. We can analyze them into their elementary concepts and, in default of *mathematics*, adopt a procedure similar to that of *chemistry*—the *separation*, by repeated experiments on common human understanding, of the empirical from the rational that may be found in them—and come to know both of them *pure* and what each can accomplish of itself.[1]

The starry heavens should be understood, on the one hand, as the immensity of the world in comparison with which human reason seems humbled, man being an inferior and limited creature, and, on the other hand, as the mathematical mastery of the world, i.e., astronomy, within the framework of the Newtonian system. The starry heavens are ultimately the symbol of immensity, in connection with the mathematical mastery of phenomena. Duty itself, intimidating, indisputable, must be treated like the starry heavens. It is the inner star. We need to have its structural setup, hence *The Critique of Practical Reason*, just as, earlier, there was *The Critique of Pure Reason*.

The new structural setup doesn't have the same functions as the previous one. Indeed, the trajectory of the *Critique of Pure Reason* began with presentational multiplicity and ended with synthesis, with the count-as-one. In the *Critique of Practical Reason*, by contrast, the aim is to produce a separation, to isolate something truly pure, and this already tells us that we're going to find the subtractive, because we're going to proceed by purification, by successive filterings, on the basis of common, ordinary moral experience. If we want to track down being in the guise of its existence, and therefore as freedom, we need to proceed by analysis, not by synthesis.

After such an analysis—which includes the will, the categorical imperative, the ontological freedom of the subject in the guise of the moral act, which connects it with the supersensible—it becomes clear that morality cannot be inferred from anything: the intrinsic structure of morality is axiomatic. This is very interesting. What's more, I think that in many respects it's true. I think, too, that the fundamental structure of politics is also axiomatic. There are initial statements in politics that are not deducible and are not transitive to anything. This is why there is something definitive about Kantian radicalism, which consists in saying that the essence of the moral will lies neither in the implication "if . . . then" nor in a calculation of means to a limited end.

If we assume a will effectively bound by a categorical imperative now, we see that this will, like being in cognitive representation, is in the realm of the subtractive. It is subtracted from causality, from any cause-and-effect relationship, from anything that produces representation. We will see why and how.

Kant will have to show that traditional religious morality is essentially implicative, of the "if . . . then" type, even if Saint Paul says that it is faith (not works) that saves. For Kant, the hypothetical imperative has nothing to do with morality. It only amounts to "prudential maxims." Ultimately, the implication "if   then," judging the end by the means, lies in representation, since the transcendental regulation of representation is precisely the relationship of cause and effect. So the hypothetical imperative is a matter of empirical experience and not of ontological subtraction. Insofar as there is a categorical imperative—an imperative that can only be represented axiomatically, that cannot be inferred—and assuming there's a will that acts in strict conformity with this imperative, thus by representation of the law and not in accordance with the laws of representation, I would say that a will of this kind is in a subtractive position since it will be subtracted from the transcendental constitution of representation through the transcendental categories, in particular through causality. It is an unfettered, free will and therefore in a subtractive position.

There is a key connection between axiomatic presentation and ontological subtraction: it is because the imperative is only representable as an axiom that the will related to this imperative is in a subtractive position with regard to its ontological position. If duty cannot be inferred, it cannot have the figure of the object, otherwise it would be represented. Since duty is noninferable, no object figure is given, and the will, in turn, is therefore unpresentable.

That's a point that should be explored.

Actually, the crucial question is whether a categorical imperative can really exist. Kant, too, uses the conditional. How can a law be binding for the will without any object being represented, without any purpose? Kant says there's a solution, namely that this law is purely formal. For the law to be formal means that it concerns only the form of the action, not its reality, because the action is in the world, so it's in representation. It follows that if my will acts in conformity with a categorical law, this conformity clearly has nothing to do with an empirical action, which, by contrast, is able to be represented, and therefore structured by the categories of cause and effect.

It is certain that, no matter what you do in the empirical world, what you do can be attributed, from outside, to relations of causality. The external representation of an action is part of the representable; it is structured by the transcendental. So it's not this that constitutes the action's conformity with the categorical imperative. The reason why we land on the shores of morality does not concern the immediately representable action, what happens and is necessarily in representation, but *the form of the action*, a parameter that is not exhausted in representation.

The form of the action is precisely the immanent representation of the law, inasmuch as this representation alone binds the will in the action. It is not the structure of the action but its metastructure. In the *Groundwork of the Metaphysics of Morals*, Kant summarizes all this in the following way:

> Finally there is one imperative that, without being based upon and having as its condition any other purpose to be attained by certain conduct, commands this conduct immediately. This imperative is **categorical**. It has to do not with the matter of the action and what is to result from it, but with the form and the principle from which the action itself follows; and the essentially good in the action consists in the disposition, let the result be what it may. This imperative may be called the imperative of **morality**.[2]

I should point out that saying that we're dealing with a psychologizing interpretation wouldn't be a good way of interpreting "the form and the principle." To be sure, the word *intention*[3] is somewhat ambiguous. Isn't judging the value of an action on the basis of the subject's intentions tantamount to returning to psychological empiricity? It should be understood that Kant uses the word *intention* with a purely pedagogical . . . intention. Obviously, there's a patent vicious circle, which "intention" covers over or conceals. It's a vicious circle because, on the one hand, the action is moral if the acting will is bound by the representation of a categorical imperative. But, on the other hand, the imperative is categorical if it prescribes nothing but acting in accordance with the representation of the law, and therefore if it is the sole axiom of the action. Consequently, the action is axiomatic if it is moral, and moral if it is axiomatic.

What will resolve the issue is the fact that the categorical imperative is what prescribes the law as law, the lawfulness of the law, which the hypothetical law conceals because it is conditioning, in the sense that "Do this" is dependent on "if you want that." So my interpretation is that the categorical imperative is not just "another" imperative. It is the imperativeness of the imperative, which, in the hypothetical imperative, is concealed and ultimately eliminated.

When its conception of the law is based on the scope of its outcome, an action is outside the sphere of morality; it is merely a prudential action. By contrast, it is moral when the will conceives of the lawfulness of the law, i.e., that the law is law, and when the pure command, the essence of any possible command, is included in the representation.

In other words, an action is good if it takes place—if the will produces it—strictly in connection with the fact that it is axiomatically bound by the representation of the fact that *there is the law*.

This, in my opinion, is something that the distinction between the hypothetical and the categorical imperative glosses over a little. I ultimately don't believe that there are two types of imperative. An action is moral when you act in accordance with the representation of the pure command. That is what will be called freedom. As regards the hypothetical imperative, the will is fettered. An "unfettered" will acts in accordance with the representation of the command as a command. This is what will ensure that the command is absolutely universal and has no objectified content.

The problem is then as follows. Since the lawfulness of the law, i.e., the categorical imperative, is what underlies the will to act, action is of course bound by a law but by the law as law. As a result, when the will is of this kind, it ex-centers the subject in relation to the supersensible. Why is this so? Well, because the law as pure law, if we're only concerned here with its lawgiving form, is something subtracted from any object representation. We can no longer say *a* law; we must instead speak of the lawfulness of *the* law. But if the moral will is bound by the law as law, it is in a subtractive position; it is exempt from any object representation and is inscribed in the supersensible. At the same time, the will is a concept of existence. Consequently, we are justified in saying that moral action *brings the existent into being*. It *super*sensibilizes the existent.

The moral will as relationship—the will is relationship since the acting will is in representation and, as the will of the subject, it is in existence—is what is subtracted from any object relation. Simultaneously, however, it occurs affirmatively, not as pure void: it exists in the world at the same time as it is inscribed in the supersensible, insofar as it is only bound by the lawfulness of the law. Moral action, if it exists, is thus in a position to bring existence into being, that is to say, to count being and existence as one.

And then, as is always the case in philosophy, insofar as we have an existential dialectic of being, a count-as-one of being and existence, and therefore a meta-count-as-one, or, in other words, a bridge between being and existence, the name for all this is *freedom*. Freedom is axiomatic action; it is also the subject, practical, as subtraction, and, last but not least, it is action with universal value.

As you can see, what's amazing about this approach is that subtracting the subject means wresting it away from the reign of necessity, from the regime of causality, but for that to happen a superior type of necessity is required, a transcendental, purely transcendental necessity, i.e., a pure command, with no content other than the command. So it would seem that we've solved our problem. The subject as existence, which is the count-as-one of a void, has a parameter, a faculty: the will. The will exists, and insofar as it allows itself to be axiomatically bound by the lawfulness of the law, and not by *a* law, since it is subtracted from the law, it is put in a subtractive position, thus in a position of being.

———⚉———

We're going to take a look at how the passage handed out to you [from the *Critique of Practical Reason*] sums all this up. This passage is both a partial summary and a significant exploration of the problem of freedom. It adopts a demonstrative structure at the beginning: the demonstration of a necessary and sufficient condition, which is then commented on.

5. PROBLEM I

Supposing that the mere lawgiving form of maxims is the only sufficient determining ground of a will: to find the constitution of a will that is determinable by it alone.

Since the mere form of a law can be represented only by reason and is therefore not an object of the senses and consequently does not belong among appearances, the representation of this form as the determining ground of the will is distinct from all determining grounds of events in nature in accordance with the law of causality, because in their case the determining grounds must themselves be appearances. But if no determining ground of the will other than that universal lawgiving form can serve as a law for it, such a will must be thought as altogether independent of the natural law of appearances in their relations to one another, namely the law of causality. But such independence is called *freedom* in the strictest, that is, in the transcendental, sense. Therefore, a will for which the mere lawgiving form of a maxim can alone serve as a law is a free will.

6. PROBLEM II

Supposing that a will is *free*: to find the law that alone is competent to determine it necessarily.

Since the matter of a practical law, that is, an object of the maxim, can never be given otherwise than empirically whereas a free will, as independent of empirical conditions (i.e., conditions belonging to the sensible world), must nevertheless be determinable, a free will must find a determining ground in the law but independently of the *matter* of the law. But, besides the matter of the law, nothing further is contained in it than the lawgiving form. The lawgiving form, insofar as this is contained in the maxim, is therefore the only thing that can constitute a determining ground of the will.

REMARK

Thus freedom and unconditional practical law reciprocally imply each other. Now I do not ask here whether they are in fact different or whether it is not much rather the case that an unconditional law is merely the self-consciousness of a pure practical reason, this being identical with the positive concept of freedom; I ask instead from what our *cognition* of the unconditionally practical *starts*, whether from freedom or from the practical law. It cannot start from freedom, for we can neither be immediately conscious of this, since the first concept of it is negative, nor can we conclude to it from experience, since experience lets us cognize only the law of appearances and hence the mechanism of nature, the direct opposite of freedom. It is therefore the *moral law*, of which we become immediately conscious (as soon as we draw up maxims of the will for ourselves), that *first* offers itself to us and, inasmuch as reason presents it as a determining ground not to be outweighed by any sensible conditions and is quite independent of them, leads directly to the concept of freedom. But how is consciousness of that moral law possible? We can become aware of pure practical laws just as we are aware of pure theoretical principles, by attending to the necessity with which reason prescribes them to us and to the setting aside of all empirical conditions to which reason directs us. The concept of a pure will arises from the first, as consciousness of a pure understanding arises from the latter. (5:29–30, pp. 26–27)

In short, for a will to be free it is necessary, and sufficient, that it be determined only by the lawgiving form of the law. There are thus two parts: it is sufficient, and it is necessary.

It is sufficient: if a will is determined only by this universal lawgiving form, it is free.

It is necessary: if the will is free, it is absolutely necessary that it be determined only by the lawgiving form of the law.

So we have a double implication, in one way and then in the other. In the first paragraph, the aim is to show that the will is free. Here, the will is an existential term, and in this sense it is, as such, a representable term. It falls under the count-as-one. I know that my will is my will because it is in the operation of original apperception. The will is a faculty. Conversely, freedom is in the position of being, but it is certainly not representable. Therefore, freedom is the unrepresentable being of the will, which *is* represented. The mediation is the lawgiving form of the law. Even in Kant's text, freedom is explicitly a subtractive term. It is a negative concept subtracted from the law of representation.

Clearly, freedom is only definable in terms of *nonempirical necessity*.

The second problem presents us with the converse of the first. If the will is free, hence subtracted, it must nonetheless be determined by a law (since there is nothing without law), and this determination must come from the form of the law.

In the *Remark*, the first sentence asserts the theory of reciprocal implication. Then, if we continue up to "independent of its conditions," the *Remark* asks a question, which is once again the question of the count-as-one. Freedom is implied by constraint, by the lawfulness of the law, and, inversely, if there is constraint, then the will is free. So Kant asks: Are these really the same thing? Does the double implication mean that the two terms can be counted as one? Mightn't the lawfulness of the law and freedom be the same thing? He asks the question, saying, I'm not really asking this question; rather, what I'm asking is what is known first, not whether they're the same thing.

The answer may seem odd: freedom is not first, because I can't be conscious of freedom. Why? Because it's a negative (subtractive) concept. To be conscious of something is to experience it. So there is no experience of freedom. What is first, what I'm conscious of, is therefore the moral law, but it is nonetheless a problem. Indeed, what is the "consciousness of the moral law" if not the consciousness of the lawfulness of the law? I understand that if there is no consciousness of the law, there is no will, but what does it mean to be immediately conscious of *the lawfulness of the law*?

This is our final problem. For the time being, this is where we are. Kant says there is a consciousness, of the lawfulness of the law, and the ontology of this consciousness is freedom. We have no consciousness of freedom but only a concept. What we lack is knowing what the specific form of the consciousness of the lawfulness of the law is. Except for this lack, our problem is solved.

We could put it this way: Is there, for the will, a representation that is both the representation of law and the representation of the lawfulness of the law? For if, by chance, there were no representation of the lawfulness of the law, we'd find here the split we were trying to avoid: there might be actions done on the basis of the lawfulness of the law, but they remain unrepresentable. Morality, like cognition, has a blind spot. It is not accessible, except as action in the world, but certainly not on the basis of existence and being. This would mean that *a good action is unconscious, as opaque to itself as being is to cognition.* If there is no representation of the lawfulness of the law, that doesn't preclude the good action, but it does preclude this being a way to count existence and being as one. Good actions will only be recognizable from God's point of view; they won't be a point of being of the subject itself.

That is why Kant will need to write a third *Critique*, after some temporary patchwork provided by the theory of respect.

So our work is cut out for us. We'll begin by examining Kant's first stab at a solution—the specific moral feeling of respect. But this won't be sufficient for there to be a representation of the lawgiving power of the law. A third structural setup will be necessary. This one will lead us into the world of the beautiful and the sublime. There, we'll learn that there are *symbolic* representations of the pure power of the law.

⎯ ⎯⎯ ⎯

We'll conclude this session with an attempt to answer a number of questions.

⎯ ⎯⎯ ⎯

The first question is: What becomes of the identity principle— which plays such an important role in mathematics—in a subtractive ontology?

For Kant, and contrary to the formalists or to Wittgenstein, mathematical judgments cannot be reduced to the identity principle. The fact that the structuring of the representation of experience through mathematizable laws cannot be reduced to the identity principle is even an absolutely initial point for him. There is a productive synthesis at work in real judgments, including in mathematical necessity. The identity principle remains a formally empty principle, incapable of incorporating the representation of natural or mathematical laws.

⎯ ⎯⎯ ⎯

The second question is: But then, in the final analysis, what is the relationship of Kant's philosophy to the sciences in their present state, to physics and mathematics?

It is important to see that these are two completely separate questions: (1) physics and (2) mathematics.

1. Physical ideas have evolved in a roughly Kantian way, especially in quantum physics, where the increasing involvement of the observer in the field of the observable can be seen. Relativity, followed by quantum physics, is moving toward an increasing relativization of phenomena that includes the observer's operations. The general thesis, according to which physical phenomena incorporate relationships with the observer, makes the actions of the observer him- or herself quite constitutive of the observable field. Post-quantum physics seems to be going in that direction, even in its Bachelardian interpretation. But I'm not sure that this idealist orientation will last for long.

2. Here, too, although not retaining Kant's vision of the synthetic, efforts to reduce mathematics to logic (a Leibnizian tendency found in Frege's and Russell's logicist efforts) have ultimately failed. The fact is, the alternative approach that regards mathematics as pure logic has been unsuccessful—hence a Kantian victory: Kant maintains the intrinsic productivity of mathematical discourse, which is not reducible to logical tautologies. In the judgment of the history of science, everything in Kant is obsolete, yet something about his general inspiration isn't—provided, that is, that we don't situate ourselves completely in idealism, even if the idealist aspect is glaringly obvious.

The third question is: What can be said about Kant's relationship with Lacan?

Lacan's interpretation is that the categorical imperative should be ascribed to the ferocious assumption of the law, hence there is a fundamental identity between Kant and Sade. It is assignable to the logic of the pure command and to its unbearable ferocity. My interpretation is different. In *Theory of the Subject*, I suggested that the truly ferocious instance is the moment when the law emerges in its essence as nonlaw, that is, in its essence as pure violence, in the realm of impossibility, the result of which is primitive violence. All the efforts of Kant, who is indeed poised on the brink of the abyss, consist in saying that the lawfulness of the law can be represented otherwise than as nonlaw, and therefore as law. The law as law is still law, in the sense of a measured or measurable law. That's the whole problem.

Kant proposes a third type of law that, formally, is pure command, but that does not make of it the ferocious regime of impossibility. He retains the lawfulness as such in the figure of the law. So it is still the law, even though this law immediately puts the subject in a subtractive position, that is, unfetters it. Clearly, the theme of the unfettered subject is a Sadean theme, which is what Lacan says: it is the subject returned to primitive archaism. Kant says the exact opposite: the unfettered subject is the existent as being, that is, the field of possible morality, of man's humanity in his assumption of the supersensible. From this point on, there are considerable difficulties for Kant. If the lawfulness of the law is itself law, how is the binding of the will carried out? We could say that if the subject is completely in a subtractive position, the lawfulness of the law is not represented, and this will lead Kant to the third *Critique*. He will speak about representation by a feeling, by another faculty: respect. This is in fact just a quick fix since respect is an illusion, even though Kant says it's a "rational feeling."

The fourth question is: What about desire?

If the word *desire* is brought into play, a terrific strain is put on the Kantian problematic. What Lacan, in the wake of Freud, calls "desire," which he says is "reciprocal to the law," Kant calls the "autonomy" of the subject. This means the subject existing purely in the law of its being, which is to say *the existent, as such*. Let me remind you here that Lacan claims that the true meaning of "not giving way on your desire" is . . . doing your duty. Antigone is there to prove him right—him, and Kant along with him.

Session 15

May 22, 1984

L et's start synthetically from the conclusions arrived at by Kant once the first two *Critiques*, the *Critique of Pure Reason* and the *Critique of Practical Reason*, were completed. Between the unity of representation (the count-as-one of representation in experience) and the supersensible (which is nothing but an empty existential index, namely, being-in-itself in a subtractive position, subtracted from representation, unpresentable) there is a connection, not a cognitive one, of course (in cognition everything is representation) but a practical one: the voluntary action, insofar as it is moral. Being-in-itself (being qua being) is subtracted from representation; representation is counted as one in the void of the existential transcendental subject; the existential transcendental subject counted as one contains the will; the will can find its form in a categorical imperative, apart from any empirical purpose, under the influence of the pure lawfulness of the law and, in doing so, the will testifies to a connection between the subject and supersensible being. Thought seems to have made a full circle.

But Kant is not satisfied. He's not sure that we've been led back to the point of departure. The circle may be just an arc of a circle leading once again to an unbridgeable gap. So the third *Critique*, the final one, will ask in substance: is the supersensible attested by the law as the moral law really the same as the supersensible that constitutes the (unrepresentable) being of the sensible? It is supersensible, freedom is supersensible, but is it really the supersensible of the sensible? Is it really this basis in being that is subtracted from representation? This is the ultimate question, the question of the count-as-one of being itself, rather than of the operations in which it is subtracted (representation and cognition) and then seems to be given (moral action).

On the one hand, we know that being in its practical determination is supersensible (the end result); it is the categoricity of action, the realization of the law as law, and without any empirical determination. Moral action is the supersensible realization of the empty point that is the existential subject. On the other hand, we also know that the being that underpins the objectivity of cognitive determinations is supersensible. But cognition is the structural organization of a representation, not the cognition of being, hence the supersensible of being is subtracted from sensible representation, which nonetheless always concerns a real being. So the problem is very clear: can these two instances of the supersensible—the one that activates the subject in moral action and the one that is subtracted in the representations of the knowing subject—be counted as one?

Where does this question come from? It comes from the fact that we have implicitly counted them as one, since we've given them the same name. The fact remains, though, that in the case of the moral action there is an absence of all objects, whereas in the case of cognition there is a nonrepresentation of what, in the realm of being, founds the objectivity of the object. Are these two negations—absence and subtraction—identical? No, because the position of negation with respect to the object differs. It's unclear whether, without confusing the concepts, we can classify, under the same word *supersensible*, the negation of any object (by the categorical imperative) and the nonrepresentation of the foundation of the objectivity of the object (by the operation of the transcendental).

There might be two distinct regions of being, one connected to the objectivity of the object, the other to the lawfulness of the law.

Ultimately, the sensible/supersensible dichotomy, the gap between existence and being, is not overcome. It is merely transferred to the supersensible itself. The danger of a radical ontological dualism won't be averted unless something indicates that what is at issue in the lawfulness of the law is homogenous with, can be counted as one with, what is at issue in the objectivity of the object. Otherwise, the point of being of cognition and that of morality will remain separate.

This question can be retranslated in a simpler form. What, in my activity in a broad sense, would indicate a rough way to unify the categorical imperative of practical reason and the objectivity of the object of pure reason?

Let's take a look now at the first of the texts handed out to you, which is a very complicated one.

> Now although there is an incalculable gulf fixed between the domain of the concept of nature, as the sensible, and the domain of the concept of freedom, as the supersensible, so that from the former to the latter (thus by means of the theoretical use of reason) no transition is possible, just as if there were so many different worlds, the first of which can have no influence on the second: yet the latter **should** have an influence on the former, namely the concept of freedom should make the end that is imposed by its laws real in the sensible world; and nature must consequently also be able to be conceived in such a way that the lawfulness of its form is at least in agreement with the possibility of the ends that are to be realized in it in accordance with the laws of freedom.—Thus there must still be a ground of the **unity** of the supersensible that grounds nature with that which the concept of freedom contains practically, the concept of which, even if it does not suffice for cognition of it either theoretically or practically, and

thus has no proper domain of its own, nevertheless makes possible
the transition from the manner of thinking in accordance with the
principles of the one to that in accordance with the principles of the
other.[1]

Kant starts off as though he were going to treat the opposition
between the sensible and the supersensible and immediately introduces the typical metaphor of the gulf and the transition. The gulf,
the chasm, lies between the concept of nature and the concept of
freedom. But, he says, there must be a transition. Yet the rest of the
passage clearly shows that the question isn't about the relationship
between the sensible and the supersensible. A little farther on, Kant
mentions the unity of the supersensible. There is in fact a transfer
from the gulf between the sensible and the supersensible, from the
count-as-one of the supersensible, to the content of freedom, which
is precisely the supersensible. In Kant's approach the sensible and
the supersensible are radically separate, but free action must be carried out in the sensible world, insofar as it is the sensible realization
of the practical supersensible. Consequently—and this is the third
point—there must be unifiability between the supersensible that's
related to the sensible and the supersensible that's related to freedom. We must be able to conceive, not of a unity of the sensible and
the supersensible but of a unity of the supersensible itself. In short,
the question is that of the relationship between the One and being.

There is absolutely no way we can know this unity of the supersensible, the unity of the being of the world and the being of the
law, either theoretically or practically, since it cannot be brought
about by either cognition or practice. So there is a gulf between the
supersensible found in moral action and the supersensible under-
pinning the objectivity of objects. In other words, there is an absolute disjunction between freedom and nature. Insofar as there is no
solution to this problem, either in terms of cognition or in terms of

the rationality of the law, we can only look for one in what intuitive anthropology seems to leave us, namely *feeling*.

So these are the formal givens of our problem. We know that in order to count the supersensible as one, to transit across the gulf and save the law, we have no recourse in terms of thought as a way, whether theoretical or practical. The solution, if it exists, will be found only in feeling in the elementary sense, the "feeling of pleasure or displeasure." It's an inferior faculty, elevated to the status of supreme faculty. How is this possible? Well, an *idea* needs to be found whose particular mode of subjective existence is to give pleasure or displeasure. For Kant, this idea is *purposiveness*—not as a category of cognition (that was typical of the old world, the world before science) nor as the representation of action in accordance with ends (which is contrary to the categorical imperative), but as an idea that produces a feeling.

Just as freedom was the name of the count-as-one of being and the existent, so, too, is purposiveness the name of the count-as-one of the supersensible. It's incidentally an excellent definition of purposiveness. Purposiveness is basically the idea that the world has a meaning with respect to the command of the law. In no way is this a category of cognition. Kant is a modern philosopher and rejects the old Aristotelian finalism. Purposiveness is "felt," not thought. Whenever we think that there's purposiveness in what is happening, whether in nature, in art, or in human history, it is a *reflective judgment*. This means a judgment that in no way represents the rationality of what causes it or relates to a categorical imperative but is rather a judgment that relates to myself, that fosters a feeling—a judgment whose existential index of the object is of the order of satisfaction or dissatisfaction, pleasure or displeasure.

Artistic objects are particularly capable of arousing such a feeling. They are sensible objects that, through the feeling of pleasure they afford owing to their purposive arrangement, are able to act as symbols of morality. Art can make me feel that certain sensible forms of nature, due to their purposive perfection, touch being as revealed by the moral law, and therefore freedom.

That is why the work of art realizes the count-as-one of the supersensible: it is ultimately the key to general ontology. The experience of art achieves the unity of being. But the purposiveness of the work of art does not determine any object of cognition. The work of art is never cognized; its ontological efficacy lies in the immediacy of the pleasure or displeasure it affords, because it represents the sensible as a symbol of morality without itself having any purpose. Indeed, art represents—the formulation is famous—a "purposiveness without a purpose." The work of art is the formal symbol of morality with no particular purpose and no particular object other than itself. It represents to us the idea of purposiveness, apart from any purpose. The point of departure is that it pleases, but this feeling of pleasure offers nothing to cognition other than the idea of purposiveness. Hence a second definition of the work of art, which is also very famous: art is "that which pleases without a concept."

A large part of the *Critique of the Power of Judgment* will be devoted to establishing this double definition and its articulation, i.e., I repeat: the work of art, on account of its beauty, is simultaneously purposiveness without a purpose and that which pleases without a concept.

This long analysis leaves us with a clearly defined feeling: the feeling of the beautiful. However, for our purposes the main point is no doubt, among the affects constituting aesthetic subjectivity and its function as count-as-one of nature and freedom, the distinction between the beautiful and the sublime. We can in fact note that, regarding the feeling of the beautiful, what was discussed was what causes pleasure, but that the negative affect, displeasure, was left aside. It will be dialectically incorporated into the feeling of the sublime. Indeed, the sublime is that in comparison with which everything else is small, and the main feeling it triggers is first and foremost enthusiasm. But this enthusiasm requires my accepting to consider myself, as an individual, a negligible quantity compared with what arouses enthusiasm. The sublime is the indirect pleasure I take in being forced to think of myself as small compared with what is immense. So I am humbled by the sublime, but there's a complex pleasure involved in this humbling. Feeling humbled is actually the opposite of abjection, which consists in thinking of oneself as being small as such. In the feeling of the sublime, I am at once humbled and distressed by my smallness and exhilarated and enthralled by the immensity.

The moral law can be immediately symbolized by sublimity. I think of it as an imperative command, which sets me in conflict with my sensory interests and of which, always too focused on these interests, I am constitutively unworthy, even if I submit to it. Indeed, my anthropological unworthiness lies in my acting in accordance with hypothetical imperatives. As a result, everything that is sublime, showing the mediocrity of calculations of interest and the grandeur of disinterestedness, is immediately a symbol of the moral law. The sublime is thus the most immediate representation of the unity of the supersensible.

The sublime is a crucial feeling for Kant, and, in a certain sense, only its existence reveals the supersensible unity of the subject. Without the sublime we would be made up of bits and pieces. The sublime is a great, quasi-insurrectionary uprising of the subject, whose inner dynamic is the dialectic of feelings of pleasure and displeasure, linked to the humbling/enthusiasm pair.

In the background, the sublimity of the French Revolution was on Kant's mind. Initially, the feeling aroused by the French Revolution in Europe and particularly in Germany was that feeling of enthusiasm, along with a feeling of powerlessness stemming from an inability to emulate the people of France and consequently to end up on the sidelines of history. This combination of enthusiasm and feeling humbled was proof of the sublimity of the event. With the sublime, then, we're dealing not only with an aesthetic figure but with a historical one as well, in the organic relationship between the sublime and the event. The evental connotation is stronger than in the case of the beautiful, which is more affected by principles of equilibrium, by the rather static unity of the supersensible. The sublime, by contrast, represents a dynamic idea. It can be aroused by a natural event—a storm, an earthquake. It can, moreover, involve and tolerate horrible things.

The feeling of displeasure is also related, when it comes to the sublime, to the fact that the lawfulness of the understanding is overwhelmed and powerless in the face of the measurelessness of the event. The event is sublime as the emergence of the principle of the supersensible as such, with the absence of all cognitive control and the appearance of the chaotic, the uncontrolled. Here we find a whole aspect of eighteenth-century thought on the sublime, including in meditations on disasters such as the Lisbon earthquake.

Let's return now to our original concept, the question of purposiveness. Purposiveness is the name of the count-as-one of the supersensible. We might wonder why Kant chose that term. As usual with him, to clarify a theoretical point he begins with a fact, with what exists, with what is given, with known types of statements. In the *Critique of Pure Reason*, he began with cognitive statements, with mathematics, reduced to their simplest, to $7 + 5 = 12$. In the *Critique of Practical Reason*, he began with the self-evidence of the distinction between good and evil acts. The third type of judgment, whose internal law is opposed to the other two, is *the reflective judgment*. The reflective judgment/determinant judgment dichotomy structures the entire *Critique of the Power of Judgment*.

Here is how Kant introduces the distinction, in the introduction to the *Critique of the Power of Judgment*:

> The power of judgment in general is the faculty for thinking of the particular as contained under the universal. If the universal (the rule, the principle, the law) is given, then the power of judgment, which subsumes the particular under it (even when, as a transcendental power of judgment, it provides the conditions *a priori* in accordance with which alone anything can be subsumed under that universal), is **determining**. If, however, only the particular is given, for which the universal is to be found, then the power of judgment is merely **reflecting**.
> . . . The reflecting power of judgment, which is under the obligation of ascending from the particular in nature to the universal, therefore requires a principle that it cannot borrow from experience, precisely because it is supposed to ground the unity of all empirical principles under equally empirical but higher principles, and is thus to ground the possibility of the systematic subordination of empirical principles under one another. (5:179–180, pp. 66–67)

So Kant starts out from a little entranceway, the way in which judgments connect the particular and the universal—"how universality is contained in particularity," as Mao will say.[2] There are two cases:

1. The universal judgment is given. The question is how the particular can be contained in it. If it's an operation of subsumption of the particular under the universal, then the judgment is determinant. It can be theoretical or practical: moral and scientific judgments are determinant. I experience how the particular can be subsumed under laws.

2. The universal (the general) must be found; it is not given. So I begin with the particular. If I extract a generality from this particular, it will never be already given (since I find it); it

is simply a generality of a type superior to the particular, a particularity of a superior type, more inclusive. I produce a particular generality with respect to a particular. If I reason a posteriori, I will never find the a priori. I remain within generalities that are hierarchized but all empirical, and I must therefore act in accordance with an idea that is the possible unity of all empirical laws. If no such unity were possible, I would never be able to proceed in this way.

In other words, if I move from the particular to the general, I necessarily hypothesize that the object laws are in the element of unity, not of an a priori unity in the universal or transcendental sense but in a principle of unifiability. But this is not a cognition, it's an idea.

There is a fundamental distinction in Kant between the idea (regulative function) and the concept (that by which I know). The reflective judgment is only for myself (it is not a cognition), for my own use; that is, I will make use of the idea of the coherence of empirical determinations to find the general in the particular.

There are three types of law for Kant:

1. The law for objects—scientific laws, causality, necessity, transcendental constitution, representation; all of it related to the count-as-one: original apperception.

2. The unconditional law—the pure lawfulness of the law, the moral law, the formal power of the categorical imperative.

3. The law for laws. This is the idea that laws (namely, the relationship between the general and the particular) are regulated elements. I can proceed inductively from there. I reflect the idea of an empirical status of laws. The law for laws doesn't give me any object to cognize, but neither is it unconditional. It's a law for internal use, due process *for me*. The idea that there's a law of laws: that's what will be called *purposiveness*.

Kant puts it in this way:

> Now this principle can be nothing other than this: that since universal
> laws of nature have their ground in our understanding, which prescribes
> them to nature (although only in accordance with the universal concept
> of it as nature), the particular empirical laws, in regard to that which is
> left undetermined in them by the former, must be considered in terms
> of the sort of unity they would have if an understanding (even if not
> ours) had likewise given them for the sake of our faculty of cognition, in
> order to make possible a system of experience in accordance with par-
> ticular laws of nature. Not as if in this way such an understanding must
> really be assumed (for it is only the reflecting power of judgment for
> which this idea serves as a principle, for reflecting, not for determining);
> rather this faculty thereby gives a law only to itself, and not to nature.
>
> Now since the concept of an object insofar as it at the same time
> contains the ground of the reality of this object is called an *end*, and
> the correspondence of a thing with that constitution of things that
> is possible only in accordance with ends is called the *purposiveness* of
> its form, thus the principle of the power of judgment in regard to
> the form of things in nature under empirical laws in general is *the
> purposiveness of nature* in its multiplicity. I.e., nature is represented
> through this concept as if an understanding contained the ground of
> the unity of the manifold of its empirical laws.
>
> The purposiveness of nature is thus a special *a priori* concept that
> has its origin strictly in the reflecting power of judgment. For we
> cannot ascribe to the products of nature anything like a relation of
> nature in them to ends, but can only use this concept in order to
> reflect on the connection of appearances in nature that are given in
> accordance with empirical laws. This concept is also entirely distinct
> from that of practical purposiveness (of human art as well as of mor-
> als), although it is certainly conceived of in terms of an analogy with
> that. (5:180–181, pp. 67–68)

Translation: if I proceed from the particular to the universal, I am dealing with complete empirical diversity. There are, to be sure, general laws that prescribe the structure of representations, their transcendental organization. But there are remnants; there is absolute particularity, which is not subsumable under the unity of laws. But doesn't it fall under any *universal*? I will in any case proceed in accordance with an integrated *coherence* of experience, which will allow me to extract particularity from the sensible otherwise than by determining it, by subsuming it under laws.

This is what the painter who paints a blade of grass does. There's not a "general" blade of grass on his canvas. There's no visibility of the universal. This is not a "Newton of the blade of grass" operation but a *subjective* process of generalization. This proves that there are types of judgment that relate the particular to the universal in a different way from that of transcendental structurings. They create this relationship *for the subject* and say nothing about the objectivity of the object.

If I suppose a law of empirical laws for myself, I reason in terms of purposiveness. I reason as if the particular phenomenon was not just based on the universal law of the understanding, as in science, but on a principle of coherence as well.

Purposiveness is the idea of a unity of particular phenomena. It is the reflective idea of unity, compared with absolute empirical diversity. But it is an idea that produces no cognition as such: I still don't cognize the unity of the world. It's an absolute presupposition that is only given in the reflective judgment. And as it is beyond cognition, its existential index—the way in which it is given in representation—the index of pure reflection, is a feeling, and could be nothing else. Let me read:

> In fact, although in the concurrence of perceptions with laws in
> accordance with universal concepts of nature (the categories) we do

not encounter the least effect on the feeling of pleasure in us nor can encounter it, because here the understanding proceeds unintentionally, in accordance with its nature, by contrast the discovered unifiability of two or more empirically heterogeneous laws of nature under a principle that comprehends them both is the ground of a very noticeable pleasure, often indeed of admiration, even of one which does not cease though one is already sufficiently familiar with its object. (5:187, pp. 73–74)

I cognize nothing more through coherence and purposiveness, but it gives me pleasure to have found the universal in the particular. When I subsume the particular under universal laws it gives me no pleasure because I am acting unintentionally: it's the anonymous structure of the transcendental subject that's at work. The third *Critique* introduces distinctions that anticipate the difference between the conscious and the unconscious: if I cognize in accordance with laws, I don't feel any pleasure, but if I think (reflect) that heterogenous laws are connectable in accordance with a higher empirical unity, then it's a great pleasure. It is very important, very convincing here, that the pleasure is the pleasure afforded by the unity contained in heterogeneity. Whenever there is invention, production, discovery of a purposiveness, the connecting of heterogeneous empirical laws, there is pleasure. It is pleasure that proves that I've done it, since there is nothing to be cognized.

The beautiful "pleases immediately without a concept." It's an immediate pleasure, without the mediation of a cognition, without a concept (no determination), but whose secret, in my own eyes, lies in the fact that I find the possibility of a unity among heterogenous principles.

The feeling of the One with regard to heterogeneity in the sensible world: it's from this that the count-as-one of the supersensible, and therefore the determination of being as One, comes into existence.

Session 16

June 19, 1984

Today I'd like to offer a sort of final assessment of Kant. If I were to try and give a bird's-eye review of my investigation of Kant, I'd say that it was done with the help of two main operators: the question of the subtractive and that of the count-as-one. These are crucial operators.

What I called "the subtractive" is a direct ontological operator, the one that indicates that the very identification of the question of being qua being avoids any presumption of presence. It is particularly appropriate for Kant, whose argument about being always consists in showing how, in fact, being is subtracted from any representation.

As for the count-as-one, it is for me the operative term for what has often been called structure. The generic essence of a structure is to count as one in given multiplicities and thereby to overcome apparent separations. For Kant, however, the work of thought always consists, first of all, in distinguishing between incompatible, irreconcilable domains. But no sooner are they identified as being separated by a chasm than the question of their count-as-one arises. In Kant, it is always the irreconcilable itself that has to be counted as one. Kantian rationalism is absolute and implacable in this respect because it is not satisfied with saying, as is obvious, that the irreconcilable is external to the cognizable. This "self-evident fact" must be deconstructed, because the thinkable is not the cognizable. We may not cognize the irreconcilable, but that doesn't prevent us from thinking reconciliation.

On the basis of these two questions, the subtractive and the count-as-one, we followed the three Kantian explorations of the human faculties: representation and cognition; action and decision; feeling. These three faculties—the cognitive, the active, and the expressive or emotional—are, for Kant, in the realm of fact. To deal with the faculties, he begins with the existent. It is the factual guarantee of the ontological approach.

Let's take again as an example the total disjunction between moral action and cognitive representations. The chasm between them seems absolute. It could be said that between morality and cognition there is the Lacanian distinction between lack and fore-closure, that is, the difference between neurosis and psychosis. In neurosis, the object of desire is missing, and this (real) lack produces symptoms. In psychosis, the name of the Father, the signifier of order, is purely and simply foreclosed, i.e., totally absent, even in the form of lack, from the subject's world.

Now, the object, in the sphere of morality, is indeed foreclosed; it is simply not there. If there is an object, a purpose, an interest, it's no longer moral; we're dealing instead with the hypothetical impera-tive. In the sphere of cognition or representation, on the other hand, the object is missing something, namely, having the potential for the presentation of its objectivity, that is, of the being that maintains that the representation is not a fiction. The subtractive's point of adherence isn't the same. In both cases we're dealing with a subtrac-tive ontology, but the subtractive isn't situated in the same way. In one case it is constructed as lack; in the other, as foreclosure. *Cogni-tion*, we might say, *is neurotic, and morality, psychotic.*

Kant is acutely aware of all this. He is almost conscious of the fact that morality is psychotic since the question of whether there is a moral action is undecidable. Because to act in accordance with the categorical imperative is truly crazy. Indeed, human nature requires us to act for a purpose, and so, when it comes to empirical acts, it's always the hypothetical imperative that's involved. Action in accordance with the categorical imperative—which *can*, certainly, exist, but whose reality remains in doubt—is so far removed from human nature that it's not unreasonable to regard it as crazy.

This double subtractive structure, either as foreclosure or as lack, leads Kant to say, as we've just seen, that one of the two subtractions (foreclosure) is not attested to in the real. In both cases there is, to be sure, a point of being, but does this point of being guarantee the unity of the supersensible? The reasonable conclusion would be to say that there are two types of supersensibility. The second *Critique* doesn't founder on the unity of the existent and being but rather on the question of the unity of being. At a given moment there are two kinds of being, two types of subtractive operations, two distinct positions of the supersensible.

So it was necessary to begin again—for that's what thought required—if a bridge was to be built across this chasm. This absolutely had to be done; otherwise, in Kant's eyes, it would mean that the unthinkable, in the strict sense of the term, existed. Not the uncognizable—there was as much of that as anyone could want. But this would mean that the supersensible was unthinkable, since it couldn't be counted as one.

Hence the third *Critique*.

Kant's aesthetics consists in the construction of a count-as-one mechanism dealing with the chasm left by the second *Critique*. It is thought, because thought is ultimately simply the ability to construct a count-as-one. That this mechanism is one of feeling makes no difference. There is, of course, a distinction between cognition and feeling, but there will be no distinction between thought and feeling. Actually, in the three *Critiques* the movement of thought continues as the movement of the count-as-one.

Let's read the passage [from the *Critique of the Power of Judgment*] that you have before you:

> Now the judgment of taste does pertain to objects of the senses, but not in order to determine a **concept** of them for the understanding, for it is not a cognitive judgment. It is thus, as an intuitive singular representation related to the feeling of pleasure, only a private judgment, and to this extent its validity would be limited to the judging individual alone: The object is an object of satisfaction **for me**, it may be different for others;—everyone has his own taste.
>
> Nevertheless, the judgment of taste doubtlessly contains an enlarged relation of the representation of the object (and at the same time of the subject), on which we base an extension of this kind of judgment, as necessary for everyone, which must thus be based on some sort of concept, but a concept that **cannot** be determined by intuition, by which nothing can be cognized, and which thus also **leads to no proof** for the judgment of taste. A concept of this kind, however, is the mere pure rational concept of the supersensible, which grounds the object (and also the judging subject) as an object of sense, consequently as an appearance. For if one did not assume such a point of view, then the claim of the judgment of taste to universal validity could not be saved; if the concept on which it is based were only a merely confused concept of the understanding, of perfection, say, to which one could, correspondingly, assign the sensible intuition of the beautiful, then it would be possible, at least in itself, to ground the judgment of taste on proofs, which contradicts the thesis.
>
> But now all contradiction vanishes if I say that the judgment of taste is based on a concept (of a general ground for the subjective purposiveness of nature for the power of judgment), from which,

however, nothing can be cognized and proved with regard to the object, because it is in itself indeterminable and unfit for cognition; yet at the same time by means of this very concept it acquires validity for everyone (in each case, to be sure, as a singular judgment immediately accompanying the intuition), because its determining ground may lie in the concept of that which can be regarded as the supersensible substratum of humanity. (5:339–340, pp. 215–216)

The judgment of taste is a judgment without a law; Kant will say: without a concept. This in no way means that it is not an operation of thought. The law was fundamental up to this point; it was crucial, first as the law or structure of representation (the transcendental), then as the purely formal categorical lawgiving power of the law (morality). The judgment of taste brings into play thought without a law, whose existential index is the feeling of pleasure or displeasure.

The relationship to the work of art, to the aesthetic object, to the beauty of nature, to major historical events is neither prescribed as a moral law nor deducible. It corresponds neither to a command nor to a cognition. It is immediate, that is, without a concept. And the existential index of the immediate is the feeling of pleasure or displeasure. Even more than the absence of law, the subtractive here is the absence of mediation, nonmediation. It is because there is no mediation that we expect the judgment of taste to act as a bridge across the divide of the supersensible, because no rational mediation can unite cognition and morality, nature and freedom.

Just as freedom was the name of the One of existence and being, purposiveness will be the name of the One of being as such, of the supersensible. Purposiveness determines nothing; it gives nothing to cognize. It is an idea of the reflective judgment (not of the determinant judgment, which deals with objects), which is a judgment in terms of ideas and not of concepts, a judgment that proves to me the unity of nature and freedom. Because the artistic object is a sensible object, of nature, but it is also a product of ideas. Here, it is related to both the subtractive of representation and the subtractive of decision. If this object pleases me, the immediate feeling I have of it connects me to the idea of purposiveness: this pleasure and this displeasure are the existential index of the One of being, of the One of human nature. The pleasure of art is simply the pleasure of this One.

The pleasure of art is the pleasure of the count-as-one of the supersensible, which never occurs other than as a "This pleases me."

Ontologically, this unity of nature and freedom is grounded in the unity of the supersensible, but formally, it's a purely symbolic unity. The cause of my pleasure is indeed the unity of the supersensible inasmuch as a representation is neither its presentation nor its representation but its symbol. Art is nothing but a sensible symbol of freedom. The proof of the unity of the supersensible, and therefore of the One of being, is simply that such a symbol is possible.

All this is obviously based on the fact that there is art. That is the ground of the universality of the judgment of taste.

Kant offers us a very detailed analysis of this whole question.

How can we say that there is universality if there is neither proof nor imperative? Will Kant abandon all universality of the arts? If there is any, it is in any case without a concept. I can therefore neither prove it nor make an imperative out of it. Such universality is invisible, unrealizable, untransmissible. So we have the concept of an *untransmissible universality*, that is, the concept of what is universal in its being and remains so, despite the fact that its transmission is impossible. This is the universality of the reflective judgment. I know (I reflect) that there is universality in the feeling of pleasure or displeasure, but this universality is never specifiable on a case-by-case basis. Transmissibility is free-floating; it is everywhere and nowhere at once. It is related to the judgment of taste without being identifiable according to precise criteria of sensible representation. It is given in a strictly sensible symbolism of freedom and admits of no proof.

Artistic feeling, Kant tells us, is the feeling of having access existentially to the One of being, which exceeds us since it exceeds both our cognition, from which it is missing, and the sphere of morality, in which no object representation gives us its reality. The pleasure of art lies in having access to the One of what exceeds us. The accent can in fact be placed either on "access" or on "excess," since the pleasure of art is marked by either one or the other. If it's marked by access, then we're dealing with the beautiful, and if it's marked by excess, then we're dealing with the sublime. Consequently, the sublime is first a displeasure, the displeasure of excess, and the beautiful, first a pleasure, the pleasure of access. Then, the pleasure of this displeasure (the access to this excess) is reintegrated into the sublime, and the displeasure of its pleasure (the excess of its access) into the beautiful. But these are in any case two forms of the feeling of the One of being. Thus, the beautiful is a contemplative and inward-looking pleasure, whereas the sublime is the painful tension of an enthusiasm. That's why the political and historical enthusiasm of the German nation for the French Revolution arises from the sublime. The beautiful is calm purposiveness, and the sublime is an agitated purposiveness.

That said, what chasm will open up once again and take us to Kant's limits this time? In my opinion it's immediately obvious in the chasm between excess and access, between the sublime and the beautiful. Between them there is only the verbal unity of a conceptual formula (the access to excess), not the real unity of a feeling. They are two distinct feelings, in which the dialectical order of pleasure and displeasure is not the same.

If you think about it, you can see that this chasm is none other than the one between the finite and the infinite. The sublime is

essentially the feeling of the infinity of being, as symbolized, for
instance, in a radical event in history. It exceeds its basis in every
respect. Excess conveys a powerful feeling of the infinity of the One
of being. The beautiful, by contrast, is the serene feeling of beautiful
finiteness because it is the pure and simple, joyful access to the fact
that the One of being exists. It provides the feeling of our finitude
being inscribed somehow in the infinity of the One of being, but
this feeling can be measured, whereas the sublime is beyond all measure. So the chasm that opens up is the chasm between the finite
and the infinite, which represents another form of the fundamental
difficulty of counting being as One.

I actually think that the root of this recurrence of the chasm is
that, at this stage, *Kant was unable to avoid the reappearance of an ontology of presence.* The subtractive here, in the beautiful and the sublime
alike, gives way to the majesty of presence, not of representational
presence but of what acts as presence for feeling.

It is important to understand that to culminate in an aesthetics
is always to end up dissolving the subtractive in presence. Whether
Kant likes it or not, pleasure and displeasure are experiences of presence. I'm not saying that pleasure and displeasure are structured
solely in accordance with the ontology of presence. But in the end,
in the power of the feeling of the beautiful and even more so in that
of the feeling of the sublime, the One of being presents itself; it
enters the picture. There is neither a representation of it nor a concept, but there is a *manifestation*, on which all the artistic symbolism,
as well as the smallness/immensity dialectic in the sublime, is based.

I for one would say that, in Kant's trajectory, the subtractive
ontology, maintained with the utmost rigor for the first time in
the history of philosophy, ends up as an emotional and aesthetic
ontology of presence. It's what I would call Kant's late romanticism.
Indeed, in his strict and rigorous trajectory, Kant himself is the

bridge between the eighteenth and nineteenth centuries, between late Classicism and early Romanticism.

From the concept to presence by way of the absolute action (morality): that's the story in a nutshell.

We can therefore establish a point of method. Whenever an obstacle to the infinite appears in a trajectory of the thinking of being, the question arises as to whether that obstacle might not be indicating a shift from the subtractive to presence. We can see it here in relation to the specific issue of the beautiful and the sublime, but a general maxim can be drawn from it.

Kant leaves us with one final thought about the subject. What happens to the infinite when it comes to maintaining a subtractive ontology? How can the infinite be maintained within the subtractive instead of being the ultimate ruse of presence? That, to my mind, is Hegel's real starting point. Hegel is the philosopher whose project is to keep the infinite within the negative, or, in other words, the philosopher who wonders how to infer the infinite from nothingness, in the hopes that such an operation won't be reducible to an aesthetic *coup de théâtre*.

Personally, I think Hegel's project, taken as a whole, failed, because he actually extracts the infinite from nothing only by putting it there in the first place. Nonetheless, his project in its detail is often remarkable, and many of his local analyses are truly . . . sublime!

———— ∞ ————

It was Mallarmé who plumbed this question in depth. He is the thinker of this issue, but his dialectic is entirely different from Hegel's. I will take three citations from Mallarmé's *Igitur*:

The infinite emerges from chance, which you have denied.[1]

Who is this "you"? Kant, perhaps, because he had in fact denied chance. In any case, all the scientistic determinists, the defenders of necessity.

And so from the Infinite constellations and the sea are separated. (92)

This means that the sublime must be separated from the infinite: what we see is the expulsion of all sublimity from the infinite. There must be an infinite that is symbolized neither by constellations nor by the sea, nor by any combination of them.

> Briefly, in an act where chance is in play, chance always accomplishes its own Idea in affirming or negating itself. Confronting its existence, negation and affirmation fail. It contains the Absurd—implies it, but in the latent state and prevents it from existing: which permits the Infinite to be. (99)

Mallarmé tells us that the infinite arises from a prevention. What allows the infinite to be is the prevention of the existence of something else, the absurd, in this case, which in its turn is related to chance. Something other than simple negation should be understood in this obstruction. Let's take a closer look. The obstruction of what? Of the absurd? But what is the absurd? A negation, no doubt, but unrepresentable, a stopping point without a concept. It is precisely what, in the Kantian sublime, causes us to be humbled, and it's this that chance prevents from existing, thereby allowing the infinite to be.

This leads to an entirely new problematic of the infinite because, for Mallarmé, the concept of the infinite is based on the idea of a repetition that stops without a concept. That's what the absurd is. It may be the same thing as death. The infinite requires that a repetition's conceptless stopping be prevented. This means that, for Mallarmé, the fundamental concepts from which this infinite arises are those of repetition, cessation, and prevention, three notions on the basis of which he declares that the infinite can be. It remains to clarify how these three concepts themselves should be related to the notion of chance.

Chance is the event, the "there is." This is the chink in Kant's armor: what is lacking in Kant is the event, not in terms of its occurrence (think of his passionate relationship to the French Revolution), but as a singular thinking, and not only in the guise of the feeling of the sublime. What Mallarmé shows us, in the first place, is that a thinking of the infinite can remain subtractive and therefore avoid lapsing into the lexicon of presence only if there is a *thinking* of the "there is" qua event.

If we were to take a shortcut (something that should never be done), we would say: the infinite is the event. That's much too simple. But it's an essential, anti-Kantian approach, since it deals with the last chasm, the one that opens up between the beautiful and the sublime, the chasm across which Kant was unable to construct a bridge.

Mallarmé reconstructs the fundamental connection between the event and the infinite through the question of repetition—with the potential absurdity of its stopping point—and the question of the prevention of this stopping point, which allows the infinite to be. That is where we should start from to write a fourth *Critique* that would be called *The Critique of Evental Reason*. The event is very complicated because it is at once the absurdity of the stopping point and the prevention of its absurdity. It is the incalculable element of any rational truth.

I'd like to conclude by writing out a mathematical inscription for you.

$$(\exists inf) \, [(\varnothing \in inf) \text{ and } (\forall x) \, [(x \in inf) \to (\{x\} \in inf)]]$$

This mumbo jumbo can be read as follows: "There exists a set *inf* such that, first, the empty set is an element of it, and, second, if x is an element of *inf*, then{x}, the singleton of x, is also an element of *inf*."

This is the axiom of infinity. A matheme of infinity is written here, a Mallarméan matheme, not a Kantian one. That's why this axiom is not sublime.

The paradox of Mallarmé is that he renders sublime his attempt to negate sublimity because he operates in the element of Poetry. Mallarmé is the exceptional poet who actually has no other task than to negate the poetics of the poem in Poetry, so as to remain subtractive and never inject presence into it. Does he succeed in this? It's hard not to attach shreds of presence to Mallarmé's poetry because the truth is, there are stopping points in his work that are immanent in poetics as such, which he does not manage to treat in the subtractive. The mathematical axiom is clearly much more relevant for that, but it is in a sense less strict, since it doesn't have to deal with that typically Mallarméan process, with the desire to desublimate the sublime, to produce the subtractive by the visible poetic operation of a desublimation of the sublime—which still requires producing the sublime, and therefore presence.

The matheme's force lies in not having to desublimate, because that's its original gesture: its gesture always begins with having desublimated, because it has abolished presence in writing. Presence is abolished here by the fact that this extraordinary symbol, ϕ, has been written. It is indeed an altogether extraordinary singular symbol, which combines the circle and the bar in order to symbolize the subtractive. Never again will there be the fullness of the circle to symbolize the assumption of presence of the closed figure—the bar has been placed on it once and for all. It is an amazing writing operation, carried out, as usual, by mathematicians with a complete lack of awareness.

Well, those will be my final words for this year.

Notes

Introduction to Alain Badiou's seminar *The One* (1983–1984)

1. Badiou presents an account of the history and form of his seminars in the "Author's General Preface to the English Edition of the Seminars of Alain Badiou."

2. In *Being and Event*, trans. Oliver Feltham (London: Continuum, 2006), Badiou will describe four meanings of the word "one": the One (that is not); the operation of count-as-one; unicity, which is a predicate of a multiple in relation to other multiples that it is other than; and the forming-into-one, through which a multiple that has been counted-as-one is *counted-again-as-one* (89–92). Badiou also discusses the concept of the "ultra-one," which he describes as the anomalous doubleness of the event in which an element of the situation is counted "once as a presented multiple, and once as a multiple presented in its own presentation" (182).

3. *Philosophy and Truth: Selections from Nietzsche's Notebooks of the Early 1870s*, trans. Daniel Breazeale (New York: Humanities, 1979), 83.

4. In *Being and Event*, Badiou also describes the operation of "forming-into-one," which is a modality or second degree of the count-as-one in which what has already been counted as one is counted again as one, as a part or "state" of a situation (91).

5. See, for example, Heidegger's 1938 lecture (published in 1950) "The Age of the World Picture," in *Off the Beaten Track*, ed. and trans. Julian Young and Kenneth Haynes (Cambridge: Cambridge University Press, 2002), 57–85. The twentieth century was violently anti-Platonic as well, and from a variety of perspectives, as Badiou details in the first session of his seminar, *Pour aujourd'hui: Platon! 2007–2010* (Paris: Fayard, 2019), 23–39.

6. For the distinction between "subjectivation" and "subjective process" in Badiou, see *Theory of the Subject*, trans. Bruno Bosteels (London: Continuum, 2009), 241–274.

7. See Meditation 4, "The Void: Proper Name of Being" (52–59).

8. In *Logics of Worlds*, trans. Alberto Toscano (London: Continuum, 2009), Badiou no longer emphasizes the concept of "naming" the event in order to avoid the implication of a preexisting subject who does the naming, prior to the faithful subjects that may arise in the pursuit of truth procedures. See *Logics of Worlds*, 361.

9. Badiou opens *Theory of the Subject* with a discussion of these two understandings of the dialectic in Hegel's *Science of Logic* (3–12).

10. Immanuel Kant, *Critique of Pure Reason*, ed. and trans. Paul Guyer (New York: Cambridge University Press, 1998), 232.

11. "Transcendental knowledge is ontological knowledge, i.e., a priori knowledge of the ontological constitution of beings. Because transcendental knowledge is ontological knowledge, Kant can equate transcendental philosophy with ontology." Martin Heidegger, *Phenomenological Interpretation of Kant's Critique of Pure Reason* (Bloomington: Indiana University Press, 1997), 127.

12. Badiou elaborates on these issues in "Kant's Subtractive Ontology," in *Briefings on Existence: A Short Treatise on Transitory Ontology*, trans. Norman Madarasz (Buffalo: State University of New York Press, 2006), 133–141.

About the 1983–84 Seminar on the One

1. Badiou's Malebranche seminar, translated by Jason E. Smith with Susan Spitzer, was published by Columbia University Press in 2019. The English translation of the Parmenides and Heidegger seminars, as well as the seminar on Infinity mentioned below, are forthcoming from Columbia University Press.

Session 1: November 11, 1983

1. See in particular Alexandre Koyré, *From the Closed World to the Infinite Universe* (Baltimore: Johns Hopkins University Press, 1968).

2. René Descartes, *Meditations on First Philosophy*, "Second Meditation," in *The Philosophical Writings of Descartes*, trans. John Cottingham, Robert Stoothoff, and Dugald Murdoch (Cambridge: Cambridge University Press, 1984), 2:16–17. Subsequent page references to this edition will be given in parentheses in the text.

3. Jacques Lacan, "Science and Truth," in *Écrits: The First Complete Edition in English*, trans. Bruce Fink (New York: Norton, 2017), 727.

4. Badiou is borrowing Lacan's distinction between "subjectivation," as the punctual moment of interruption that inaugurates the subject, and "subjective process," as the extended time in which a subject gains consistency and durability. See Badiou's account of this in part 5 of *Theory of the Subject*, trans. Bruno Bosteels (London: Continuum, 2009), 241–274.

Session 2: December 6, 1983

1. Baruch Spinoza, *Treatise on the Emendation of the Intellect*, in *Spinoza: Complete Works*, ed. Michael L. Morgan, trans. Samuel Shirley (Indianapolis, IN: Hackett, 2002), 10.

2. *The Leibniz-Arnauld Correspondence*, ed. and trans. H. T. Mason (Manchester, UK: Manchester University Press, 1967), 121.

3. Blaise Pascal, *Pensées and Other Writings*, ed. Anthony Levi, trans. Honor Levi (Oxford: Oxford University Press, 1995), 105.

Session 3: December 13, 1983

1. In Descartes's original Latin, there are indeed *Postulata*. But while this is translated as "Postulates" in the English edition, in French it is translated as "Demandes"—hence Badiou's statement that there are no "postulates" in this passage. According to the editor of the English edition, "Descartes is here playing on words, since what follows is not a set of postulates in the Euclidian sense, but a number of informal requests." *The Philosophical Writings of Descartes*, trans. John Cottingham, Robert Stoothof, and Dugall Murdoch (Cambridge: Cambridge University Press, 1984), 2:114, note 3.

2. "Anxiety, superego, courage, and justice hereby come to name the four fundamental concepts in any theory of the subject." Translator's introduction to Alain Badiou, *Theory of the Subject*, trans. Bruno Bosteels (London: Bloomsbury, 2013), xvii.

Session 5: January 10, 1984

1. Jacques Lacan, *Le séminaire, Livre XVIII: D'un discours qui ne serait pas du semblant* (Paris: Éditions du Seuil, 2006).

2. Plato, *The Sophist* in *Theaetetus* and *Sophist*, trans. Christopher Rowe (Cambridge: Cambridge University Press, 2015), 139.

3. Translated as "The Point of the Signifier," in *Concept and Form: Key Texts from the* Cahiers pour l'Analyse, ed. Peter Hallward and Knox Peden (London: Verso, 2012), 1:107–118.

Session 7: January 31, 1984

1. "Difference" is the translation used here for what the French text has as "*l'autre*." Where this term is used in Badiou's discussion, we have chosen to retain "the other."

Session 9: February 28, 1984

1. Plato, *The Dialogues of Plato*, vol. 4: *Plato's Parmenides*, trans. R. E. Allen (New Haven, CT: Yale University Press, 1997), 165.
2. Translated by Peter Hallward and Knox Peden as "Dialectic of Epistemologies," in *Concept and Form: Key Texts from the* Cahiers pour l'Analyse, ed. Peter Hallward and Knox Peden (London: Verso, 2012), 2:119–150.

Session 10: March 13, 1984

1. Parmenides, "Parmenides' *Poem*," fragment 8, ll. 22–25, in *Parmenides and Presocratic Philosophy*, by John Palmer (Oxford: Oxford University Press, 2013), 369.
2. Jean-Paul Sartre, *Being and Nothingness*, trans. Hazel Barnes (New York: Citadel, 2001), lxvi.
3. Beginning in 1982 and continuing through 1984, the Talbot-Poissy automobile factory was the site of workers' strikes, many of them violently put down by the police. Badiou returns to these strikes a number of times (for instance, at length in *Peut-on penser la politique* [1985] and in his commentary on Sylvain Lazarus, in *Metapolitics*), but the events at Talbot press upon him especially during the period in which he is giving this seminar. In January–February 1984, the bimonthly journal *Le Perroquet*, coedited by Badiou and Natacha Michel, published an issue devoted to "La grève ouvrière de Talbot (Poissy): décembre 1983–janvier 1984" [The Talbot (Poissy) strike: December 1983–January 1984].

Session 11: March 20, 1984

1. Immanuel Kant, *Critique of Pure Reason*, ed. and trans. Paul Guyer and Allen Wood (Cambridge: Cambridge University Press, 1997), A 340; B 389,

pp. 409–410. Subsequent references to this edition will be given in parentheses in the text.

Session 13: April 17, 1984

1. Immanuel Kant, *Groundwork of the Metaphysics of Morals*, trans. Mary Gregor (Cambridge: Cambridge University Press, 1997), 4:408, pp. 20–21. Subsequent page references to this edition will be given in parentheses in the text.

Session 14: May 15, 1984

1. Immanuel Kant, *Critique of Practical Reason*, 2nd ed., ed. and trans. Mary J. Gregor (Cambridge: Cambridge University Press, 2015), 5:161–163, p. 129. Subsequent references to this edition will be given in parentheses in the text.
2. Immanuel Kant, *Groundwork of the Metaphysics of Morals*, ed. and trans. Mary J. Gregor (Cambridge: Cambridge University Press, 1998), 4:416, p. 27.
3. The French word *intention* is rendered as "disposition" in Gregor's translation, but we are using "intention" here as it expresses Badiou's point more clearly.

Session 15: May 22, 1984

1. Immanuel Kant, *Critique of the Power of Judgment*, ed. Paul Guyer, trans. Paul Guyer and Eric Matthews (Cambridge: Cambridge University Press, 2000), 5:175–176, p. 63. Subsequent page references to this edition will be given in parentheses in the text.
2. "Since the particular is united with the universal and since the universality as well as the particularity of contradiction is inherent in everything—universality residing in particularity—we should, when studying an object, try to discover both the particular and the universal and their interconnection." Mao Zedong, "On Contradiction," in *On Practice and Contradiction* (New York: Verso, 2007), 85.

Session 16: June 19, 1984

1. Stéphane Mallarmé, "Igitur," in *Selected Prose and Poetry*, ed. and trans. Mary Ann Caws (New York: New Directions, 1982), 91. Subsequent page references to this edition will be given in parentheses in the text.

Index

absoluteness, One and, 123–124
abyss function, of Other, 101–102
analysis, synthesis compared to, 37–38
anthropology, Kantian, 189
apperception, transcendental, 172–175
a priori synthetic judgments, 186;
    existence of mathematics and, 181;
    experience and, 161; mathematics
    and, 159
Archimedes, 8–10
Aristoteles, 129–131
Aristotle, 26, 32–33; on causality of
    motion, 62; on substance, 50
Arnauld, Antoine, 34–35
art, 178; count-as-one of supersensible
    and, 210; feeling and, 225; judgment
    of taste and, 222–223; nature and,
    223–224; pleasure of, 224–225;
    purposiveness and, 209–210
atheism, 59; nonbeing as One in, 111;
    principle of sufficient reason and, 63
atomism, xxvii, 35
Austin, J. L., 14
axioms: on causality and difference,
    66–67; on causality and existence
    of God, 61–65; on existence of God,
    43, 60–62; hierarchical construction
    of, 69–70; meaning of, 44, 57; of
    objective reality of ideas, 67–69;

principle of sufficient reason and,
    60–61, 66; truth of, 57

beautiful, feeling of, 210
being: body and, 52; causality and, 67;
    class represented by, 106; count-as-
    one of, 146, 195; difference and, 93–94;
    event compared to, xxvi, xxx–xxxi,
    15–16; existence and, 180–181, 187;
    guarantee of, 164; identification
    and differentiation of, 95; lack of,
    xxiv; language, One and, 80–82;
    mathematics and, 52–53; mixing
    ideas with, 90; One and, xxxii–
    xxxiii, 124–125, 131; ontology and, 53,
    164–165; Parmenides on, 117–118; Plato
    on, xxviii–xxix, 86–87; representation
    and subtraction of, 178–179, 205; rest,
    motion and, 87; same compared to,
    96–98; subject and, 188; substance
    and, 50; supersensible of, 206–207; of
    thought, 167–168; truth and, 78; as
    unpresentable, 139–140; void in,
    xxix–xxx, 131–132, 137
Being and Event (Badiou), xxi–xxiii,
    xxx–xxxi, xxxv, 231n2
Being and Nothingness (Sartre), 51, 131–132
body: being and, 52; constraints of, 63;
    materialism and, 83

Index 241

repetition and, 228–229; sublime and, 228; subtraction and, 227; unlimited and, 136–137, 139–140 inscrutable God, 64 intelligible multiplicity, 85–86 intention, 235n3; idea as, 47; of subject, 193
"I think": "I am" compared to, xxv; Kant on, 147, 149; subject and, 149

Jansenist movement, 34–35
judgment of taste, 222–223
Jung, Carl, 13

Kant, Immanuel, xxxvii, 116, 143; on a priori synthetic judgments, 159; anthropology of, 189; Badiou's work and importance of, xxiv–xxv; on being subtracted from representation, 178–179, 205; bibliographic references for, 156–157; on Cartesian subject, 144–146, 152; on categorical imperative, 186; on cognition and thought, 166–167; on condition of experience, 149–150; on consciousness and freedom, 199; on consistency and subject, 148–149; Continental current on subject and, 157; on "Copernican Revolution," 161; count-as-one and, 169, 219–220; critical philosophy of, 160; on Descartes, 146–149; Descartes on subject compared to, 161–164; on desire, 203; on dogmatism, 155; on duty, 181–182; empirical consciousness and, 150, 159; event and, 229; on existence and being, 180–181; extraordinary life of, 154–155; on feeling and art, 225; on feeling and purposiveness, 209–210; on freedom, xxxiii, 181, 196–198; on gulf and transition, 207–208; Heidegger on, 164–165, 174; idealism and, 165; on identity principle and mathematics, 200; on

"I think," 147, 149; on judgment of taste, 222–223; Lacan and, 201–203; on lawfulness of law, 199, 202; on law types, 214–215; materialism of, 174; mathematics and, 158–159; on mathematics and language, 189; on mathematics and logic, 201; on moral action and cognition, 220–221; on object and experience, 165–166; on objectivity of object, 166, 179; on object representation, 188; on One and being, xxxii–xxxiii; ontology and being and, 164–165; ontology of, 174; ontology of presence and, 226–227; on place, xxxii; on power of form in action, 186; predecessors of, 154; psychoanalysis development and, 175; quantum physics and, 201; radicalism of, 191; on rational psychology, 147–148, 175; on recovery of One, 177; on reflective judgment/determinant judgment, 212–214; structuralism and, 153; on subject, xxxi–xxxii; on subject as One, 167–169, 179–180; on sublime, 211–212; subtraction and, 219–220; on transcendental apperception, 172–175; on unity of supersensible, 208; on universality in particularity, 213–217; universality of judgment in, 163–164; on will, xxxiii, 183
knowledge: dead, 14; as process, 84; synthesis and, 38; truth and, 13, 20–21

Lacan, Jacques, xi, xviii, 13, 145; on Cartesian subject, xxv; on desire, 203; Freud and, 143, 146; Kant and, 201–203; on lack-of-being, xxiv; on primary repression, 140–141; on S1/S2 matrix of subject, 140–142; on subject of desire, xxvii; theory of dysfunction and, 141
lack: of being, xxiv; causality of, 67, 70–71

106, 115; Parmenides and, 112; *Sophist*
on, 75, 78
non-self-identity, Other and, 99–101

object: experience and, 165–166; law for,
214; mathematics and, 52; objectivity
of, 166, 174, 179; One of, 171, 173;
representation and, 183–184, 188;
transcendental, 173–174; unity of,
170–171, 173
objections to Descartes: by Arnauld,
34–35; by Caterus, 32–33; *disputatio*
tradition and, 32; by Father
Mersenne, 34, 36–37; by Gassendi,
35–36; by Hobbes, 34; replies to,
31–32; by Sorbonne group, 36
objective reality of an idea, 42, 47–49,
67–69
objectivity: cognition and, 167; of object,
166, 174, 179; One in, 172
One: absoluteness and, 123–124; being
and, xxxii–xxxiii, 124–125, 131; *Being
and Event* on, xxi–xxiii; of change as
instantaneousness, 124; count-as-one
and, xxiii, xxxiv–xxxvi; existence
linked to, 29, 123–124; language, being
and, 80–82; Many and, 127–128;
meanings of, 231n2; nonbeing as,
110–111; of object, 171, 173; in objectivity,
172; as operator, 140; *Parmenides* on,
118, 123–125, 129–131; participation
in, 137–139; point of, 11; recovery of,
177; relation to, 123–124; self-identity
and, 131; subject as, 167–169, 179–180;
subjectivation and, 169; Two and,
xxvi–xxvii, 28–31; uncertainties about,
xxxvii; void and, 132; Whole compared
to, xxviii–xxix, 80, 82–83, 128, 135–136
One, The (Badiou), xxi; concept of,
xxxvi; on subject, xxiii–xxiv. *See also*
Descartes, René; Kant, Immanuel;
Plato
ontological subtraction, 191–192
ontology: being and, 53, 164–165;
Descartes on, 50–51; of ideas, 47;

of Kant, 174; mobilistic, 110; of
presence, 226–227; of transcendental
subject, 179
oral presentation, in seminars of Badiou,
xviii–xix
order of reasons: Descartes using, 5–8,
29; truth and, 20
Other: abyss function of, 101–102; being
compared to, xxix, 96, 99–101;
delimitation function of, 101; double
status of, 106; empty class and, 101–102,
106; gap and, 104, 107; God as, 16;
hierarchy of ideas and, 48; "I am" and,
28; identification and differentiation
of, 95–96; as meta-idea, 95, 102;
mixing ideas with, 93–94; nonbeing
and, 106, 115; non-self-identity and,
99–101; politics and, 104; presence of,
103–104; repetition forbidden by, 99;
subject and, 30, 74, 115–116

Parmenides, xxiii–xxiv, 96, 103;
challenge to, 111–116; as father of
Greek philosophy, xxvii–xxviii; gap
and, 131; nonbeing and, 112; parricide
and, 113–115
Parmenides (Plato), xxvii–xxviii, xxxvii,
80; aim of, 126–127; as aporetic
dialogue, 118; on being, 117–118;
characters in, 121; dialectic of One
and Many in, 127–128; hypotheses in,
119–120, 123–125; mastery in, 117, 118,
121; on One, 118, 123–125, 129–131; on
One compared to Whole, 128; *Sophist*
compared to, 125–126; structural
remove in, 122–123; temporal remove
in, 121–122; uniqueness of, 117; weak
interlocutors in, 123
parricide, in *Sophist*, 113–115
participation: in ideas, 89, 93; in One,
137–139; theory of, 89
particularity, universality in, 213–217,
235n2
Pascal, Blaise, 34–35, 63–64; on infinite,
73–74

List of the seminars
(*in chronological order*)